Mystagogus

Josephine McCarthy

Published by TaDehent Books 2022
Exeter UK

Hardback ISBN: 9781911134718
Paperback ISBN: 9781911134725
Ebook ISBN: 9781911134732

Cover image by Stuart Littlejohn
Typeset by Michael Sheppard

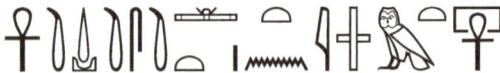

TaDehent Books

Dedicated to Stuart Littlejohn, my wonderful husband and co-conspirator.

This deck project started on the cusp of the Covid pandemic and was worked on throughout successive lockdowns for two years. During that time, I lost friends, family and fellow magicians to the virus, and many more suffered life-changing effects from serious infection. This project is also dedicated to all who were affected in so many different ways by this terrible situation.

...the most pre-eminent kind of human is he who has realized perfection in the intuition of the theoretical intellect, such that he is completely free of need of a human teacher; and has (attained skill) in his practical divinatory ability such that he witnesses 'the realm of the soul'[1] and that which therein relates to the states of the lower world, establishing them whilst awake so that the imagination completely performs its action for him to witness them in a specific way, as we have already explained, and the power of his soul exerts its effect throughout the natural world.

— Avicenna[2] (980-1037 CE)

[1] *al-ʿālam al-nafsānī*: magicians would read this as 'inner realm'.
[2] Avicenna Ibn Sina. *Aḥwāl al-nafs*, as translated by Noble (2020: 198).

Contents

Card Index

1 Progenitor

2 Fate Creation

3 Fate Weavers

4 Harvester

5 Awakening

6 Student

7 Path

8 Daimon

9 Purification

10 Dreams

11 Wheel

12 Perception

13 Magic

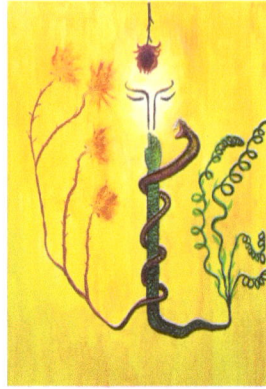
14 Silence

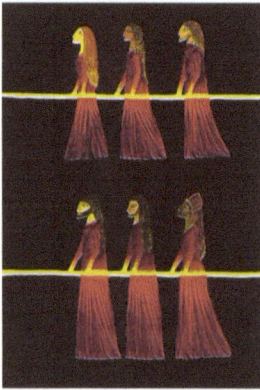
15 Service

16 Healing

17 Defence

18 Stargazers

19 Utterance

20 Creating

21 Loadsharer

22 Dead End

23 Four Creatures

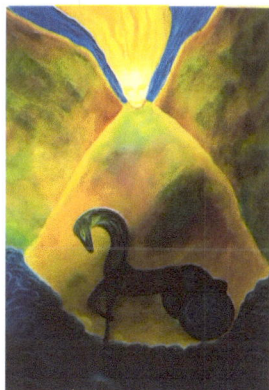

24 Chariot

25 Leadership

26 Hidden Knowledge

27 Inner Desert

28 Test

29 Wisdom

30 Phanos

31 Akh

32 Foundation Stone

33 East Gate

34 South Gate

35 West Gate

36 North Gate

37 Profane Place

38 Hearth

39 Obscure Path

40 Inner Library

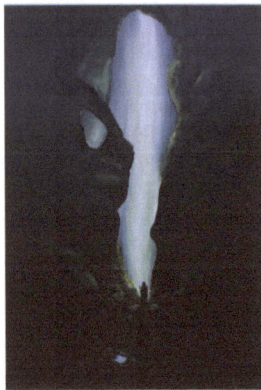

41 Sanctuary

42 Nature

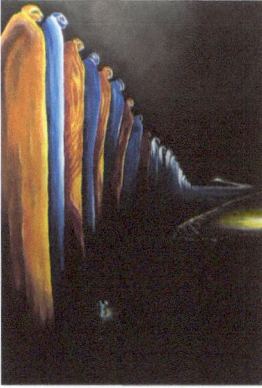

43 Underworld

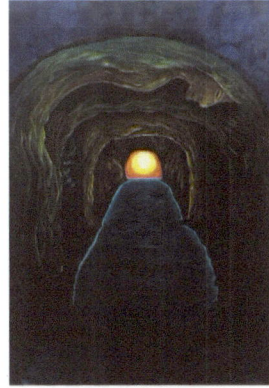

44 Sacred Place

45 Wind Spirits

46 Firestorm

47 Water of Life

48 Balance

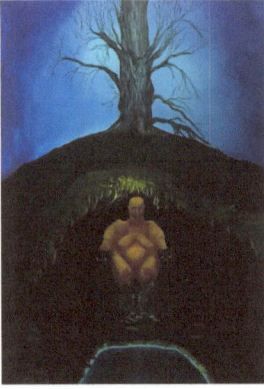

49 Ancient One

50 Companions

51 Secret Commonwealth

52 Threshold Guardians

53 Light Bearer

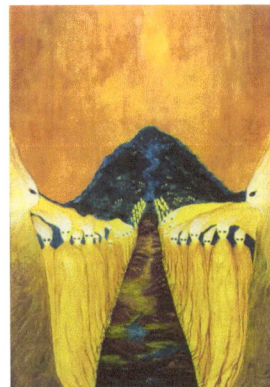

54 Divine Servants

55 Oracle

56 College

57 Ghost

58 Parasite

59 Choppers

60 Partnership

61 Separation

62 Limiter

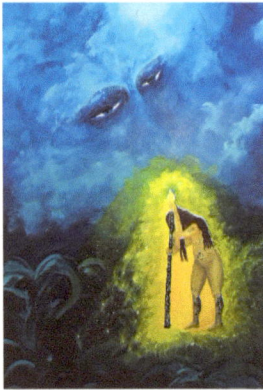

63 Endurance

64 Voice of Truth

65 Gift

66 Lightning Strike

67 Splendour

68 True Justice

69 Unraveller

70 Defeat

71 Voice of Untruth

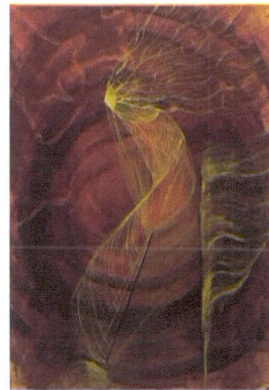
72 Binder

73 Danger

74 Fall

75 Serpent of Chaos

76 Destruction

77 Magical Death

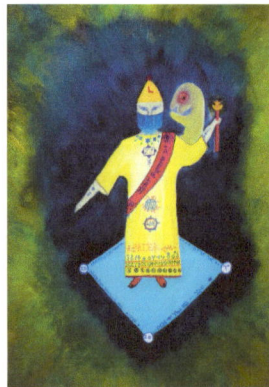

78 Empty Vessel

About Mystagogus: how to use this deck and book

A contacted magical deck for the lone practitioner

A Mystagogus was a priest in the classical world who prepared people for initiation into the Greater Mysteries. This deck is magically designed and created to act as a guide, advisor, and source of divination to someone who is walking their magical path alone. In a world that is increasingly difficult, we all need someone or something to turn to when we have exhausted our own intuitions, or don't know which way to turn.

This deck started to build up as an inner pattern just before the pandemic hit. It started towards the end of December of 2019, with one painting that I had an urge to do. By the end of January 2020 I was getting the idea that a deck was sat waiting for me to catch up with it. I had dreams, and inner contacts nudging me daily: *something is coming, you need to lie low, here, paint this, make yourself useful.* It took me a little while to figure out what was really being asked of me, but I got it eventually. I mapped it out, bought in some paints and canvases, and spent the following two years painting and learning.

The deck is designed around an ancient magical pattern of inner self evolution. It has embedded within it the steps of development inherent to any magical path that seeks greater union with the deeper self, and with the hidden inner worlds that flow through and around the physical world. It can be used as a learning tool as well as a guide and divination tool for those who pay attention.

Each of the cards, even the simplest ones, have layers of meaning that can either be taken at face value for mundane divination or can be explored for their deeper magical meaning. Each one is a power, dynamic, place, or action that the magician bumps up against on their magical journey through life.

The majority of the cards have simple, common names that express the power or dynamics behind them. A few have names that are specific, due to the power that flows through them. Each image is a 'contacted' image in that the painting process was also a magical process that drew on certain power dynamics and 'fixed' it into the image. Each painting was also consecrated to ensure its inner magical focus and clarity.

There are 78 cards in the deck, and it is not based on the tarot system: it is itself. A final contacted and consecrated painting was done for the card back of an angelic power that protects through catching and tangling. This ensures that the cards stay tuned and are not 'infested' by any being or magic that would seek to

1

interfere with the relationship between the magician and the deck. It also acts as a 'web' that upholds the family of the deck as one whole. The deck is not designed in a colour-coded or stylistic way: each card is itself, just like us humans.

This book that accompanies the deck is not only an 'about each card' book: it also teaches about the magical aspects of the powers, beings, places and dynamics expressed in the paintings. I have also included 'extras' for some cards: analogies from science, history, religion, philosophy, etc. I originally did this for each card, but the book got too long, and on reflection such extras were not always necessary. But the analogies where I have used them are there to not only say, 'it is like this' or 'it comes from here', but also to show how magical learning often includes looking and learning from non-magical subjects and sources.

The book is freely available to download on the Quareia website (www.quareia.com). You don't need to buy a deck to access the book: it is a free download for anyone who is interested in it. The book can be used as a learning tool by itself, and also as an oracle book: you can use dice to select a page, or just open the book at random, once a specific question has formed in your mind. There is a section on book divination in the layouts chapter of this book.

As you work with the deck, over time you will find that some of the images form a meaning that is unique to you. This is where, at a deep level, you start to form your own inner dialogue with the power that flows through a card, and it adapts to you. Always trust your instinct, but never let your 'wants' rule such a dialogue: some images are difficult and challenging, and it is easy to try and soften their meaning, but that would be an injustice both to them and to you. Rather, if you have such reactions to some of the images, it is better to learn what their power feels like. That way, you will develop an early warning instinct when such a power creeps around you in your everyday life, threatening and unseen. You will pick up on it, know it, and learn how to dodge, dissipate, or reject its power.

I. The Core Fate Powers

1 PROGENITOR

> An intelligible unknown, a unique being who has no equal, something sought but not comprehended.
>
> — Secundus the Silent[1]

MEANING

The Progenitor is the conscious Divine power at the root of all things here on our Earth. This card has many layers of meaning to it, and the deeper into mysticism or magic a person goes, the more the layers of this consciousness reveal themselves. It is a depiction of the land, the sky/sun, and the serpent power that flows between the two.

This card's layers of meaning flow though our concepts of the Divine, and what that means to each individual reader is different depending on their beliefs and experiences. It can mean 'God', it can mean the Divine that all deities flow from, it can mean the consciousness of the planet and the sun that gives us life, and the conscious inner energy that runs through everything that exists in our world...it is the 'inner glue' that holds everything together.

The deeper into inner experiences the magician goes, the more our ideas and perceptions change. We often start out with a very clear idea that 'god is up there' or 'the gods are out there', and we give names, attributes, and powers to this idea. But as we journey deeper beyond the mundane world, over time our certainties and dogmatic structures slowly fall away as we develop. We start to get glimpses of something that is hard to grasp, hard to define, and this fluidity seeps around our rigid thinking until it starts to crack it open.

What we are left with are moments of recognition: the face of a person, the side of a mountain, a raindrop, the billions of stars all around us, an insect, a tree...all of these things shine with a light we recognize but cannot name. And slowly, slowly,

---

[1] Secundus the Silent: a 2nd century A.D. Neopythagorean philosopher of Athens. Quote source: Cairo Genizah, magical texts (T-S K1.115), translated by Bohak, 2006: 360.

we come to see it within ourselves.

The Progenitor is the power that awakens the potential of a goddess in a tree, or a god in a storm. It is the power that flows through fate, through substance, through destruction and creation, and through life and death: *I am within you and all around you.*

Magicians, mystics, artists and 'inspired ones' have the potential to 'awaken' that power within something, be it music, statues, magical patterns, or some other art, and that 'something' can then become an interface through which we can commune and interact with the deities, nature, etc.

The Progenitor is our collective universal starting point from which everything flows. It is not 'this god' or 'that god': it is the source from which they all flow, and the source that flows through our conception, our lives, and our deaths. The ancient cultures depicted this power as a goddess because we all come from a mother, but in truth it is a power that has all genders and none. Sometimes this power expresses itself in a very male way on certain lands when we tap into that land magically, and sometimes it expresses as a female power, but these are its superficial filters or 'skins'. Once we dig deeper into that power, we find that it is itself—undefinable.

Divination

This is the most complex card to read when it falls in a reading, and for each person the meaning or intent will be slightly different. The more you work with the deck, the more your unique understanding of this card will grow through direct experience.

But overall, the position where the Progenitor card falls in a layout (e.g. dreams, home, relationships) indicates an aspect of the situation being read for where this Divine power is potentially active.

For example, suppose you are planning a round of magical work, and you do a reading to check if your magical plan is balanced properly and has the potential to do its job. Say that the Progenitor falls in a position that indicates inner magical work, but the cards around it are difficult, and the outcome looks obscure or hidden. If the Progenitor had not appeared anywhere in the layout, then the difficult cards and obscure outcome would indicate that you are missing something, or it is the wrong timing, or the work is unbalanced, and you need to rethink.

But when the Progenitor card appears somewhere in the reading, and particularly in a magical position, then it is saying, 'however difficult this work will be, however unbalanced it may appear, Divine power will flow through it'. Either for you, or for whatever/whoever is connected to the magical working, the Progenitor will become a bridge that Divine power can actively flow through in order to achieve something that may be way beyond your initial understanding.

It does not mean that you will not possibly get blowback from doing unbalanced magical work; rather it means the working and the outcome will achieve something that cannot happen without this power being active within it, and it will not become active if you don't do the work. It may, for instance, be a situation whereby, through the messy magical work, you have a deep experience that awakens you to this Divine power within everything which totally changes your view of the world, your work and your life. Sometimes those experiences come quickly and sometimes they come much later, but the catalyst for that later experience is the work you are doing now. Such experiences can often take decades to understand, but they change us to our core.

And sometimes it is not about us, but what we do acts as trigger to catalyse that power to awaken in something or someone else, or triggers a series of events that Divine power and fate can flow through to achieve something.

The bottom line with the appearance of this card is that for good or bad, the event needs to happen unless it appears in a restricted position. If this card falls in a layout position of restriction or negation, then it is saying, *there is nothing Divine in this*. For example if you have an experience with a deity in a church or temple and you decide to do a reading about it, and if this card appears in the negative position, then it is telling you that there is nothing actively 'Divine' in that situation. The deity is not actually a deity; it is something else.

Another meaning this card can have for you, depending upon what the reading is about, is: 'you are not alone in this'. If you are in a situation of despair or have found yourself in the bottom of a dark hole, or have reached the limit of your endurance in something, and you are doing a reading to get insight into how to step forward or cope with it, remember: *I am within you and all around you*. You are not alone in this: the Divine Presence is active and is with you. You will get through this as the Divine Presence is all around you, willing you to step forward: take a deep breath, and know that you can get through this.

Formulate your meaning for this card in a way that works for your understanding of Universal Divine, and bear in mind that over time and practice, that understanding will change, deepen and become even more inexpressible. You will understand it deeply in your bones rather than through your intellect, but you will find it hard to explain it to someone else.

KEYS

Idea forming, Divine presence, preconception, before dawn.

EXTRA

> The Tao that can be trodden is not the enduring and unchanging Tao. The name that can be named is not the enduring and unchanging name. Conceived of as having no name, it is the Originator of heaven and earth; conceived of as having a name, it is the Mother of all things.
>
> — Lao-Tzu, *The Tao Te Ching*[1]

---

[1] Legge, 1891: ch.1.

2 FATE CREATION

MEANING

In magic, all power, all energy, and all being starts with a complete single that subdivides into two. This creates a polarization of positive and negative that in turn allows that power to be worked with. That polarization, depending on whether it is power, a consciousness, a being, and so forth, creates a tension that triggers formation, because where there is polarization and tension, boundaries and patterns start to form. This is the basic foundational principle in magic.

What is interesting to observe in magic is that the creative principle also holds the 'coding', for want of a better word, of destruction within it. The destructive aspect is dormant, and the creative aspect is dominant. The reverse is also true: an active destructive power also has the dormant potential for creative power. *The seeds of regeneration are always found in destruction, and the seeds of destruction are always found in creation.*

The power of Fate Creation is the very beginning of something new. It is the fertilized egg, not the animal or person it will become. It is the idea that eventually becomes a finished project. It is the light that awakens in the depths of darkness. Its meaning is very close to the tarot trump card The Star: the new beginning that starts to emerge out of the darkness.

When walking a magical path, there are times when we fall into despair after a long struggle against a destructive force, be it through our magical work or just through the rigours of life. If we allow that despair to overtake us for more than a brief period, then magically we start to shut down. However, if we remember that the seeds of creation, of regeneration and awakening, nestle silently within that destruction, then it not only gives us a rope of hope to cling to, but it can also awaken that first shaft of light that becomes creative and eventually manifests into a new path. It is a creative force, and a light that illuminates our way ahead.

This is why doing something creative (like art, dance, singing, acting, making something, or redecorating) helps to begin the lifting process of that heavy burden of destruction. When we have our 'dark night of the soul' as magicians we understand that it is the midnight before the dawn. Midnight is the start of the new day, and yet it is the time of deepest darkness. The measurement of the new day starting at midnight can be traced back to at least New Kingdom Ancient Egypt with their use of sundials and shadow clocks. But deeper than that, they also understood this profound magical dynamic of the new starting in the depths of the darkness. This can be seen illustrated in the funerary texts where the Benu Bird, the herald of new creation and new life, appears in the deepest, darkest point of the Underworld/Duat.

Fate Creation is a trigger, a catalyst that allows a fate path to form, unfold and become active. While we each have an overall fate pattern, like everything else that is alive, we also have 'cycles' of fate within that pattern. These cycles can be long or short, and are highly adaptive: they are constantly shifting, developing and changing according to our actions, choices, and interactions with the fate paths of others.

DIVINATION

When Fate Creation appears in a reading, it heralds the very beginning of a new phase. It indicates a new 'something' that will not be apparent to you at present, but is a hidden seed that is starting to wake up. Where it falls in a layout should be a big hint of what the new beginning is all about. For instance, if the card falls in a 'home/hearth' position, then it could indicate a new home or something new coming into the home, or potentially a child. It is a 'newness' that changes the overall pattern of the home and family in some way.

If it falls in a position of magical/inner work, then it can indicate a new long-term phase of learning, a new project, or new magical work. If it falls in the position of self, then it can indicate that a whole new cycle of fate is forming itself. Throughout our lives we have various cycles of fate that come and go and at times overlap; however, when this card indicates a new fate pattern, it will be a longer-term one, not a short or limited fate event.

This card is one of new beginnings, and whatever the new beginning is when it dawns, it will either directly or indirectly take you on a longer-term path of fate: years or decades, as opposed to months or a couple of years. (Shorter term fate changes are indicated by the Wheel card.) This power often catalyses through actions and events, and while the event may be short but meaningful, the way it changes a fate path is longer term.

The fate will often (but not always) be gestated through a series of polarisations, and occasionally some reductive division, before the new path is complete and ready for you to walk. These are the 'dark hours of the night between midnight and dawn'. When we realize this while we are in the darkness and struggle, we can look around and start to see the reductive division. People, things, jobs, or firmly-held beliefs can fall away from us and leave us floundering. But once we understand what is happening we can take those divisions in our stride, knowing that they are parts of the process of creation before the dawn and rebirth.

This card can also indicate a 'dawning of the mind' and an awakening of the soul. This is the deeper aspect of this card, and when it appears in a reading about the long-term fate of a magician, it can indicate the 'Great Awakening', where everything we thought we knew about the world, about magic, and about the powers of the Divine, begins to crumble and fall away, leaving us standing alone in the rubble.

The key word at that point is *trust*. Trust in yourself and have faith in yourself and in the process of fate creation: the drop of water that awakens the seed. As that seed starts to grow, you will start to see yourself and the world around you in a very different and more powerful way.

In a mundane reading, this card always indicates a new and important beginning.

Keys

New beginning, major changes ahead, creative power, birth and rebirth, a new path, a new life.

3 Fate Weavers

Know that celestial forces do not affect preternatural events without the bringing together of passive receptive elemental forces with earthly psychic forces, and this is the talisman.

— Rāzī, *Sharḥ al-Ishārāt*[1]

Meaning

The nine figures are the planetary spirits of Pluto, Neptune, Uranus, Saturn, Jupiter, Mars, Venus, Mercury, and the Sun. The planetary spirits are the inner consciousness of the physical planet, just as we magicians see Gaia[2] as the goddess or inner spirit of our planet. They weave threads of creation and destruction in loops through which runs a thread of time, and all of those threads are drawn from within the body of each planetary spirit. Brought together, those 'chains of fate' set out on a pathway of influence, upheld by the deeper and more powerful web of fate, depicted in the painting as a faint blue net behind and around the figures: this net upholds the planetary spirits.

The image is a way of depicting the complexity of how the inner consciousness and inner qualities of each planet, including our own, affect life, fate, and tides. The qualities and energy of each planetary spirit intermingle to form a 'soup' of inner influence that affects everything on our planet (and probably on all the other

---

[1]Noble, 2020: 22.

[2]Gaia Gaea: an ancient Greek goddess who personified the earth planet. The oracle at Delphi was thought to have first been an oracle of Gaia before it became an oracle and temple of Apollo. The oracle shrine was a simple cave and was connected to Gaia's son Python, a vast snake. The prophetess would go into the cave to hear the words of Gaia and Python.

planets around our sun). As an aside, it is an interesting magical question to ask what inner consciousness and qualities our planet mediates outwards as an influence. The influences are constantly moving, interacting and affecting each other and everything in their path, and that process affects us as individuals on an inner level, not only at our conception and birth, but throughout our lives.

Their influence adds to the bigger and more complex web of fate that everything flows through and is connected to. It is a mistake to think of fate and influences as fixed and immovable; there is rather a constantly evolving process of creative and destructive energies weaving themselves as influences into the pattern of time.

When we (everything that is living) are conceived and born, the moment of our birth is a key point where those planetary influences 'lock in' to our fate pattern, and the timing of that moment is a crucial element of that. That 'locking in' creates a unique pattern of influence that becomes a response mechanism for our fate and life. How we approach and deal with the various challenges and joys our life and fate throws at us is up to us, but the planetary influences are gifts we can choose to draw upon, or deficits we can choose to overcome. They are tools that are at our disposal as we navigate life and death. The web of fate is a deeper and more profound complex dynamic that weaves time with vast fate patterns, and it is a dynamic that functions in layers. One layer is the overall pattern for the planet, another is a layer that operates across landmasses and all the living beings that dwell on them, and other layers are individual to each living being. The influences of the planets 'soaks' into those layers and influences them.

What does all of this mean for the magician? The Weavers of Fate not only contribute to the overall life fate of the individual (hence the development of astrology) but their power also contributes to the various cycles of fate within the lifespan of the person (or creature). The various cycles within a person's life are a mixture of their own actions and choices, planetary influences, the overall pattern of time, and important junction points of different fates coming together and influencing each other. The planetary spirits are an influence on the qualities we will have at our disposal to deal with fate events in our lives, and how/when those fate events will trigger and unfold.

Whether we make use of these qualities, both good and difficult, depends on us and our choices, and especially how we choose to navigate the important junction points in our fate patterns. We are given 'tools' to use and develop through our lives, but we must take up those tools and use them.

Overall, this card indicates an ongoing fate pattern. It is up to the individual to decide how much they are going to engage with the fate pattern to harvest the most experience and resources from it. An ongoing fate pattern that is not engaged with is a wasted resource and a lost opportunity.

Knowing about the complexity of the weaves and patterns of fate, and the influences of the planets, helps us as magicians to look at the long-term patterns that are playing out not only in our own lives but in the fates of nations, events, and upon the land itself. This in turn informs our magic. If we know the dynamics playing out in a situation, from individual ones to the situations of nations and communities, then we can focus our magical work in a more informed way.

Divination

The message of this card is to use the potentials of the planetary spirits' influences to navigate your own story. Your fate pattern is a weave of power and influence, and the planetary spirits play a major part in how that pattern is constructed. Learning how to understand that influence and engage with it is the beginning of learning how fate works, and how you can work with fate as opposed to being at its mercy.

For magicians, this means being able to grasp the basics of astrology. Even a rudimentary understanding of the planets' influences in one's own chart is invaluable in magical practice. If you think of the dynamics that each planet brings to a chart, and then understand that each planet also has a planetary spirit that we are energetically connected to, and then reflect upon those dynamics in terms of your own personality and life, then you will begin to see how these powers can be engaged with.

When this card appears in a reading, pay close attention to where it has landed and what is around it. The place where it lands in a layout indicates where the anchor potentially is for the fate pattern you are currently living in. For example, if this card falls in the position of hearth, which is home/family/community, then, even if your question is a magical one, the current fate 'weather' you are experiencing is influenced by the dynamics of your home and/or community. If you then look at your fourth house in your astrological chart and see what is going on there, then it might give you a wider insight into your current question/situation.

If this card falls in a layout position of 'current fate pattern', the position and the card strengthen each other. This indicates that whatever your question is about, it is a very fateful situation or time. Decisions you make and actions you take at this time with regards to your question/situation can have long-reaching effects for you/the situation. Even if the situation you are reading about is a bad one, it is also a very fateful one, and is likely one of those situations where good things, regeneration, or even greatness can spring from a difficult period.

If the question is about a choice of action in life or magic and this card appears, then it indicates that the choice is an important one and that it is a time of catalysts, opportunities, and development. What you might presume is a small decision could end up changing your life, and if this card is well positioned in the layout, then that change will be good.

If the card lands in a negative or withheld position, then whatever the question is about, it is saying that this path holds no fate for you, and that if you carry on down this path, you are likely to be pushing against the natural flow of your fate and future. It is saying, 'this option is not for you'. If the question is about if something is going to happen and this card is in the negative/withheld position, then there is no power in event and it will likely not come to much in terms of long-term influence.

When the reading is about someone who is being magically attacked and this card falls in a withheld position, then the attack is being successful and it is blocking the person's future fate and also the helpful influence of the planets. However, if in the same situation the card is in a positive or future position, then whatever the attack is, the person has planetary spirits helping them, and they will not only survive the attack, but it will strengthen them.

In positive positions, this card shows help from the spirits, and the good energy that comes when you have clicked into the right path at the right time. In negative positions, the subject of the reading is fighting against a force that cannot be vanquished. It is like trying to turn a raging storm back with a puff of wind. In such cases, a change in approach or changing one's circumstances or intentions can be enough to release the block on the useful connections that flow from these powers.

When this card appears in the near or distant future positions then it tells of fate development, of an expansion of life, and a coming-together of forces to help you along your path. The influence of these planetary powers will flow around you in a helpful way.

In mundane readings it can also indicate any group of powerful people who hold the power to change lives, such as decision-making committees, helpful organizations, and governments.

KEYS

Helpful influence, gifts of fate, upholders of your fate, protection, fateful event, long term influence.

EXTRA

The following is an extract from *Al-Sirr al-Maktūm* (The Hidden Secret), written by the 12th century Muslim philosopher and theologian, Fakhr al-Dīn al-Rāzī'.[1] *Al-Sirr al-Maktūm* is a study of the Sabians of Hurran and their work with the planetary spirits.

> (...) as for the spirits which govern the celestial bodies (planets), then the most apparent is that the spheres for them are like the bodies, the planets are like the hearts, and the lines of rays which emanate from the bodies of the planets flow in the manner of subtle luminescent bodies which emanate from the heart and brain to reach the rest of the organs. Moreover, just as there is for each body one soul, from which emanates to every part of the body a power that governs it (...)

---

[1] Fakhr al-Dīn al-Rāzī' (1149-1209 CE). Born in Ray, Iran and died in Herat, Afghanistan, he was a polymath and prolific Muslim scholar who wrote on subjects including philosophy, theology, history, alchemy, natural sciences, astronomy, physics, and law.

11

The Sabians took idols for these heavenly bodies for every purpose that could be sought such as love, hate, sickness, health, ill-fortune and good- luck. And they turned themselves in their worship and they occupied their eyes with gazing at those statues; their tongues with the recitation of incantations which comprised mention of their attributes and influence until the forms reached their souls twice; for a man cannot describe something with his tongue unless its meaning occurs to his mind; then when he expresses it with his tongue, that sound reaches his ear and the soul understands the meaning of that speech, so he perceives that object of description once more. So the remembrance of the tongue is preserved by two conceptualizations. One prior and one posterior. And so when it occurs that the senses are drawn in a concerted way to the spirits of those heavenly bodies, the soul becomes connected with them and the soul, when it perseveres in these acts, reaches a level close in rank to that soul innately disposed towards this special occult power.[1]

4 HARVESTER

MEANING

This is a complex card with many magical layers. It is the power that people fear the most, and yet it can be a major friend and protector of the magician if they understand it and learn to work with it.

The Harvester is a power that brings things to conclusions and 'harvests the crop': be that crop a life, a cycle of fate, learning, or time, or the end of something that is causing restriction and degeneration. It is a natural power that is a part of the cycle of creation and destruction, and creation cannot sprout and grow if the deadwood has not been cut away.

As magicians, the onus is on us to spot where overgrowth or degeneration is happening in our lives and for us to instigate the cutting away for ourselves. If we do not and we cling to something or refuse to end something that it is truly necessary for us to let go of, then the harvester power will start to push in on our lives and work. First comes the unravelling power, and if we do not spot that and act

---

[1] Noble, 2020: 192.

upon it, then we will be unravelled enough to make us wide open to the harvesting power which will then cut away whatever we have clung to.

The Harvester is a power of major change, and when we do not recognize it making an appearance in our lives, then it can start to trigger series of disasters, failures and blockages. These are outer manifestations of a deeper festering within that needs to break free and compost. Once we recognize it and start to let go of what we are clinging to (jobs, homes, relationships, magical paths, identities, belongings, wealth, etc.) then the fate cycles can come to a natural healthy conclusion so that new ones can start to form. If we resist change or refuse to let go, then at its worst, the blade of the Harvester will cut everything away.

It is a power of death in its most obvious form, but we suffer many smaller deaths in life before our bodies are finally harvested. And if we engage with those smaller deaths and let things go, then we find a new strength that flows to us as a direct result of facing change. The process of this power is put wonderfully in this quote:

> Once the storm is over you won't remember how you made it through, how you managed to survive. You won't even be sure, in fact, whether the storm is really over. But one thing is certain. When you come out of the storm you won't be the same person who walked in. That's what this storm's all about..

> —Haruki Murakami, *Kafka on the Shore*[1]

The Harvester rules over death, fate, time, and liberation. It is also a power of awakening. We awaken to our reality out of a slumber of fantasy. If we can face that reality without looking away, no matter how terrifying it is, then we will learn the beauty of this power. It is the one power above all others that can bring us to *know ourselves*. This involves a constant series of awakenings in our lives, and is a process that is critical to the adept magician. If you do not know even parts of yourself in truth, then you cannot truly know magic or operate successfully within it.

The final layer of this power is bloodlust. When something has become so very rotten that it has no chance of regeneration, then the Harvester sets to work destroying. But there is an element of this destruction that can tip beyond balance and can destroy everything and everyone in its path. This is a power dynamic that was well understood in the ancient world and is illustrated in the story of The Heavenly Cow from New Kingdom Egypt, where Sekhmet rampages across the land killing everything in her path.

This out-of-control power is also illustrated in the story of Kali,[2] the Hindu goddess who is the personification of the rage of the goddess Durga. While battling demons, Durga was pushed to her limits and the goddess Kali emerged from within

---

[1] Murakami, 2006.

[2] *The Devi Mahatmyam*: Sanskrit, 5ᵗʰ century A.D.: a Hindu philosophical text that forms part of the *Markandeya Purana* texts.

her. Kali slayed the demons but in her rage she could not stop killing. It is that moment in the story, the emergence of that power, that this card illustrates.

Hence the illustration of this card is closely aligned with the imagery of the goddess Kali: the dark face (Kali means dark, and also time) and the lolling tongue.

Divination

When this card appears it is talking about an end that is coming or needs to happen, unless it is in a withheld or past position in the layout. The change or ending that this card heralds is often a major life change in one form or another, or it can indicate the death of a belief or magical practice that is now holding you back. It is not a card of little changes and adjustments. Once the change or death has happened, there is no going back. The change this card heralds is permanent change or loss. How this card is read depends upon the question and the layout.

Because it is such a major change in fate, the timing of this process can be difficult to pin down in a reading. Because it is such a major event, it can show up in readings a couple of years or more before the actual events start to unfold. The more fateful the event is for the subject of the reading, the earlier it will become fixed in their fate and thus start to show in readings. This can be terrifying, but it is also good as it often (not always) gives the magician advanced warning so that they can prepare and engage with the power of letting things go before fate does it for them. If you engage with that power in advance, so that some of the heavy work of letting go has already been done, then when the actual event or process hits it will be much easier to navigate it and survive intact.

If the card appears in a reading about health and indicates a possible physical death, then the magician can ascertain through readings if the death has already set in the fate pattern and is immovable, or if it can be avoided by changing something. There are times when our fate lines run close to a death pattern, and if we do not change our course, behaviour, or intentions, then we are likely to risk actual death. Most people will not see that coming and death will take them unless some basic intuition kicks in to trigger change and avoidance. However, we magicians have divination. We can see a death pattern coming and sidestep it by changing something that in turn steers our fate away from it. The change could be as simple as deciding not to go somewhere, or as obvious as stopping a certain behaviour that is walking us quietly into death. It can be a prompt to get medical help, or to not drive on a certain freeway on a certain day.

Lastly, this card can indicate a loss of control and a rage that will destroy everything in its path. Instead of heralding death or an end, this card then indicates that the subject of the reading could *become the destroyer*. If this card appears in a reading about an issue where loss of control is a possibility, such as in a magical working that involves handling a lot of power, then it could be warning that the power levels could get out of control and trigger the destruction of everything in the path of the magical pattern or the magician themselves. Such a loss of control is akin to bloodlust, where the warrior cannot stop killing as their mind rages in a storm of destruction.

Using focused questions and choosing the layout carefully will assist in pinning down this difficult card to get its meaning for a specific reading in a clear and understandable way.

KEYS

Death, change, liberation, closing, limited time, letting go, end of a fate cycle, loss of control that destroys.

II. The Magical Path

5 AWAKENING

MEANING

There is a point within life and death that a person awakens and becomes aware of their deeper self. In life it is the moment that a person realizes that their mundane life is as sleeping. A person can sleepwalk their way through a mundane life and never awaken to the Mysteries around them. The awakening can come in a fleeting moment and be dramatic, or it can be a slow, steady awakening to the inner worlds around them.

It is not an awakening of intellect, or accumulated knowledge, or the subconscious; rather it is a sudden glimpse of something indescribable that awakens the sleeping soul within us. We can spend the rest of our lives searching for a way to return to that experience. Some stumble across a path that their soul recognizes as taking them to full awakening. Such a path can lead us through different spiritual, magical or mystical 'forests', and in each one we gain another fragment of the mysteries, until we find our own true and unique individual path.

> And it is He who placed the stars for you, so that by them you will
> guide yourself across the darkness of the earth and the sea.[1]

Although the above quote is from a set religious path, it hides a deeper truth for a magical or mystical traveller. Once you awaken, then inner and outer life will guide you if you pay attention.

There is no 'one path' or 'one training' in magic: there is only the path of the individual, and no two paths are the same. We start out on the magical path for a variety of reasons, and we may learn skills and techniques, but we remain trapped in the darkness of the mundane until one day we yearn for more. Not more skills, or power, or prestige, but for something that we cannot name or identify. That is

---

[1] *Quran* Surah *Al-An'am*. 6:97

the moment we start walking towards our own personal awakening.

Then one day we have an experience (or series of experiences) that shows us that there is far more around us than what we can see with our eyes. There is an unknowable 'something' that we reach for, that drives us, and our spirit recognises it even if our intellect does not. That something is not found in magical training, but the magical training of any decent system, or our own wanderings, experiments and practice, can move us closer to that doorway that only ourselves as individuals can step through. We have discussions, revelations, dreams, a breath that flows into our hearts and awakens it. We become surrounded by signs that speak to us, and we begin to see the inner brightness that flows out of everything.

The Awakening card shows our step forward into the realization of the inner worlds, and of the consciousness that flows through every living thing. We take our place within that flow and actively work with it. That is magic.

Divination

At its highest level, this card speaks of awakening, emergence, and becoming aware of the true depths of the Mysteries. But as a divination card it has various levels of meaning, all of which speak to an awakening of some kind. It can be an awakening to misunderstanding: perhaps realizing you are being 'glamoured' by something that seems great and wonderful on the surface but which is empty or rotten beneath. It can be an awakening to the lies and misdirections that we inflict upon ourselves, or it can be an awakening out of a period of stasis, lack of energy, or 'incubation'.

Magical incubation is a period in our magical lives where everything seems to shut down and nothing works, or we are blocked from working magically in one way or another. It can be a short period or it can be a long one that can last a couple of years or more. While we feel magically useless and trapped during that time, it is nevertheless often a time where immersion in the mundane is necessary to support deep changes and developments happening within us at a magical level. It is a time of transformation.

And that is the key of the Awakening card at its depth. When we awaken, whatever we are awakening from, we are changed at a deep level. We emerge stronger, wiser, and more aware of the myriad of powers around us that pass unseen to most eyes.

If this card appears in an otherwise difficult reading, then it either points to an awakening that emerges out of a struggle you are going through, or it indicates an emergence and awakening that shakes your worldview to such an extent that you feel you are no longer stood on solid ground.

If this card falls in a withheld position, it points to 'being asleep', not seeing what needs to be seen, not being present, or wallowing in the dark.

If this card falls as the outcome card in a reading about what you need to do, or what action needs to be taken, and the cards around it are negative or difficult, then it can indicate the need to wake up and see beyond the surface presentation of something, or to look more carefully at what is being planned. However, if the question is about what is coming, or whether something will work, and this card falls in the outcome or near future position, then it points to you being on the cusp of a new awakening, of energy coming back in, or of seeing things properly for the first time.

The Awakening card can also represent a literal awakening. It can indicate that something is waking up and becoming active, be it a person, a mountain volcano, etc. It can also indicate a birth. Where fate creation shows us conception, awakening shows us the baby emerging out of the darkness of the womb and blinking in the light.

When the reading is about magical tools, statues etc., then the Awakening card indicates the point where the vessel has been made, cleansed, and consecrated, and the inner gates within it have started to open. It has come into its own: it is awake and no longer a tool, but a being in its own right. As such it must be treated with the respect and care afforded to all living beings, physical or non-physical. It is no longer something that you just use or direct with or to your will; it is a consciousness that has its own will, its own fate pattern. The magician must learn to work cooperatively in partnership and respect with this power within a vessel.

If you are looking at something in a reading and this card falls in a withheld or past position, then it would indicate that the subject of your reading has not awakened. In any other position of the layout it indicates that the subject of the reading is indeed awake in some form.

If the reading is about looking to see if someone is alive or dead, such as a missing person, and this card appears, then it indicates that they are alive (unless the card lands in the withheld, past, or inner worlds positions).

KEYS

Waking up, emerging, alive, conscious, revelation, awakening to power, facing the truth.

EXTRA

The inspiration for the painting of this card came from a scene in the Egyptian funerary text, *The Book of Gates*.[1] This little known esoteric funerary text is slowly becoming more widely known in magical circles. The scene is from the ninth hour, and is a scene in the Duat Underworld where the souls of the dead are floating, swimming, sinking, or emerging from a deep, dark water. The Barque of Re passes through the darkness and the bright solar light of Re falls upon those who are in the water, waking them up and encouraging them to move, to swim, to follow. Like a lot of things in *The Book of Gates*, this has multiple layers of meaning, and relates

---

[1] For a translation of this text with magical commentary, see McCarthy, Sheppard, and Littlejohn, 2022.

not only to the dead but also to the living. What we see as the process of the soul of the dead person navigating the Underworld is the same process we also navigate in life. And the deepest mystery is that the navigation in life and death are both happening at once. As we awaken in life we also awaken in the Duat, and *vice versa*.

Here is the text from scene 58, middle register, 9th hour:

> Swimmers in the Nu
>
> Says to them Re:
>
> A coming forth for your heads those who are diving, plying for your arms those who are slack, swiftness for your hurrying those who are golden swimmers, breath for your noses those who are expanded.
>
> A coming into power for you through your water; be you at peace in your cold refreshment. Your setting out is of the Nu; your strides are of a stream.
>
> Your presences, which are on earth they are at peace, meaning they breathe, there is no destruction for them.
>
> Their extension is the peace of the earth.
>
> Now, putting forth what is theirs on earth means coming into power of one's peace on earth.

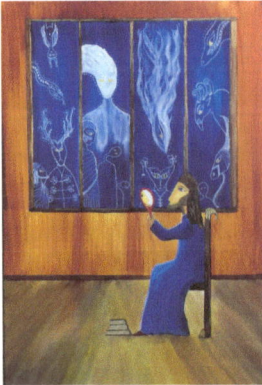

6 Student

Meaning

The gaze of the student into the mirror is not one of ego or narcissism, it is one of learning. He is examining himself in truth, without hiding anything from himself. It is only through recognising and accepting ourselves that we can begin to emerge upon a magical path of power and evolution.

The empty room is his lack of experience, and the books at his feet are his only reference point at this time. The beings wait patiently, unseen, waiting for the student to first see himself, and then to see the beings who are an integral part of magic, and who are beyond the student's material world.

When we first venture out into magic through reading books, listening to teachers, and starting our own tentative experiments in magical practice, we are often unaware of ourselves as we truly are. Psychological counselling can help open that door, but it still relies on another person or process to facilitate the awakening of self. In magic it is vitally important that we open that door and walk through that process for ourselves through direct experience and self-reflection as much as we can. It is a process that is lifelong. We never really reach the bottom of learning about ourselves in truth.

But once we have triggered that process ourselves and we begin to see our own bullshit and how we lie to ourselves, then we start to see ourselves in glimpses. And once our eyes are open to the glimpses of self, they also become opened to the glimpsing of beings and worlds that are not physical, and that are not of ourselves. We start to see and experience the non-physical universe that is all around us, along with the many different types of beings that inhabit it. Some inner beings, like us, also have bodies that are the anchor of their inner existence in the physical world, but many do not.

A person becomes a true magical student not when they start studying or training, but only when they start to open their awareness of self and beyond. That can come through an experience within themselves, or by experiencing something outside of themselves that confirms to them that there is more to the world than what they can see and touch. Some in magical training never reach that potential. They become locked in orthodoxies, rules, rituals, identities, hierarchies, glamours, and ego-boosting acts of control. But for others the path triggers the mirror process at a deep level, particularly if the training is actual magical training and not just learning a system. They start to question themselves and find they can no longer hide from themselves or others.

Through that process the student magician learns that it is not the path system that teaches them, but rather their own experiences and subsequent evolution of understanding. Thus they slowly become liberated from the orthodoxy and are no longer bound to it. They choose whether to stay within the training with a new understanding and freedom, or to walk away to forge their own path through action and experience. Either is valid: both work.

The more the student starts to connect with the unseeable, the inner, and the many beings that flow around them, and the more the student engages in magical work that benefits everything around them, the more the student changes and evolves. And the more the student changes and evolves, the more the magician effects changes and evolution around them not by intention but by nature of their presence. This is wonderfully highlighted in the teachings of the Kasdānian Sabians:

> Therefore do not deny that some souls have this power such that they act on bodies other than their own and that such bodies react to these souls as the bodies of these souls do.[1]

In truth in magic, the magical student is always a student, always learning and

---

[1] Forget, 1892.

21

developing: it is a process that never ends. That is not to say that a magical student must spend a lifetime in training and in subservience to a teacher. That is not learning: that is arresting one's development. Rather, once the student has learned the skills that they need, it is their own practice and where it takes them which teaches them through direct experience, and that is a lifetime of work.

Divination

When this card appears in a reading it either points out a dynamic in your life or magical work that will teach you something important, or it gives you a caution: "your skill set is not yet strong enough or deep enough to take something on fully: either rethink your intentions, or proceed with caution". Knowing your own limits is a major part of knowing yourself, which is a cornerstone skill in magic.

If your question is about whether you should do something, and the Student card appears in an action position, then it is telling you to tread with caution and be aware of your limitations, since you do not yet have a full understanding of the situation for the magic that you are planning. If the card falls in a warning position, then it is saying that you do not have the understanding and skill to do what you intend to do, and you are likely to arrest your own development though thoughtless action if you proceed.

If the card appears in a withheld position then it signifies that you will not gain anything or learn anything. (In this position in a mundane reading, it may simply mean that you will not be a student or accepted as a student somewhere.)

If the card is in an outcome position, whatever the question is, then it is pointing to you learning and evolving through a situation or action. Where you may feel that you are skilled and not a student, the appearance of this card as an outcome says that you will learn a great deal and realize what it is that you did not know you didn't know. Even for experienced magical adepts, the learning process never stops! The card in this position can also point to learning a new skill though your actions, a skill that you didn't intend to learn, but learning it will add greatly to your collection of skills.

Often, walking a magical path through life teaches us not only magic, but also introduces us to all sorts of different opportunities to learn skills, be they arts, music, study, languages, history, or practical skills. A magical life is one that is full of learning new skills, many of which are not directly magical at all but that add to our magical lives. And when this card appears in a reading, it most often indicates learning something new.

In mundane readings this card represents someone who is unskilled or who is learning skills. It can also represent a student, a young person, or a person who is immature. If the card falls in a past or withheld position then it indicates either that a learning phase has passed, or that learning cannot be gained from whatever you are looking at in the reading. It is a sign to move on from something.

If the reading is about a place, then it can indicate that the building or land is young, is going through the early stages of development, or is not complete. It is a card of starting points and early evolution, of youth, and also of innocence.

Keys

Learning, still developing, immature, innocence, youth, unfinished, new skill, training, in process.

Extra

The following is an excerpt of the Abstract of a dissertation by Myungjoon Lee, that looks at the ancient and classical Greek system of education and society. What is true for education and learning in society is also true for learning and education in magic. The founding principles of learning, and how that learning affects the society of the individual and collective, both apply not only in general education and nations, but also in any focused learning and community. Reading it in the context of magical learning, and of today's magical communities, highlights these deeper principles.

> Plato regards education as a means to achieve justice, both individual justice and social justice. According to Plato, individual justice can be obtained when each individual develops his or her ability to the fullest. In this sense, justice means excellence.

> For the Greeks and Plato, excellence is virtue (being just). According to Socrates, virtue is knowledge. Thus, knowledge is required to be just. From this Plato concludes that virtue can be obtained through three stages of development of knowledge: knowledge of one's own job, self-knowledge, and knowledge of the Idea of the Good.

> According to Plato, social justice can be achieved when all social classes in a society, workers, warriors, and rulers are in a harmonious relationship. Plato believes that all people can easily exist in harmony when society gives them equal educational opportunity from an early age to compete fairly with each other. Without equal educational opportunity, an unjust society appears since the political system is run by unqualified people; timocracy, oligarchy, defective democracy, or tyranny will result.[1]

---

[1] Myungjoon Lee, 1994.

7 Path

Forget not the Path that leads to Truth

Meaning

A traveller on the Path pauses and looks at the narrowing steps before them. The steps rise steeply above the traveller, and beyond the steps is a bright opening of sunlight. There is a hint that the path continues, maybe around a corner, but where the path leads cannot be seen. Above the steps is a cave roof with overgrown vines, giving the impression that the traveller is emerging out of a cave as the path goes from semi-shade to brightness. The land on either side of the steps is barren rock formations and in places near the opening, old tree roots.

The traveller has flowers behind them and where they have just trodden, greenery appears. Life flourishes in their footsteps. In their left hand is a staff with a forked end, and around the staff is a snake that has wound itself around and around, its small head almost level with the traveller's. They are companions and fellow travellers on this journey.

The walker does not see the flowers that bloom in their footsteps as they are focused on moving forward. The walker cannot see beyond the top of the steps, but there is a hint of something beyond.

The Path, in magic, is the point when the aspiring magician steps onto what will likely be a lifetime of magical life and learning. This can come in different ways to different people. For some it is a calling or a sense of coming home: often such people will have been quite young when they first realized that there was something more to life, and they will have searched tirelessly until fate finally put them in a place, or the presence of a person, where their magical life starts to open up. For others, the magical life begins as an interest that they read around, and they find themselves drawn to the fashion, the alternative community, and the ideas through books and discussion. For some of these people, eventually the dabbling and reading is not enough: they need to *know* and *be*. That is the point where the Path begins to open up.

So what is it? The Path is a way of living magically, of learning magically, and of the evolution of the soul. That can immediately trigger ideas of aesthetic religious life in some people, and they envisage a life of dressing and acting in a certain way: this is not what the Path is about. Living a magical life and treading the magical

Path is where, through magical acts and learning, a person's mind, soul, and body become tools for learning the Mysteries. The person begins to realise that there is far more around them than can be seen by the eye, and as they interact with these unseen powers, it facilitates change within the person.

That change is a constant process throughout the life of the magician, where their weaknesses are challenged and their strengths are put to work. Fate speeds up for such a person, and they are confronted by situations and powers that expose to them their stupidity, ignorance, greed and cowardice. This is a process of coming to know oneself and coming to know that these weaknesses are in everyone. It is not about morality or being bad or good, but about being confronted with what is 'bad' for you and what is good for you as an individual.

One very interesting dynamic of the magical Path is that it also teaches us that we are not separate units (nor is any being). As we work with inner spirits, being around them and connecting with them brings change to us—and also to them. And as we develop as magicians and evolve as people, we start to effect change around us simply by showing up and being present. This is something that was understood from early ancient times in Sabian and Egyptian cultures and was the mark of a *Magi*. The nature of the elder magician triggers change by their presence. They don't *do* magic, they *are* magic.

DIVINATION

The Path appears in readings for several reasons. One is that it can be indicating the path ahead of you, the path you are currently walking on in terms of fate, events, etc. And with that it is linked to the fate cycle or pattern you are currently moving through.

If you are questioning in a reading whether you are on the right track, and this card appears in an answer position, or in a near future or a present position, the answer is *yes*. Regardless of what is going on around you and whatever challenges you face, you are on the right path for what your need to achieve, even if it doesn't currently look like it. Where this card lands in the layout can indicate where the focus needs to be or where the next step of the Path can be found.

In both magical and mundane readings, the Path is a card of action, of doing, of developing, learning, serving, moving forward and of being challenged. It can be a hint that you need to get moving, get serious, and get on with something.

If the card falls in a distant past position then it indicates that a path (be it magical, or a job, etc.) or *choice* of path has now gone and will not return. If it falls in a near past position, then that path is drifting into the past and while it can still present itself in the situation, its power has gone, and it is best to let it go.

If it falls in a withheld position, depending on the question it can either indicate that this is not the path for you at this time, or that in your current situation there is no way forward for you, so you need to rethink your options and potentially change direction or approach.

Overall, in both mundane and magical readings, this is a good card that indicates a fateful moving forward and good development. Where it lands in a layout can highlight where the current strength of your path lies.

Keys

Important fate path, trust, yes, correct, way ahead, action, move forward.

Extra

The following is a short extract from *The Golden Ass* (*Metamorphoses*, 11:20-23) by Lucius Apuleius (124–170 CE). *The Golden Ass* is a tale of magic, transformation, idiocy and of coming to know oneself, all of which are features of the Path. It is a tale which ends in acceptance into the Greater Mysteries.

> I shall speak only of what can be revealed to the minds of the uninitiated without need for subsequent atonement, things which though you have heard them, you may well not understand. So listen, and believe in what is true. I reached the very gates of death and, treading Proserpine's threshold, yet passed through all the elements and returned. I have seen the sun at midnight shining brightly. I have entered the presence of the gods below and the presence of the gods above, and I have paid due reverence before them.[1]

8 Daimon

Meaning

The word *daimon* comes from Greek[2] and means an attending spirit, guarding spirit, or the provider or divider of destiny.[3] In the Christianised culture of the west, the understanding of these beings has morphed from being spirits to 'angels' and they are worked with in magic as the 'Holy Guardian Angel'.

However, these beings are not angelic, and

---

[1] Kline, 2013.
[2] δαίμων.
[3] Cresswell, 2014: 146.

they are often deeply misunderstood in magic. The Greeks and Egyptians had a much better understanding of these beings in that *personal daimon* was a job description, not a type of being. There are many different types of beings that can become one's personal daimon: land spirits, ancestral spirits, deities, angelic beings, inner contacts[1]...For example, to the Greeks, some ancient heroes could become personal daimons, along with localised nature powers.

The misunderstanding of the nature of personal daimons as personal guardian angels is something we can trace back to Honorius Augustodunesis,[2] a 12th century theologian who was a prolific writer and whose writing style appealed to the everyday person. While the idea that angels could intervene on behalf of a human to help them or save them traces back to the Septuagint,[3] none of the Biblical references point to a single guardian angel assigned to an individual person. But the 12th century writing of Augustodunesis specifically indicates the angelic human assignment for the first time. Later the concept of the guardian angel seeped into magical grimoires and eventually morphed into the Holy Guardian Angel.

The Daimon is a being that is with you from birth until death and the early stages beyond death. Learning to communicate to some extent with that being is an important endeavour. When a magician starts to work in depth in magic there comes a point where the magician becomes aware of the spirit that guards them, and learns to recognise when that being is active, is drawing close, or is trying to communicate a warning or advice. And we must learn how to listen, to recognise, and to understand.

There is never a true conversation as such between the magician and the Daimon: it is more like the magician communicates, and the Daimon responds through dreams, inner senses, visions, and inner knowing. Communication can also appear through external signs and hints. The Daimon also 'nudges' you gently, sometimes physically, when you need to do something or get out of the way of something that could seriously harm you. But that only happens when it is a situation that your fate does not depend upon. Sometimes we have to go through difficult or painful situations in order to learn, grow and change fate directions.

But because a 'conversation with the Holy Guardian Angel' became such a thing in magic, it has set people up for inner contact with a parasitical being who will very willingly take on that appearance and role, and feed the person whatever they want to hear, and it will happily get into inner and visionary conversations with the magician. That way it can feed off the magician.

The reason for lack of true communication, such as the sorts of conversations adepts have with inner contacts, is that it deeply interferes with the actual work

---

[1] The spirit of an evolved now dead human, known as a saint in Christianity, and an Akh in Dynastic Egypt.

[2] Honorius Augustodunesis or Honorius of Atun (1080-1140) student of Aslem of Canterbury, who towards the end of his life was a monk at the Benedictine Abbey of St James in Regensburg, Bavaria, Germany.

[3] The Greek Old Testament approx. 250-132 BCE, translated from Hebrew for the Egyptian Jewish community.

and function of the Daimon. They are not teachers, parents, or friends to the lonely. They have a specific function and are best left to get on with it. Their main function is to witness, and they intervene or connect when necessary, in fateful or dangerous circumstances. They also draw close when a person has reached their limit of endurance or is defeated. They witness and wait. If the person tries to pick themselves back up again then the Daimon will intervene if needed to open doors, give you a push, or to let you know you are not alone.

You will know the measure of the magician by the Daimon that keeps them.

DIVINATION

The appearance of this card in a reading can herald a few different things at the same time. It points to the active drawing close of this being, which in turn can mean that an important part of a person's fate is about to unfold.

Most people have a fairly tame fate with two or three major events in their lifetimes, but some have strong and active fate patterns where there are quite a few major fateful events. And for magicians who delve seriously into magic in practice (not just study and dabbling) their fate can become condensed with a lot of powerful and important fateful events. It is sometimes like a series of life-lessons are being compressed into one life.

When one of those fate events or changes in your path is about to trigger, the Daimon draws close to work with you as you navigate your way through the events. And when this card turns up in a reading, it can point to one of these important times. It does not mean that each event is difficult: sometimes it can be wonderful things that happen. However, how the magician navigates their way through these events has a deep bearing upon the evolution of their soul. Hence the Daimon becomes active. The Daimon is ultimately more focused on your soul than they are on your mundane life.

So when this card appears in a reading, regardless of what is going on for you and be it good or bad, it indicates that how you deal with challenges or abundance that has come or is coming your way will have a direct influence on your future fate and also your deep soul. Tread carefully with balance and truth and look carefully at what is happening, as there is something deeply important about the choices and actions you make at this time.

The Daimon not only guides but guards when necessary. As such, this card is linked to the card 'Defence', which illustrates the Personal Daimon around the magician. If the reading is about a difficult situation and this card appears, then it suggests that there is some danger for you, but the Daimon has your back. So long as you do what is right and true, while also taking responsibility for yourself, this being will protect and uphold you. If you act with stupidity and aggression, then the Daimon will step back and let you take the blows.

The position this card lands in can tell you where the Daimon is active in your life. This can also tell you where any potential difficulty is coming from, but it is a difficulty that you most likely need to go through for your own development. The Daimon tries to steer you away from unnecessary difficulty, but will stand beside you when the difficulty is something you need to go through.

If this card falls in a difficult position in a layout, then it can indicate that the subject of the reading has strayed badly from their path of evolution and the Daimon has withdrawn to take a passive 'witness' position in your fate position. This is explained more in the card 'Defeat'. However, the Daimon can also take a passive witness stance if you are in a very difficult situation that you need to get yourself out of, and the effort it takes to get out of it is a major learning or strengthening process for you. This can be strongly indicated if both the Daimon card and the Defeat card come up in the same reading.

But for the most part wherever this card appears in a reading layout, the Daimon card is telling you that you are truly not alone and that the Daimon walks silently beside you.

In terms of readings and interpretation, it is worth noting that nations have a Daimon, as do long term focused communities. Monastic orders (of any religion) that are fully formed and stable, monarchies, magical systems and lodges that are properly formed and stable, all of these over time and stability form fate paths that in turn attract and open the door for a Daimon.

The same can also be said of consecrated buildings like churches, temples, etc. It does not happen with all of them, but I have stumbled across such guardian Daimons that are personal to the fate pattern of a place, a building, or a long-term group. I have also found that there are many such places and groups that do not have a personal Daimon, and I have not as yet figured out why some have them and some do not. If your reading is about the fate of a building, place, group or nation and the Daimon card is in a withheld position, then it is likely such does not have a Daimon.

KEYS

Tread carefully, pay attention, you are not alone, witness, guide, fateful, yes, choose wisely and honestly.

EXTRA

Porphyry relates that an Egyptian priest invited (or challenged) Plotinus to come to the Iseion, a temple devoted to Isis in Rome, and for Plotinus to succeed in making his daimon appear. The priest insisted that the ritual was done at the Iseion, as it was 'the only clean place in Rome'.

When the daimon was summoned to appear, a deity came and not a being of the daimon order. The Egyptian priest said, "Blessed are you, who have a god for your daimon and not a companion of the subordinate order."[1]

---

[1] Porphyry (234-305AD) *Life of Plotinus*.

9 Purification

To make sacred

Meaning

Ritually purifying is a magical 'step up' from cleansing a space. Cleansing a space briefly drives out minor infestations of parasitic and other unwanted beings by nature of smell through smudging or incense. Ritual purification strips a space or object of all accumulated degenerating energy, parasitic or any other type of being that is unhealthy for the space, fragmenting magical patterns, magical attacks, and any destructive energy that has come into a space. It not only purifies a space, it also tunes a space in a simple way which then makes it far easier to do a stronger ritual tuning. It is for this reason that ritual purification was used in temples in the ancient world, and that ancient ritual action was adopted and adapted within some strands of Christianity, and especially Catholicism.

The reason it works far more strongly than cleansing is the nature of what is used and how it is used. Where cleansing uses scent, smoke and salt, ritual purification uses the elements of earth, water and utterance in a very specific way. The earth (salt) and water are first themselves ritually stripped of all imbalance and impurity, and then they are consecrated, which is to say the Divine within all substance is awakened within those substances: they are made sacred. Whatever that mixture touches, is therefore touched by a substance that is Divinely active.

That Divinely-awakened mix is then sprinkled around every part of the space while ritual utterances, using Divine names, exorcize any beings in the space that should not be there. It also removes, by way of the utterance, decaying energies, and any unwanted or aggressively sent magical patterns such as attacks. Some purification rituals will have a ritual element that not only drives out all of these things from the space, but also directs where they should go. This is an important part of purification. If you simply tell everything to leave, then it just steps out of the area you are cleaning and waits for you to finish before coming straight back in again. To be magically effective, you must also send them somewhere whence they will not return easily.

The religion of the magician is irrelevant, as is the religious structure of the purification. There is a big difference between the recognition of the unknowable Divine power, and a religion that is basically a man-made power structure. If the ritual is an old embedded one, it will work regardless. Why? A properly constructed magical and sacred (Divine power enlivened within it) ritual will run on 'autopilot' if that is the intention embedded within it.

So anyone regardless of their knowledge or ability, or lack of, can switch it on and make it work. So long as the Divine element is balanced and properly recognised in the construction, it will awaken within the ritual. This is why a magician who recognises the Universal Divine power within everything can operate within all religions and none. The religion is just a vocabulary and man-made structure that the power can flow through. That means, for the magician, being able to step away from the concept of the Divine as a man with long white hair and a beard, wearing a white frock and sandals, sitting on a throne (a throwback to Zeus) and stepping towards an understanding that the Divine is a power and intelligence that flows through everything and which we cannot really truly understand, but only experience.

The other thing to think about with this concept of making sacred as a way of purifying is that anything can be made sacred or have the Divine within it awakened. When we do purification rituals, we 'deep clean' the space. Only the elements that we use (earth salt and water) are awakened with Divine consecration. It is those awakened substances that clean and rebalance whatever they touch. You can consecrate a space, but it then becomes a vessel for Divine power and must be treated very carefully on a regular basis. It becomes a place that is outside the mundane and will remain that way unless it is then stripped of its consecration, which is much harder to do. However, what magicians can do is to construct and consecrate an inner space that is then 'seated' within a mundane space. That consecrated inner energetic space can then be 'rolled up' and moved, to be inserted into another mundane space. This enables the easier movement of a magical working space. However, to use an inner space such as this means that the mundane physical space must be kept ritually purified, as it contains a Divine construction.

DIVINATION

When this card appears, its message depends very much on what the reading is about, what layout you use, and where it falls in that layout. For instance, if your question is about a magical working or project, then it says that you should first purify yourself and/or the space where you will be working. If you are setting up a magical working space and this card appears, then it could mean simply to purify the space first, or it could indicate the need either to actually consecrate it, or alternatively to construct an inner working space that is consecrated and that will then be seated in the physical space. That can be deduced from further readings with a simple layout.

Staying with a question reading about a places or spaces, if this card falls in a difficult position, then it could indicate that there is something in the space, be it an object, image, statue, magical tool etc, or bit of furniture that is potentially seriously unbalanced, and that purifying the space or working living in that space will not be wholly successful until whatever it is that is unbalanced has been dealt with. For instance, if a statue has been previously tuned and holds a being that with an unbalanced destructive power, then purifying it will only take the dirt and any parasites off it: it will not rid it of its destructive element. To get rid of the issue, whatever object that is causing the problem either needs to be destroyed or removed. Such an object can be identified using short yes/no readings where each suspected object is checked to see if it is a major problem. Often when doing such readings not only do you identify the offending object, but you also find that some other objects around the space are a potential issue as well. Sometimes moving or stripping them magically is enough. Sometimes they just have to go. A magical space in general should be clean, balanced, and only have objects in it that are a part of the functioning magical pattern.

If the card falls in a position that indicates your home space, then it is saying that the space is degenerating energetically and needs purifying. If the card falls in the position of the indicator ground zero and the reading is about you, then it is saying you need to take a ritual bath and get cleaned up. We all collect energetic dirt, parasites, etc. just by walking around in the mundane world: that is normal. This card falling on the ground zero indicator position can also indicate the need to ritually clean if you have been magically attacked.

A ritual purification done properly and regularly will strip off any magical attack pattern that is aimed at an individual person. Hence it is pointless spending tons of energy defending or deflecting magical attacks. Simply wipe it off once it comes in and then get on with your life. Each time it comes in, wipe it off. It takes little energy to do such ritual purifications, but the magicians who are throwing the shit at you will be using up a lot of energy. Let them exhaust themselves and then have to live with the realization that they failed miserably. There is no greater punishment for a person than to realize they are truly ineffective and powerless.

This card can also indicate a sacred space that is being regularly upkept. There are sacred spaces that have fallen into disuse and are dormant but still sacred, just as there are natural sacred spaces (see Sacred Space card). But then there are also sacred spaces that are kept ritually clean and active. This can be handy information to have if you are working as an exorcist or are looking for a place of sacred sanctuary that is active, a place where you can rest and gather your energy and thoughts.

On a mundane level, the appearance of this card can indicate the need to clean up, whether that is cleaning your home, cleaning yourself up, or cleaning up how you eat, sleep, work etc. Such warnings come in when the general energy tides that flow around us are getting dirty, unhealthy, or stagnant, and while we may not need ritual cleaning, a physical clean up can make a big difference and get healthier energy flowing around us.

KEYS

Ritual cleansing, purify, consecrate, bathe, tidy up, clean space, make sacred.

10 Dreams

Meaning

Our dreams have many functions, some of which are to 'sort out our filing cabinet' of daily experiences and for the brain to go through a series of clearing, sorting, and rebooting processes. The dream-state is also where our subconscious rises to process deeply embedded experiences. The most important function for a magician, in terms of dreams, is the bridge that they give us into the inner realms. This allows for communication, magical insight, and also warnings from inner beings. It is also a state whereby our consciousness takes a back seat which gives our own inner 'seeing' capacity to work through our imagination. Our ability to see into the future can surface in the form of prophetic dreams. The more visionary magical work the magician does and the more skilled in this aspect of magic they become, the more the dreamscape is able to not only do necessary simple processing, but also to become an inner extension of our spirit. A visionary magician is far more likely to have prophetic dreams, warning dreams, and learning dreams where dormant patterns of magical patterns and skills can come alive.

Over the last hundred years or so it has become fashionable to force lucid dreaming and magical dreaming in order to gain certain experiences and knowledge or contact. But such forcing of the dreamscape by direct training and exercises often either does not work, or does not work effectively, and the damage it can do to the dream health of a person far outweighs any benefit. Allowing the brain and immune system to do its necessary processing through sleep and dreams is really important for a magician, even more so than for the average person. Sleep health is a necessary cornerstone of magical strength. The other issue with forced magical dreaming is the control issue. People want not only to trigger magical or lucid dreaming, but also to control it, when it happens, what it does, etc. This is a backward step in real magic, as we focus our control based on a limited understanding of inner realms and contact. This creates a barrier for more obscure and important contact. One of the first real lessons a student has to learn in magic is to relinquish control in many aspects. Think of it like a toddler trying to control a household based on their limited understanding.

What the magician can do is first learn the difference between a processing dream and a magical dream. That is done by journaling your dreams, and through paying attention to the feel of the dream as you emerge from it. Often, magical dreams are far stronger than processing dreams, and are easier to remember: they often also have a particular 'feel' to them. Over time, through observance and journaling, the magician starts to recognise the feel and 'signature' of a magical dream. Working in this more natural way allows for the health of the mind and body to be upheld, while also slowly building the recognition and freedom of magical dreaming. When allowed to work naturally, the dreamscape tips into magical dreaming when it is necessary, not when you are curious. That allows deep and powerful contact, action and connection to occur.

Another aspect of magical dreaming (and another very good reason to not try and control the inner dreamscape) is working magically in one's sleep. Early practitioners of magic assume that the ritual or magical working they have done finishes when they close the ritual or working down. But magic doesn't work like that. Once a pattern is triggered, it will continue working until it has completed the task it was created for. Often there are so many unseen variables within a magical working that is active that the time span of the working can stretch far beyond what we would expect. When the magical working triggers, it draws upon the spirit and energy of the magician, and at times the magician's spirit will continue that magical working in the dreamscape.

This is all the more intense if the magician also uses visionary magic, as visionary magic and magical dreamscapes are inextricably linked. This manifests as wild or crazy complex dreams and waking up exhausted the following morning. If the magical work was profound in its reach and scope, then often the magician cannot remember their dreams, but will wake up battered, bruised, and exhausted each morning for a length of time. They will have spent night after night working in their sleep. This particularly happens if the contact or work has a reach far beyond the magician, for example if it is magic for the fate of a landmass, area, or nation, or for a person who has a strong fate path, as the magic triggers points on the fate pattern and when that happens the magician's spirit is pulled into action. Our spirits work independently of our conscious minds far more than is realized.

Journaling dreams that stand out as unusual or complex is an important thing for magicians to do, particularly if there is a specific message in the dream, or if it appears to reach into the future. It might seem like a crazy dream at the time, but writing it down for future reference is like writing your own textbook of magic. One day you will go back and reread that dream you had forgotten about, and it will all make sense.

DIVINATION

In magical divination, the Dream card can literally indicate dreams, or it can indicate visionary work. It can also indicate sleep and sleep health.

When this card appears in a reading, depending on the subject matter of the reading and the position it lands in, it can indicate that your dreamscape is connecting in with the issue, and may give you insights into the issue. If the layout you are using has a position for dreams, look to what falls in that position, and look at where the actual Dream card has fallen, and read the two cards and positions together.

For example (and this is a real, recent example) if the dream card falls in a difficult endurance position, and in the layout position of dreams falls a card that indicates a being, it is saying that there is a being that is causing issues related to the subject matter of the reading. My partner had a strong, vivid dream of a troublesome child in the house that was poking and attacking him. I did a reading which indicated that a faery being had come home with us after we had been out on the high moors. We gave the being a place in the garden to hang out, and the issue stopped.

If the Dream card falls in a position of inner realms, then it indicates that you are working or learning in your sleep. Pay attention to any dreams you remember. Write them down as soon as you wake up, as details can fade quickly without you realizing it.

If the reading is about choosing a magical method to deal with an issue or situation, or to look for the best way to learn something magical, and the Dream card comes up in a relevant position, then it can be indicating the need to work with visionary magic. Sometimes vision work is the best way to approach something, particularly if the work needs the involvement of spirits/beings.

If you have been having troubled sleep or problems getting to sleep or staying asleep, and this card appears, then look at the position where it has fallen: this can give insight into what underlying issue is interfering with your sleep. We often deal with energetic issues through our dreamscape, and once we recognize the issue and deal with it, the troubled sleep goes away.

Constantly waking up or not being able to get into a deep sleep can have inner magical reasons as well as physical health ones. A magician can become a very sensitive sleeper. For example, intrusion by a being into your space, or a human energetic vampire drawing close, can trigger your inner warning system, which will wake you up. Some people without intent or realization can wander about in spirit while they are asleep, looking for another human to energetically feed from. If this happens, often your dreamscape will warn you, or you will wake up.

If you are having problems with sleep and suspect that it may have a magical cause, then do a reading with a layout that has a dream position, and look at what appears in that position, along with what appears in an inner realm position, and in the ground zero (physical body) position. Also look to see if the Dream card itself appears in the reading.

If the Dream card falls in a past position, then depending on the question it could indicate that what you are dreaming about is something from the past, or that it is about a long dead person or ancestor. If the card is in a withheld position and the reading is about a magical question, then it can indicate that using vision or dreamwork would not be the best way forward.

In a mundane reading if the Dream card is in a withheld position, it can indicate insomnia or problems with sleep health.

Keys

Dreaming, sleep, vision, dream communication, need for rest.

Extra

In ancient Egypt, dreams appear in texts dating from the First Intermediate period, from approximately 2150 B.C. to the late New Kingdom. These early recordings of dreams appear in 'Letters to the Dead', messages that were written on papyrus, linen, or on bowls, and left in or near a tomb or mortuary temple. Fifteen of these 'letters to the dead' have survived, and they were found in various places across the Egyptian territory.

Some of these letters mention dreams, where the living person had a dream about the dead person and it worried them. An example of this is a letter written by a priest to his dead overseer priest called Meru. In the letter, the younger priest tells of a dream he had where he was walking in the city with his overseer priest. Having a dream about his dead overseer distressed the priest as he seemed to be worried that the overseer was angry at him.

This letter among others was analysed by William Kelly Simpson, Professor of Egyptology at Yale University, and published in the Journal of Egyptian Archaeology.[1] In the letter, Meru pointed out something that caught my eye as a magician. It was a sentence that states: "the breath of the mouth (the utterance of the speaker) is beneficial to the dead and causes no fatigue to the speaker". To magicians who are used to doing visionary work and or magical utterance, when working with a lot of power, a simple act such as magical utterance can completely exhaust a magician, sometimes for days afterwards. The inner energy it takes to release such magic causes physical exhaustion. This line from a priest to his old teacher stating the lack of fatigue while uttering is an important point for magicians, because it underlines that they also experienced the same exhaustion while using magical utterance with power. In the dynastic Egyptian religion, magic and magical acts were an integral part of the work of a priest.

[1]Simpson, 1966.

11 Wheel

Meaning

The Wheel refers to what became known
through tarot as the Wheel of Fortune, or
the turning of fate. It was named such after
Rota Fortuna, the wheel of the Roman goddess
Fortuna. The Romans, and many philosophers
since, considered fate to be fickle, unpredictable,
and cruel: a feeling that is still prevalent today.

However, the Ancient Egyptians, who had
magic as a central part of their temple religion,
considered magic a gift of the gods given to humanity as a way to navigate and avoid
the sometimes harshness of fate. And that is one of the ways that we work with
magic today. To spot the disasters that come at us over the horizon so that we can
dodge the unnecessary ones, while accepting the necessary ones.

The Wheel of Fate as a power is closely linked with the Four Creatures and the
Chariot, powers and concepts that appear in tarot cards and also in magic. They
are all aspects of the constantly shifting patterns of fate: the beings that guide
and protect you, the pattern that forms as a 'vehicle', and the magician who is the
charioteer who navigates through fate in order to rise like a star or the morning sun.

Fate is not random or fickle: this is something that adept magicians learn by
direct experience, observation, and magical work. It can be cruel at times, yes,
but not random, and certainly not fickle. Think of fate like a living conscious
multidimensional web that is made up of many smaller webs that are constantly
interacting with each other, and each interaction can trigger a change. That is like
a 'backroom' peek at fate.

Now think of it this way: fate is about energy, actions, and switches. Cause and
effect. Once you understand this and see fate's effects around you, then you will
learn how to 'charioteer' your own fate: magic just brings this into sharp focus. Fate
is not about reward and punishment; it is about necessity: how your actions line
up with the necessity of your path through fate, and how those actions can trigger
a subtle but far-reaching cascade of effects which causes shifts and changes of the
patterns of fate.

Divination

When the Wheel card appears in a reading, it is telling of a change that is either
already in process, or that is coming. If you think of your life as a series of 'seasons',

each season is pattern and period of fate that starts, runs, and ends. In some layouts, there is a position for the Wheel, and whatever falls in that position tells you what the 'season' of fate you are currently in is about.

The position in which the Wheel card falls in a reading will tell you what area of your life the change manifests through. For example, if it falls in the Hearth position, it is most likely a change either to your home or your family. If it falls in the position of Endurance, then the change will likely be hard work in its early stages, or it may mean that through enduring and keeping going the change will be born. If you have been going through a long period of endurance and it lands in the endurance layout position, then this can indicate that such difficulty is now changing. Deciding which it is depends upon the rest of the layout and the question posed.

If the Wheel card falls in a past position, then the change of fate has already done its job and you are in a period of a stability. If the Wheel lands in a withheld position in a layout, it is saying that regarding whatever you are asking a question about, change will not happen. If you are trying to trigger change and it appears in that withheld position, then you will need to rethink your approach to the issue. Different options can be looked at with readings posing questions about the different approaches, but if a card that reflects change momentum, or the Wheel card itself, continues to fall in the withheld position, then it is likely that your fate needs to play out in some way before change can happen. Often our greatest times are born out of difficult times.

If the Wheel falls in the relationship position, then depending upon the rest of the reading and the question, either there is change coming to a relationship that the subject of the reading is in, or the subject of the reading has triggered a change in fate and that change has now arrived to directly influence them. They are in a relationship with the change of fate.

If, by the layout of the reading the change coming is not a good one (which can be indicated if the near or distant future cards are negative), then it is wise to stop and think about the path decisions you are currently working through. Using divination, you can look at different options and see what comes out in the readings.

For the most part, none of us like change, but when the Wheel appears it is wise to remember that it is a card of fate, and that fate needs to keep moving in order to stay strong and healthy.

Keys

Change, growth, decisions, maturing, moving, expansion.

12 PERCEPTION

MEANING

Seven people stand out on a moorland in night-time moonlight and look upwards at something. One of the seers, dressed in blue, picks up on the feeling that someone is looking at her, and she turns her eye to look at you.

Perception is one of the two most important skills for the magician, the other being magic. Without both of these skills the magician is sorely lacking. Magic is the action, and Perception is the ability to spot dangers, intrusions, appearances, energies, mistruths, and the subtle unmistakable early signs of creeping destruction or chaos.

The deepest meaning behind the word perception is *truth*. We can all see something, but only a few can see the truth behind a façade. A magician needs to be able to look beyond a surface presentation of something and see deeply into the truth of whatever is there. Until the magician can see the hidden truth of something, it is unwise to act magically.

In the magical religion of dynastic Egypt, the understanding of the necessity for both of these skills was highlighted in the magical and funerary texts, and the two powers of magic and Perception were personified as deities[1]. It was these two skills or powers that protected the solar barque as it travelled through the Underworld.

Perception for a magician is a distinct skill: paying attention in the finest detail. Paying attention is paramount in magic, as often the powers, beings, spirits and elements give off tiny signals or signs that guide or warn the magician in their actions. And by using true perception, by looking past the surface presentation or what is half hidden, then the magician can get to the real truth of something. In today's world of mistruths, half-truths, and agendas, true perception is an extremely important skill to have. If you act in magic without proper perception, then you are likely to miscalculate, misjudge, or to potentially harm the innocent. Truth is a delicate treasure which must be protected and always fostered by the magician.

Perception is the early warning system of the magician and is also the magician's guide. If they are on the right track and yet they question themselves, the magician will look around them as they go about their daily life for signs to confirm they are on the right track, or to warn them that they are incorrect and need to adapt something.

---

[1] Heka (Magic) and Sia (Perception).

It can also be a skill that is used instead of divination, when the magician needs to go 'under the radar' and not been seen for a specific reason. In some cases, magic and divination can make the magician visible, and so perception is the skill they fall back on. The inner contacts and spirits that work with the magician often nudge the magician towards certain signs, instincts, or occurrences that the magician can draw advice and information from.

Each individual magician has their own unique way in how their inner perception works. We all have our own body signals for our 'inner radar' but we also have individual or cultural signals in the world around us that perception can work through. The vocabulary of messages can be animal behaviour, or the wind elements, or numbers, or odd things happening which mirror cultural stories, and they often occur with irony or humour.

DIVINATION

The appearance of the Perception card in a reading tells you that you need to pay attention, that you are missing something. Where it falls in a layout can indicate what area of your life you need to look more closely at. The card is nudging you to *open your eyes and see.*

The vocabulary of perception is something that is built up in a magician over time with practice, and when this card appears in a reading, it can be pointing to the need to develop that skill better.

It can also appear in a reading if you are looking for the best way to magically approach an issue or a change of direction. If Perception appears, it indicates that you shouldn't work with magic at this time, but just use perception and follow the guidance it gives you. Look for the truth.

If Perception falls in a withheld or negative position in a layout, it is saying you are not seeing the truth or you are not using that skill and you need to. Sometimes stress or lifestyle can dampen our perceptions which essentially means our radar is offline.

Occasionally this card in a withheld position can indicate that our perception is off. Some people, particularly ones who suffer from a lot of anxiety, can see signs where there are none, and that can get worse with stress. If someone suffers from this issue, then being aware that sometimes their perceptions are off can help a person to learn to distinguish between what is a real communication from signs, and what is our own subconscious playing tricks.

That is all a part of the main rule for the magician, which is: *know thyself.* If you know you have a tendency to anxiety and reading more into things than is there when under stress, then you can learn to modify, filter, and discern far better. Eventually you will come to notice that real warnings or inner signs have a particular depth and feel to them that ones from your own imagination or subconscious do not.

KEYS

Pay attention, a sign, warning, exposing hidden information, precognition, prophecy, awareness, truth, understanding the truth, seeing what others do not see, seeing what is veiled.

EXTRA

A teaching of Ibn al-'Arabi,[1] the great Sufi scholar of the 13th century:

> A true believer is one who sees the Divine and everything else with 'two eyes' (*dhu'l-'aynayn*). With one eye, he sees the Divine as utterly transcendent, a mystery we cannot understand, a force that is beyond words. The same believer sees the Divine with his other eye as here and now, flowing through everything we can see; for everything that is created is Divine, and the light of the Divine shines out of everything around us including ourselves.

Ibn al-'Arabi states that it is only by seeing the Divine with two eyes that we can begin to recognise the Truth in everything: what we see with two eyes is not two different things, but the completion of Divine truth.

13 MAGIC

I am a skilful lector priest who knows his utterance, and I know all the skilful magic by which he becomes an Akh in the necropolis.

—Tjetu I (late sixth dynasty, Giza)

MEANING

Magic is often thought to be something done with wands, swords, altars, and ceremonies, but that is mostly early training behaviour. Deep magic reaches into the elements and powers around you, and that power is drawn upon, formed by the mind, and bridged through word and mind into whatever you are working on.

In this image the woman draws upon power from the wind and is using the ·

---

[1] Abū 'Abd Allāh Muḥammad ibn 'Alī ibn Muḥammad ibn al-'Arabī al-Ḥātimī al-Ṭā'ī al-Andalusī al-Mursī al-Dimashqī; also known as Ibn al-Arabi (1165-1240 CE): an Arab Andalusian Muslim Scholar.

strength of the full moon for her work. She is working with an ancient spirit creature, a snake that is known as the 'Mother of Ants'.[1] She is called such because the deadly serpent commands a vast army of deadly spirits. In Greek mythology, Mother of Ants was spawned from the blood of Medusa, which points to a much older tale that would have been ancient by the Greek classical era.

The woman is using utterance; hence she is weaving the wind and using the act of magic to call up this spirit and ask it for help. To ask such a being for help, she is summoning a spirit army and is asking for the cooperation of the Mother of Ants, leader of the vast army, to help her achieve something that is important for the survival of her people.

This card demonstrates a different narrative to the usual 'magician in a robe with a wand and sword at an altar'. Instead, it offers a glimpse into adept magic, where the land, elements, spirits, creatures and magician are a working cooperative. When the spirits or land need help, they ask the magician; and when the magician needs help, they ask the land and spirits. The woman in the image carries no magical tools. *She* is the tool, she is the bridge of power, and her mind and words form the magic.

After years of training and practice, the skills embed into the magician and they *become* magic. The mind and utterance, the hand and foot: those are the working tools of the magician. The body of the magician becomes a bridge through which power passes and is woven by the magician into the act of magic.

Learning to work with the powers of the night and day, the moon and sun, the seasons, the land, trees, air, and the many ancient spirits that reside in the land, the Underworld and the stars are the skills of the true magician. Such skills need work and development; they cannot be read and learned from books and classes.

DIVINATION

This is a card that indicates active magic. It is the magic of skills, knowledge, wisdom and practice, not the magic of the dilettante. It can indicate the need for a more serious approach to your magic, or it can indicate the need to apply magic to a situation or place. Its interpretation depends heavily upon your question and its placement in the layout, but its overarching message is one of true magic that reaches into inner worlds and nature, that uses the skills of the magician, as opposed to recipe-style 'spell' magic.

If in the reading the card is in a withheld position then it is saying, depending on the question, 'do not use magic' or, 'it is not magic'. For example, if suddenly you suspect that certain events in your life or health are the result of being targeted by magic, and this card falls in a withheld position, then it is saying, 'no, this situation is not coming from someone using magic against you', or that magic, even your own, did not cause the situation. Even if, however, the reading does indicate that magic is a contributing factor to a situation, do not automatically assume it is caused by

---

[1] Ants move like an army and attack anything that threatens them, hence Mother of Ants. This being is also known as the Amphisbaena.

someone attacking you. In a high percentage of people affected by magic, the cause is often either their own practice acts, or their everyday behaviour in life clashing with the magic they are practising.

Its highest meaning is the adept magic of the open hand, and if you are asking advice about your own path and this card appears, then you are being advised to delve deeper into your practice and take it more seriously, or to step away from the surface glamour of magic and step towards the deeper, more powerful practice.

In a reading about a place or a patch of land or a building, this card can indicate that such a place was either a site for magical or ritual behaviour or is a place where such behaviour affected the balance of the site.

In more mundane readings, it can indicate a doctor or scientist, or the need for a doctor, one who by their knowledge and skill can effect change.

KEYS

Magic, magical activity, a ritual site, a person of great knowledge and skill, using skills to benefit others.

EXTRA

Magic at its core is the act of collaboration with the consciousness in everything physical and nonphysical to effect a change. Magic weaves power, time, and fate in conjunction with spirits to bring about a shift in fate or to tune something back into balance and thus reestablish its fate expression.

In the known ancient world, magic was often an integral part of the culture and religion of nations. The two most prominent ones, which also heavily influenced magic as we know it today, were Mesopotamia and Egypt.

In Mesopotamia, the magician priest was often known as *Ašipu*. The magician priest was often the one called upon as a healer, exorcist, diviner, and sacred advisor to the king. In Egypt the word for magic was Heka[1] and it was something practiced, like in Mesopotamia, as an integral part of the priesthood and religion. In the 'Teaching for Merikare the King',[2] a treatise on kingship from the old king to the new, it says "He (god) made for them magic as weapons to ward off the blow of events".

---

[1] *ḥk3w*
[2] Translated by Lichtheim (2006 [1975]: 97–109).

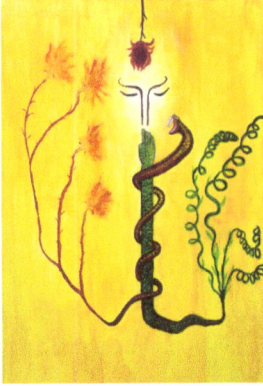

14 Silence

Meaning

The red rose hanging above the face is the key to this painting. The face is *sub rosa*, which means under the rose. Under the Rose is a term that has been used in magic and societies since the Hellenistic period in Greek culture, and the Roman Empire, and its origins lay in the tale of Cupid who gave a rose to Harpocrates, the god of silence, as a bribe so he would keep silent about the indiscretions of Venus.

Vows of silence are often taken in magical groups, often on the pain of magical attack if the vow is broken. Yet such a vow exposes the immaturity of the magicians and the magical structure. Magic always hides in plain sight and has no need of vows and attacks. If a magician needs to be under fear of attack from his peers in order to keep silent, then such a magician has no real understanding of magic at all.

Rather, Magical Silence is such where the magician knows that breaking a particular silence or revealing more than could be properly understood could cause terrible damage to others. True magic can be like a powerful nuclear reactor. In the right hands it can generate power efficiently, but in the wrong hands it could bring total destruction.

Magic protects itself by nature of the dynamics and patterns that run through magic. If a magician reveals more than necessary or to the point where it would harm the receiver of the information, the protective mechanisms within magic itself kick in. There are two main forms of these defensive mechanisms which flow through all magic regardless of the culture or system. If the magical secret being shared is powerful enough to destroy a soul's fate path or soul expression, then the system kicks in and destroys or silences the offending magician. One form is known in Kabbalah as the 'Lashes of Fire', and the other is the 'binder that silences'. Different systems have different names for the same dynamic. Wherever there is real power, these two mechanisms show up.

The lashes of fire burn the magician when they start to stray into territory they should not. It is a warning shot across the bow, to warn the magician to back off. Often the simple burning happens when the magician is not intentionally revealing something, but enables or teaches too much, and the burning reminds them to be silent. If the magician is intentionally revealing hidden knowledge or information that would lead the receiver to ruin, or if the magician unleashes powerful magic that would destroy without necessity, then the lashes of fire destroy the magician's ability in magic.

The binder of silence is another power that destroys, not by fire, but by binding the mind, energy and magic of a person up until they are unable to act or even think. When a magician has unintentionally overstepped in their passing on of knowledge or through their magical actions, the binder power will kick in and start to tangle their thoughts and words. Again, like the fire, this power gives warning shots to teach the magician and to make them step back from their actions. If the action or deeds of the magician are intentional, then the binder will tighten around them, literally squeezing the life out of them. It will affect their bodily functions in a suppressive way, and it will tangle their minds so that they cannot think or express themselves. In Kabbalah this is the power of Gevurah, the Strength of G-D.

If you look at the image, you will see hints that the wand is partially serpentine, along with the snake wound around it. These are the two snakes that work through the staff of the adept magician. They are beings that work with the magician as co-workers, and they also guard the integrity of magic. They will turn on the magician if the magician becomes corrupt, power-mad, or vindictive.

Why is the passing on of knowledge so terrible? In magic, the surface information is of no harm and either people understand it or they do not. This is how it hides in plain sight: only those with *eyes to see* can see the depths of what is written. However, if an adept magician directly assists a student or person in a magical action that would open the student up to more power or knowledge than they could have found alone, that potentially exposes the student to major power impacts or revelations that would destroy them. As such the magician is responsible for the destruction of that person, and the cause vs. effect dynamic in magic kicks in. Such exposure also limits the development of the student: we learn from finding and experiencing, not through being enabled, and to limit the magical evolution of a soul by enabling or overexposing is the greatest magical crime of all.

If the mistakes are unintentional or done in ignorance, then the mechanism does not destroy; rather it teaches.

DIVINATION

The appearance of this card is a warning to keep silent or to not act on something. It is warning you that you are treading into dangerous territory, even if you do not realize it, and that your actions could have consequences far beyond your comprehension.

If you are trying to find something out in your divination and this card appears as the answer, then it is saying that you do not need to know, and that knowing would harm you. How? If what you wanted to know was revealed, you would potentially make choices that would harm you badly in the long term. There is a process happening and you need to make your decision based on what you already know. That decision and acting on that decision will take you on a journey that you need to walk in order to experience certain things.

If this card falls in a withheld position, it is saying, 'do not hold your tongue, you need to speak out', or it could also mean, depending on the question, that there is no secret, there is no mystery.

Its appearance in a reading either points to a secret or the need to keep a secret, or to not speak as there will be unseen consequences. Where it lands in the layout, and what the subject of the question is, can have a strong bearing on how to interpret this card. If, for example, it falls in the fate wheel position, then it indicates that whatever you are going through or working on at this time, you should keep it under wraps for now, as speaking out could harm you. If it lands in the dream or inner worlds position, then either it is saying, 'do not speak of your magical work or dreams', or more likely it is saying that you are learning of hidden things in your dreams, visions, and magical work.

It can appear in the relationship position when someone is having an affair or keeping a secret from those close to them, or their partner is.

If it lands in the first position, which is the position of the subject of the reading, then it can be a warning to stay under the radar, to keep plans silent, or to not speak to others about the issue that the reading is about.

Depending on the question this card can also indicate a secret group working behind the scenes in something, be it magic or mundane.

It is also a prompt to guard your words, not because of secrets, but because your words could inadvertently harm. So another reading of this card, depending upon the question and situation, and where the card falls in a layout, would be: do you really need to speak? What is the purpose of your words?

Keys

Be silent, do not act, you do not need to know, do not ask, think before speaking, secrets and keeping secrets.

Extra

> No word uttered has helped as much as many held in silence. For it is possible to say later what has been kept silent, but certainly not to render silent what has been said—that has been poured out and has wandered far afield. This is why I think that we have men as teachers of speech, but gods as teachers of silence, since we maintain quiet in their sacrifices and rites. A fool is known by their speech; and a wise person by silence.[1]

---

[1] Plutarch. *De Garrulitate* 505f-506e.

15 SERVICE

The purpose of life is not to be happy. It is to be useful, to be honourable, to be compassionate, to have it make some difference that you have lived and lived well.

— Ralph Waldo Emerson

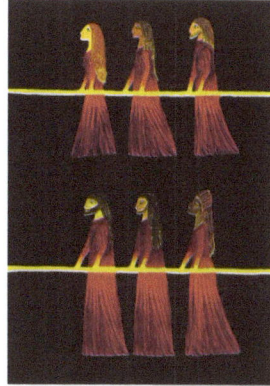

MEANING

Magical service is a major part of magical development, not only in terms of maturity but also in terms of magical power. In the painting, we see two rows of three people all working equally to achieve something. We do not get to see what they are towing nor where they are going. All we see is that they are all joined together by nature of the rope of light that their hands merge with.

A lot of magical service is like that. We often do not get to see what the ultimate outcome of the service is. It can be a difficult path to walk at times, as the root of magical service is to be a mediator, a bridge for power to flow through as necessary, or a catalyst or loadsharer. And all of this is done while the magician continues with daily mundane life such as jobs and family. For the most part the magician does not get to choose the 'when, where and why' of service. It just happens.

Magical service spans a great many things from simply tending to a shrine or a patch of land, feeding birds or picking up trash, to working to uphold or protect the fate of person or nation for an allotted time, or to heal, or exorcize, or to protect a community. It is also magical service to teach for the necessity of teaching (rather than commercial necessity), or to leave behind new writing that guides the next generation.

There is also a form of magical service that happens at a deep level, usually with magicians of skill who are also energetic empaths. An example of that for a magician would be that you open the west magical gate in a ritual, and a huge amount of power unexpectedly builds up, and you can feel a great deal going on. The west is among other things a direction of bridging from life into death. There may have been a buildup of souls of recently dead people who did not know what to do or where to go so, they ended up in limbo. By triggering the West Gate just at the right time and place, fate can link up that gate to the souls in limbo. Suddenly they can see a way forward and they begin to stream through the gate and onwards in their journey through death. You may have just intended to tune a space by triggering the gates, but it turned into an act of service to the dead.

The other thing to remember when doing service is that while you are working, what you need (rather than want) will come to you if necessary, whether that is resources, energy, guidance, or space. Everyone gets what they need, and everyone moves forward.

Divination

When this card appears, it tells of a situation where service is needed, or being given, or is currently being done. For example, if you are doing your regular magical work and suddenly a lot of power comes in unexpectedly, or it feels like really hard work when it should not, and this card appears in a reading afterwards, it is saying that what you are doing is going far beyond what you intended, because it is serving a bigger purpose.

In divination it is also a card of teamwork where everyone pulls together to achieve something that benefits others. If the question is choosing a magical approach to something and this card appears, then it is saying that it will need a team effort, not the work of an individual. However, with the same question if this card falls in a withheld position, it is saying that you need to do things alone and not with a group.

If the card falls in the position of hearth/home then it is reflecting the old wisdom of 'it takes a village to raise a child', which is to say that there is a need within the family or community for everyone to help. Depending upon the question, it could be saying, 'yes, this will work but it will need cooperation from the family community', or it can be saying, 'you need to join in and help in something'.

If the card falls in the inner worlds position in a layout, it is saying that whatever you are doing a reading about, you are part of an inner group effort, i.e. beings, spirits, inner contacts, angelic beings etc, or that these beings will step up and help you.

If it appears in the dreams position, then it is a strong indicator that you are working in your sleep. If you are a magician, then your magical work is continuing in your sleep, or you are being pulled while in sleep to join in a major service effort in something. If you are not a magician, then it is likely you are a natural psychic or energetically sensitive and your deeper spirit is joining in a group effort in your sleep. This can happen when there is great risk or danger coming over the horizon somewhere, often far away from where you are, and your spirit is joining in to help. This can happen if you are connected energetically to a place, person, or thing.

If the card lands in a withheld or negative position in a layout, it is saying that whatever you are asking about, it serves no purpose, or that some service you had been doing has now ended.

This card can also represent a magical group (or any group) that feels that what they do is a vocation or is special. Sometimes this can mean groups that are extremist or fundamentalist, and if this card falls in a difficult reading in a hostile position, it can be an indication that a group is trying to affect you or limit you because they feel duty bound to do so. This can be of particular importance to magicians who are the target of religious groups.

In mundane readings where it falls in a hostile position, it can indicate a group that is hostile to who you are because of their beliefs, such as an extremist or religious groups targeting someone for their gender identity or simply their gender, or because of their political beliefs, etc.

If the reading is for a mundane person in a mundane situation, this card can mean a job where service is a part of it: nursing, guarding, feeding people, and so forth. It is a job, paid or volunteer work that helps others and that is a team effort.

Keys

Serving, the Great Work, teamwork, helping, maturing, supporting, selflessness, taking responsibility.

Extra

Here is a short biographical excerpt on the magician, priestess and author, Dion Fortune, which summarises this card perfectly.

> She defined magic as the art of causing changes to occur in consciousness. It was (and is) an evolutionary art, but she insisted upon an attitude and approach toward magic that has now been lost, or corrupted: magic is about service. Unless her pupils could earnestly say: I desire to know in order to serve, they would never get through the first portal. Simply put, here is a soul you can trust...and fall in love with.
>
> By any reckoning, power oozed from her. She had the sort of wisdom and knowledge that transformed the magical arts and worked through to change the world at large. If she was not the most loving of souls, in the accepted sense, then she had a rare beauty that made people follow her into other dimensions. If there was a fight you would want her on your side. If you were in trouble, you could turn to her for uncompromising advice.[1]

---

[1] Richardson, 2009.

16 Healing

Meaning

I chose this type of image to paint for healing, as healing is not passively accepted: it is something that requires active participation, particularly for a magician. Healing and learning the basics of how to heal yourself are important aspects of a magical life, since magic can put a strain on the body as well as the mind and spirit. It can also bring to the surface hidden imbalances in our lifestyle, our diet, and how we manage our bodies. Once magic starts to flow through us in any real volume of power, any weaknesses in the body become more visible so that we can attend to them.

The body and mind are the vessels through which magic passes, and that vessel must be kept in relatively good condition so that it does not buckle under the strain of such power. It does not mean that the magician needs to be an athlete or obsessed with their health; what it does mean is that a working magician cannot 'get away with' abusing the body and mind through bad diet, taking in substances that badly affect the body, or using the mind in ways that are not conducive to its health and balance.

The other health issue with magicians is that once a magician starts to walk a serious path of magic, that the body can in some people manifest a condition or illness that can limit the magician in everyday life. Often the illness is either a physical crisis that must be overcome, or it is a long term condition that the magician needs to manage, often in unconventional ways.

This type of illness is often triggered either by fate or by the magician's work. But it can serve many purposes from a magical perspective. It teaches the magician about their own body and its limitations, it forces the magician to face their own prospect of death and all the soul-searching that such a prospect can trigger, and it also brings the magician to a barrier over which they have little control. At that point the magician turns, for the first real time, to the inner worlds and spirits for help. We can all pretend that we are immersed in the spirit world when things are fine, but when your life is on the line, that is when we truly confront our deepest held beliefs. Do we fold in on ourselves? Or do we reach into fate, into the inner worlds, and into our own spirit to fight for our lives? This sort of crisis, in shamanic cultures, is the 'making or breaking' of the potential magician, as it separates out the true magician from the dilettante.

For the magician, healing skills are a necessary companion when working in certain aspects of magic, for example exorcism, clearing, and triggering. In today's world of specialization, everything has become so specialized with skills that often a person has no general skills beyond what they have been trained to do. A magician needs a wide collection of skills. Many of these will be applied in various ways, and each skill will overlap others. And many of those skills are deployed when healing is necessary.

DIVINATION

When this card appears in a reading it is talking about healing and regeneration, be that physical healing, a restoration of something, or a rebuilding that will regenerate something.

If the card lands in a position of endurance, it is stating that the healing process will take time and effort and may also need discipline. It can also indicate that the person may need to endure tiredness, but that this is part of the healing process.

If the Healing card lands in an inner position, then the form of healing needed or happening involves inner or magical techniques as opposed to medicines or herbs. This would include visionary work, 'shamanic' approaches, and the help of spirits inner beings.

If the Healing card lands in a withheld position, depending upon the question, then it can be saying that the choice of actions you are deciding upon via divination will not trigger healing and may be detrimental to the overall health of the magician. It is essentially saying 'no, not that'.

If the reading is not about healing and the healing card comes up in the withheld position, then it is saying that whatever the question is about, it is not a good option and the situation will not 'heal' (resolve itself); or it is a situation that is detrimental to the person or place that the reading is about. The reverse is true if this card falls in a positive position.

If the card appears in a past position, then the healing process has passed or is not necessary at this point. If it appears in a distant past position, depending upon the question, then it can indicate ancestral healing, i.e., that the magic that is being looked at can trigger the deep healing of past events or patterns that bear influence on the present and future. In this position, if the reading is about a magical healing, then it can indicate that an ancient ancestor or powers from the Underworld can or will be a part of the healing process.

It is a positive card, so if it appears as an outcome to a question that is not about healing, it can be read as a 'yes', or 'correct choice', and 'regeneration' or 'it will get fixed'. If it is in a withheld position then it can be read as 'no, not here, or 'degeneration', or 'broken'.

In some readings, it can indicate the need to be proactive, to engage and work with something to bring regeneration and balance. Or when you are looking at a situation or a patch of land or group of people, depending on whether it falls in a positive or negative position, it can be saying, 'yes, all is good, it is doing its thing and it is regenerating' or in negative withheld positions 'it cannot regenerate or it cannot be active because it is broken or damaged'.

This card can also indicate a doctor, nurse, healer, or someone who will help a person to get back into good health.

Keys

Health, regeneration, healing process, yes, medicine, fixing something, stabilising, making whole.

Extra

The following is an extract from a research paper written by Danish anthropologist Benedikte M Kristensen who lived among the Duha Tuvinians of Northern Mongolia[1].

This is part of the story BatZajah told me about his sacrificial tree:

> My father was the shaman Gompo. His mother was also a shaman. Her sacrificial tree is far away in the south-west. My father's sacrificial tree is situated here (pointing to the west) close to the river Xaramat Gol. My father was a very good and strong shaman. You see; he even knew when he was going to die. He took off all his clothes and lay down. Then he told us that it was his time to die, and told us that when he had passed away we should place his shamanic gear beside this tree. Then he died, you see he really knew when he would die. So his *ongods*[2] are at that place. Good white *ongods*. We are linked to them. One of us (the children of Gompo) had to become a shaman. **My sister went ill. Ambii said it was the shamanic disease, so she was to become a shaman, and she did.**

This story exemplifies how the history of a shamanic lineage is remembered through the land, where each sacrificial tree represents a single shaman and her or his life and deeds, and where the totality of sacrificial trees represents the entire history of the shamanic lineage.

For more information on techniques in magical healing, please see McCarthy (2020b).

---

[1] Kristensen, 2004.
[2] Good spirits.

17 DEFENCE

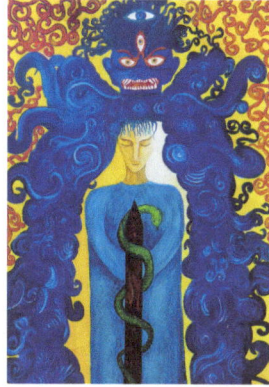

> You have often heard me speak of an oracle or sign which comes to me...This sign I have had ever since I was a child. The sign is a voice which comes to me and always forbids me to do something which I am going to do, but never commands me to do anything, and this is what stands in the way of my being a politician.[1]

— Socrates

MEANING

There is an old saying: 'judge me by those who keep me'. This saying hides a great deal of wisdom behind it. In magic, people often think that defence comes from ritual acts, talismans, magical tools, and magical utterances. While that is true to some extent, as the magician grows and matures in themselves and their practice, such external expressions of protection become less important. This is particularly true if the magician has developed their work in co-operation with inner beings and does work to serve the overall pattern of creation, stasis and destruction, also known as magical service.

As the magician steps onto a path of magical service, they are challenged and tested many times, and the response to the magician who does not flop over at their first major challenge is one of protection. The protection is not just from one being, but it is a return of service from many other types of beings including deities, angelic beings, land beings, ancestors, and so forth. What I have found, both in my own practice and when observing other magicians working in similar ways, is that the magician's daimon becomes more active and acts like a manager, calling in extra help when it is needed.

If the magician is working on something which serves fate, and all their energy is going into that work, then they are given protection while they work. No matter what is thrown to magically attack the working magician, the beings/deity/ancestor that is/are actively protecting the magician will deal with the dangerous parts of any attack. The rest is removed by the magician through regular ritual cleaning and maintenance. The same is true of natural threats like inner destructive tides. The

---

[1] Plato: Apology of Socrates 40b.

magician's fate pattern is matched up with events, places, and things that will protect them.

Ultimately it is the development, evolution, and conscious decision-making of the magician coupled with an inner response of guardianship that defends the magician. The older and more experienced the magician becomes, the less they have to intentionally trigger magic to protect themselves. However, should the magician attack someone or something for whatever reason, then the inner protection disengages. As a magician you defend powerfully, and walk your path. The moment you 'output' magic as an act of aggression towards someone or something else, the complex patterns of fate and protection are broken, and you are left to swim with the sharks. You are on your own. The inner defender mechanism is reliant upon your ethics and maturity, and your willingness to serve as and when necessary.

DIVINATION

The appearance of the Defence card has two base meanings that can be read according to the question, and the subject matter of the reading. One is 'you are defended', and the other is 'you need to defend yourself'.

If for example you are worried about a particular danger and this card falls in the first position that indicates 'ground zero' i.e., you, then it is saying 'you have protection, so tread carefully, do your work, and do not stray from your ethics and path'.

If this card falls in a negative withheld position in a layout then it is indicated that you have no defence and you need to smarten up, use divination to identify the type of threat and take appropriate steps to avoid the situation or to put up defences. The card appearing in this position for a magician also indicates that you are potentially working in an unbalanced or destructive way and the spirits around you have stepped back and are unwilling to protect you.

If this card falls in the inner worlds position of a layout, it is saying, 'you are protected from inner threat by inner beings and potentially a deity'. If it appears in the dream position, then you are protected in your sleep.

If it appears in the relationship position, it is showing the being that is protecting you has drawn close and is very active. In such a situation it often means there is great physical or inner danger around you. And while the being 'has your back', you also need to tighten up on your own defences. (For example, if you have gotten out of the habit of checking your home security before you go to bed.) The defence card in this position of relationship is a warning and an assurance, so make sure you smarten up and pay attention to what is around you, and don't take risks either with your own security, or with your safety out in the world. And most importantly, listen to that quiet inner voice or instinct. If you get a bad feeling about something, don't do it. One of the ways your daimon and the beings that protect you warn you, is through a subtle feeling, instinct, or an inner voice. But they cannot protect you if you do not step up and also take responsibility for yourself.

If the question posed is one of 'what should I do about x?' and the defence card is highlighted in the reading, then one of the things you need to do is protect yourself in all things until a danger has passed.

If the question posed is one of 'will I get through this?' and this card is prominent in the reading, then the answer is yes. It also brings with it the deeper meaning of the card. If you do what you are supposed to be doing and are acting in a balanced, truthful, and mature way, then you will get through and be just fine.

In anything to do with magic, if you are not sure of the concept you are looking at, find an analogy in everyday life. For example, magical protection will only go so far, particularly if you act without proper care and due thought: it is like a bulletproof vest. If you are in a war zone or a dangerous situation with guns around, a bulletproof vest will only protect your torso. If you walk around in such a situation without care and caution, someone could shoot you in the head. It is the same with magical defence. You bear half the responsibility of self-protection. If you simply expect magic and inner beings to protect you, and you make no effort yourself, then you have no real defence.

KEYS

Protection, guardian, immune response, check your defences, defence, defender, make clean, honour.

EXTRA

An interesting and very ancient look at magical defence in a different setting is a good way to expand our potential understanding of this dynamic while also learning something.

A good place to look is in the State of Sarawak, which sits on the northwest coastline of Borneo Island[1]. This is a place that has a long history of human habitation; cave paintings found in the cave of Lubang Jeriji Saleh date back at least forty-four thousand years.

In this area can be found the Iban of Sarawak, an indigenous tribe that has an oral history of origins from the Kapuas River on Borneo Island. The Iban are a wider tribal group that can also be found in Sumatra and surrounding areas, but the Iban of Sarawak have some interesting individual totemism that has interesting magical parallels that are pertinent to this card.

For the Iban of Sarawak, the spirit protector of an individual often first presents in dreams as a spirit of an ancestor or dead relative, so sometimes a nonhuman spirit (nature being for example) who presents themselves as a protector to the individual. Often the Iban individual in search of a spirit helper will sleep on a grave or in

---

[1] Borneo Island is divided between three nations: Malaysia and Brunei in the north, and Indonesia in the south.

a wild and quiet place, or in a forest grove to trigger dreams of a potential spirit helper. In the dream the spirit will identify themselves and state their willingness to protect the individual. The spirit then identifies a creature or sometimes an object or natural feature through which the protective spirit can manifest to the living human. The combination of the spirit and the animal it can manifest through becomes the Ngarong, or 'secret helper' of the person.

The Iban individual then spends time observing the creature, be it a bird, animal or serpent, or natural feature. They watch the mannerisms, peculiarities, and general behaviour of the creature (both as an individual and as a species) as that becomes the vocabulary for augury, communication and warnings between the spirit and the individual. The person not only reveres the individual creature that the spirit manifests through, but the whole species. They may carry something with them from that species (a feather, a claw, a tooth etc) as an added protection, and the whole species is treated with the utmost respect. They become 'part of the family' to the individual who will protect them: they will not eat or hunt that species, and they will actively discourage others around them to harm that species in any way.

III. The Magical Path II

18 STARGAZERS (FELLOWSHIP)

MEANING

The image of the Stargazers is an artistic interpretation of ancient adepts who practiced the skills of star watching, medicine, alchemy, divination, magic, and the deeper Mysteries. It is their fellowship that is the main theme of the card. A community of people who are immersed in the Mysteries. As true adepts, they become as stars, thus the reflection in the water of the three stars who are the light of the three adepts.

In some systems of magic, there is a dynamic that magicians work with called 'inner contacts' and within that dynamic are inner adepts or inner guides. They are worked with in vision and in visionary ritual, and they are people who were once alive and who now are not. They are not ancestors; rather they are people who were priestly magicians who upon their death and completion of the death process, began acting as guides and teachers in service to the living. They consciously step out of the cycle of death and rebirth. To some they are known as the Fellowship. They do not interfere with the general life path and fate of an individual, but when a magician steps onto a path of magical service, the Fellowship of inner contacts draws close. They will inspire, warn, reveal, and guide in a subtle and understated way. These are not inner contacts that someone can have a chatty conversation with, nor do they appear in vision in any sort of grandeur, nor do they identify themselves or declare their greatness. Such behaviour is that of an inner parasite.

A deeper layer of meaning to this card is that of the magical Mysteries. This layer of meaning is not about groups or people, but approaches and knowledge. There are many magicians of all different approaches in magic: for some it is a business, for some it is a lifestyle choice, or a curiosity, and for others it is a path that has always been there for them since childhood, and they walk a magical path because that is who they are. There are some who have navigated through some or all the different approaches and then find a path within themselves that takes them deep into the magical Mysteries. When that happens, the path becomes one of evolution of mind, body and soul, and that in turn changes them and everything around them. A magician on that path can effect change simply by showing up and changing the space—not by a magical working, but by the balanced magic that flows from them and through them.

In the story of the Christian Nativity, there are three Magi who come to visit, and in the story they give three gifts to the baby Jesus: frankincense, gold, and myrrh. If you read that story as an adept magician, what you see is three Magi (stargazers) who by their very presence either trigger, or recognise a fate of becoming as gold; this is the path of the Mysteries which is walked in a priestly way, not in a Christian priest way, but in a true priestly way where the magical person keeps themselves clean and balanced so that the power of the gods can flow through them and out into the world. Frankincense is the incense of the gods and thus the priest. It is a difficult path to walk, but by becoming a bridge for the gods, change is constantly happening around them as the power flows through them. This is a path of magical service. Such a person is an upholder, a mediator and bridge, a catalyst and a load-sharer: these are many burdens indeed, and myrrh is the resin that eases the pain of burden.

Divination

When this card appears, it can indicate a few different things: a group of living magicians, or the fellowship of inner adepts, or in mundane readings it can occasionally indicate a group of people who are of benefit to the subject of the reading. (Such as a student group at college, for example.) It can also indicate a magical lodge group that is truly magical (not a dressing-up drinking club with rituals).

For a magician, depending upon the subject of the reading and where this card falls in a layout, this card indicates inner support. If the magician is under a harsh energetic burden or is struggling to keep going and this card appears in a reading, then it is saying, you do not carry this burden alone, we are with you.

As with all cards, context of the question and position in the layout have a strong bearing on how a card should be read. This card can also be a prompt for your own magical work, as it's message is 'dig deeper into the mysteries'. So look at the stars and commune with the planetary spirits, learn the magic within substance (alchemy), delve deep into the mysteries and look at your own inner power potential. Your star reflects in the pool of water, so recognise it, and nurture that potential into maturity through balanced work.

If it falls in a withheld position, read it in the context of the question. For 'is this a good magical group for me to study with?', the answer would be 'no, true magic is not with these people or this person', or simply 'this is not the group for you'. For 'is this the right magical approach for what I am trying to achieve?', the answer would be 'no, that magical approach does not have the skill or wisdom within it to achieve what you need'.

If the question is about choosing a specific approach to something in magic, and this card appears, then it can be a prompt to look at astrology, or to work with the planetary spirits.

If the magician is doing a reading to look at how they need to move forward in their magical life, and this card appears in a positive position, it is saying, 'tread lightly and tread slowly, but put your foot on the path to becoming as gold'. It is a prompt to look deeper within yourself and also look deeper into the mysteries of magic beyond the surface, as that is where you path ahead lies.

In a mundane reading, it indicates a group of people or teachers who are involved in things like medicine, science, and architecture: people that you can learn a great deal from. It can also be a prompt to study and improve yourself. If this card appears in a mundane reading for a person, it can indicate potentials in the person that need to be developed through study.

KEYS

Fellowship, the Mysteries, the Path of Gold, alchemy, you are not alone, astrology, stars and planets, guidance, great learning, wise people.

EXTRA

One of the most fascinating groups of priest magicians in the ancient and classical world were the Sabian priests of Hurran. There is little we know about them, and the history of the Sabians is complicated by the fact that Pagans in the early Islamic territories would claim to be Sabians in order to avoid forced conversion or death. In the Holy Quran, the Sabians are marked out as being *ahl al-kitāb*[1] (people of the book). However, there is much confusion among historians and scholars as to who exactly they were, with the result that the word Sabian has been linked with various different historical communities. We can find fragments of details about the Sabians in various Arabic writings, which give a fascinating insight into a priestly cast who worked with planetary spirits, stars, divination, utterance, and visionary magic.

One interesting source of details regarding the Sabians can be found in the writings of the Muslim philosopher and theologian, Fakhr al-Dīn al-Rāzi',[2] in particular his work *Al-Sirr al-Maktūm (The Hidden Secret)*. In this work, al-Razi explores and recounts the religion and practices of the Sabians of Harran[3], one of the last remaining Pagan priesthood groups surviving in Upper Mesopotamia. Here is a long quote from Razi's al-Sirr. I think some of you will recognise what is being described by al-Razi, where he speaks of the skills of The Masters of Talismans.

---

[1] *Quran* 5:69.

[2] Fakhr al-Dīn al-Rāzī' (1149-1209 CE), born in Ray, Iran and died in Herat, Afghanistan. A polymath and prolific Muslim scholar who wrote on subjects including philosophy, theology, history, alchemy, natural sciences, astronomy, physics, and law.

[3] Harran was in the area which is now known as the district of Sanliurfa in Southeast Turkey.

Indeed there are no means to attain the images, unknown characters, and incantations which the masters of talismans prescribe except by means of inspiration. Tinkūlūshā claimed that many matters were revealed to him whilst he was sleeping in the temples of the heavenly bodies (planets), having offered acts of obeisance and sacrifices (...) Know that the doctrine of these Sabians is that these heavenly bodies are living, intelligent and rational, capable of action; and they are agreed that each one of the spirits of these heavenly bodies can become manifest to man at any time and reveal to him these characters and incantations: they are the names of these spirits and their adjutants. All their books contain this assertion. Moreover it is not unlikely that it be said that these incantations, which are unknown to us, consist of meaningful words, but they are uttered in languages which have in our day become archaic, for most of this knowledge is transmitted from the Kasdānians who lived in ancient times. As for now, these languages have become extinct and so it comes as no surprise that these words remain obscure.[1]

19 UTTERANCE

MEANING

Utterance is probably the most powerful tool for the magician, but for the utterance to trigger magically it must have power behind it. Sometimes magical utterance comes from within the magician, and sometimes the magician is a vessel through which the utterance passes from another being. In the card image an angelic being utters into the ear of the magician, and the magician speaks or sings a human translation of the Word.

Magical utterance takes power and gives it form. It becomes a trigger like an 'on switch' and the utterance instructs the power in how to take form, where to go and what to do. For it to truly work requires the strength, knowledge and skill of the magician, as the magician is both the bridge and the translator of that power.

The work of magical utterance starts when the magician is an apprentice magician and they learn how to use utterance along with ritual and vision, often

---

[1] Noble, 2020: 204–205.

in ways that carry no real power. It is a sandbox for the magician to learn their skill, and to learn the difference between magical utterance and simply speaking. Many budding magicians make the mistake of thinking that magical utterance needs flourish or drama, or a dramatic voice, or that what is uttered needs to be exotic or foreign or arcane. But such thinking is incorrect: emotion, theatre and drama have only a minor place in the early shallows of magic, and once the magician moves beyond the shallow paddling pool and into the deeper waters of magic, such 'performance' has no purpose. It is not the outer presentation that gives power to the utterance; rather, it is a magician who is rooted in contact and power that forms a magical pattern of words and releases it.

The utterance is any form of words that brings power and contact to a situation. It instructs, it informs, it communes, and it creates or destroys. It is used in ritual, in vision, and in other magical acts, it also is used in teaching, writing, and in magical protection. It is used to communicate with inner beings, and it is used in art that will act as a catalyst.

So what is the difference between speaking and uttering? Uttering is where the 'power switch' is turned on, and at times also the 'inner contact switch'. The words used are 'bare': i.e., the words are what is necessary, and no more. Why? Because magical utterance when switched on properly by a skilled magician is one of the most dangerous skills in magic: it is like a bullet with a guidance system. Properly used, it will do its job. Therefore, the formation of the power into words needs to be clean, precise, and carefully measured: it must be a clear lens for the power to flow through correctly. Any additional words that are not necessary or any dramatic flourishes or words of obscurity that the magician does not understand will create a muddy and confused pattern that the power cannot flow through properly.

However, like many things in magic, there are pitfalls and dead ends. What magical utterance is *not* is speaking in tongues, or 'channelling', or 'freeform ranting'. Words are a major manipulator of people, and people are very vulnerable to that manipulation. A good measure of real utterance is its simplicity and focus. If there is drama, flourishes, and emotion, then it is likely not true magical utterance. But there are exceptions. The inner power of utterance can flow unexpectedly through a dramatic non-magical recitation. The right person at the right time utters the right thing and power switches on to flow through that utterance. This can happen in ritual, but most often happens in theatre or even in a noisy bar at midnight.

DIVINATION

When this card appears in a magical reading, it indicates that magical utterance is needed for the situation, as opposed to ritual or vision, or other magical approaches. Or it can indicate that utterance is a major part of what is necessary.

It can also indicate learning. If the question is about the development of the magician, then it can indicate that power is being uttered to the magician. It can be a situation where the magician writes, and then reads that writing back to themselves and realizes that those words did not come from them, but from outside of them. They are learning, they are being taught.

If the card falls in a withheld position, then utterance and the word should not be used. It can also be a prompt to stay silent on something, or to not act.

If the card falls in the near or distant future, depending on the question, then it can indicate the need to speak, to teach, to write, or to utter magically. Or it indicates that this is what they will be doing in the future. Speaking and writing are the same thing when it comes to magical utterance. It is the communication of power and knowledge that is the important dynamic, not the method by which those words pass from one person to the other.

If the card falls in the crossed relationship position in a reading, then someone or some being is trying to communicate with the subject of the reading, or the person is writing or speaking and something other than the person is speaking through them.

Sometimes this card can be a prompt for words that need to be said. For magicians that often means that the magician needs to communicate with inner contacts or beings, or they need to externalize a power by speaking that power out into the world using words, written or spoken. Such uttering of words doesn't necessarily need to be aimed at humans or inner beings, creatures etc.: it can also be aimed at buildings and places. The Word can awaken a place, it can clean a place through words of exorcism, it can tune a place, and it can make a place sacred. Hence utterance is the most powerful magical tool.

Sometimes, depending on the question and subject matter of the reading, the appearance of this card can indicate the need for reciting a sacred text in a space, either for the person's own protection or for the sacredness of the words to embed into a space. Some sacred texts were born through inner utterance that was transformed into the written word which is then recited. The original power flows through the words and out into the world.

In a reading about a mundane subject, the appearance of this card can point to the need to communicate, to speak out, or to negotiate. Words need to be said, and words need to be heard. It can also indicate writing, public speaking, and discussion.

Keys

Communication, use of words, sacred utterance, magical writing or recitation, contacted writing, prayer.

20 Creating

Meaning

Once a magician steps past the first few outer courts of the temple of magical knowledge, they stand at the threshold of the inner temple, which houses the inner sanctum where the Divine in all its forms flows through the magic. Magic is a part of the Divine pattern of creation. This is the point where the magician ceases their quest for their 'will', which is deeply misunderstood in magic, and starts to ask, 'how may I serve?'

Everything that an adept magician does is a bridge for Divine fate, and any act a magician does, no matter how simple and mundane, becomes a sacred act. One of the most powerful acts is to create. Painting, sculpture, song, the written word, music...these are all expressions of the Divine that power can flow through. And the magician comes to realize through doing these creative acts that they are not the creator but merely a conduit, a bridge through which the creative power can express itself. Hence there are sacred utterances half-hidden upon and around the beings in the painting of this card.

The practical meaning of this card for magicians is that creating is a part of the magical life and work and is a way of serving. By bringing images, music, text, and shapes into the world, they are drawing a veil back for those who can potentially see. These works of art are breadcrumbs that create a path that triggers awakening in a person who is searching. Things like a line of text, a painting on the wall, a beautiful or powerful piece of music, are all things that inspire, awaken and strengthen a person on their path of magical discovery.

When the art in whatever form is contacted art, i.e., done magically with the technique of bridging power into it, that art becomes a magical tool or vessel that can be worked with, either actively or passively. Then it is consecrated so that no unhealthy being or energy can step into it. Once it is finished both physically and magically, it is either worked with by the magician for a specific reason, or it is sent out into the world. That means it is either given away at random, or left somewhere for someone to find, or it is sold at a price that is reasonable so that the right person can access the right vessel for them. Sometimes the magician recognizes that the art, song, or word needs to go a particular person, but they have no money so it is given to them freely. However, the creation itself is never ever done just for the sake of money: the first most important thing is that it is done because it needs doing.

It is irrelevant if the magician gets compensation for it or not.

And there are some magical creations that must be kept hidden away as they are doing a specific job, and they need a hidden space in which to operate. Once that work is done, the art is usually destroyed, or wrapped up and put away. It can never become a non-magical piece.

Sometimes a piece of contacted art is created with the direct intention to destroy it. First what needs destroying is drawn into the painting and fixed there. Then it is pinned and burned.

Divination

If this card appears in a reading which is general, it is prompting you to be more creative, to draw on the power of creation and put it into something. That is usually because there is a surplus of creative energy that needs putting into something, or because something specific needs creating, whether it is making a painting, or writing a book, or making an icon or statue, or composing music, etc.

The creative act is a major part of magic in many ways, but many modern magicians forget this or are unaware of it. By doing something creative, it allows that power to flow through you which in turn can balance you out, but if it is not let out it can start to block you up and cause damage.

If your question is a specific magical question, depending on where it falls, this card indicates that a creative act is part of the solution. If it lands in a difficult position, it can be saying that the root of the magical issue is a created vessel (statue, sigil, object) or window (a drawing, painting or icon), or, if you are currently working on creating something, it can be saying that the way you are depicting something is likely unbalanced or too controlled, or that something has moved into it and is causing problems.

If this card falls in a withheld position, it is advising against doing a creative act at this time. This means it would likely work against the current energetic tide which would cause you struggles and exhaustion or would likely expose you to danger. Magical art is not always a safe pursuit and is something that should be taken seriously and considered carefully. It is a powerful act, and you are responsible for what you create. This can be a particular problem with people who are naturally magical but who have little training or understanding. They can inadvertently create chaos by doing a work of art that creates a bridge for beings to pass into it, but the image itself is so unbalanced that it can give a destructive being access to the physical world. Another issue is when a painting allows a parasite to move into it: this gives it access to the humans who live or work around that piece of art.

In mundane divination, this is an action card. It is a prompt to bring creativity into your life, not only by passively enjoying looking, or listening, but by actually doing it. Even if you feel you are not a creative person, doing painting or drawing, drama, music, dance, sculpture, etc. allows inner energy to flow through you, which in turn can trigger regeneration, healing and growth.

This is why art is such a wonderful therapy, not only psychologically and physically, but also in terms of fate and your own spirit. When the power of creation flows through you, your whole body bathes in that energy. In religion we see creation as a 'one-off' event, which is incorrect. Creation (and destruction) is constantly happening from the smallest thing to the existence of the universe. By creating something, you mirror the foundational act of creation itself. It doesn't matter if what you have created is not up to the 'acceptable' standards of others: it is the *act* of creation, the process itself that is important, not what it looks like.

This card can also identify something that looks mundane but is actually a consecrated magical work of art or tool. If you are trying to discern if something is a real artifact or a fake, this card along with some other key cards can indicate 'yes, this is a real artefact'.

KEYS

Creating, painting, writing, sacred art, consecrated art, sacred words, creative service, music, drama, the creative act.

EXTRA

> What we call music in our everyday language is only a miniature, which our intelligence has grasped from that music or harmony of the whole universe which is working behind everything, and which is the source and origin of nature. It is because of this that the wise of all ages have considered music to be a sacred art. For in music the seer can see the picture of the whole universe; and the wise can interpret the secret and nature of the working of the whole universe in the realm of music.
>
> — Hazrat Inayat Khan[1] (1882-1927)

---

[1] Khan, 1996: 16.

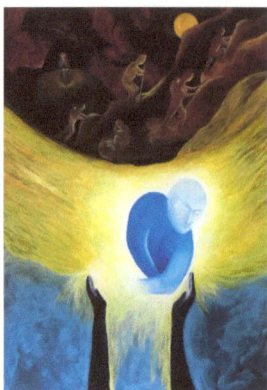

21 Loadsharer

Meaning

In the image, the sleeping figure is what is known in magic as a 'loadsharer': an empath who shares some of the energetic burdens of those who struggle. Two arms reach up to support the loadsharer, arms of inner contacts or beings that in turn uphold the loadsharer in their work.

Magical load-sharing is a step further on from an empath and is more focused. It is where the magician's energy is shared out with other magicians when a person or a group of magicians have triggered a long-term magical working in service that is critical to the fate of many.

This can also happen when a magician who works in service has their energy 'borrowed' by the inner beings that uphold and maintain complex critical fate patterns that affect nations or large events over time. In such cases, the magician usually has a connection to the complex fate pattern either by nature of their work, where they live, or their bloodlines. And sometimes a magician is both a natural empath and also a fate worker, so they can sometimes end up carrying large loads during critical times: they often find they become exhausted when some major events in the world are unfolding or building up ready to unfold.

Their energy stretches out to uphold those who are in the midst of the event, to ensure that whoever they are upholding can do what they need to do or get to where they need to be. When very fateful events happen out in the world, often different empaths and magicians around the world find that their energy is suddenly stretching out to 'join in' with the event for whatever reason.

How does it manifest for a person? When someone is load-sharing they will feel continuously tired or drained of energy, they may dream vividly and have a sense that they are 'doing something'. Their body may ache as though it is carrying a heavy weight, or they may feel like 'their tide has gone out'. There are a lot of physical conditions and illnesses that can also cause these symptoms, but if the person is a magician, and medical tests show nothing is wrong, then divination may show that the condition is because of working or load-sharing. It can be important to use divination to get to the bottom of it, just in case it is a physical illness or condition that has not yet been spotted. Always assume a physical reason before going looking for a magical cause.

It is one of the hardest and most unglamourous sides of deeper and powerful magic, where the magician's energy works very hard to protect or uphold those whose fates and actions are very important at key times. Often it is about keeping someone safe or alive during an important junction point in time, events, or fate. And it is often an unconditional service, meaning that the empathic magician does not know who they are helping or why, just that the call for help went out and the magician's deeper self has responded without a conscious decision. It is unglamourous because the magician cannot lay claim to have helped and cannot pride themselves on a job well done.

Sometimes the magician has no idea whom they have helped, and at other times it becomes obvious what they are working on. When many magicians around the world are experiencing the same thing, and then a major change happens in the world, the magician will do a reading to ascertain if that world event is what is taking their energy. If the reading confirms their suspicions, then they know to stop all other work and to rest so that the important load-sharing can do its thing and they will not get too overloaded.

What cannot be done is *intentional* load-sharing. If the magician makes a conscious decision to load-share for a person, that action is often blocked. When we see someone who we feel is struggling, we do not see the wider picture. They may need to go through a period of struggle, or there may be other elements involved in the situation that we cannot see. Making a conscious decision to load-share often comes from an emotional response to a situation, and not from a response of necessity. We can often do more harm than good when we fiddle with people's lives, and that can be a hard lesson to learn for some magicians.

The whole concept of load-sharing in magic is one of those avenues of magic that is complex, but it is also one that can be a fascinating area of learning through observation. It is not a subject to study from a theoretical perspective, even though it is often written about by magicians or philosophers who have not directly experienced it, but who simply have theories. It is far better to learn from direct personal experience or through observing such action over a span of time and paying attention to events that the magician is connected to in one way or another.

Divination

When this card appears, it is a clear message that your inner energy or the inner energy of the subject of the reading is doing something that is upholding a person, a place, or a fate event. It can be unintentional (a natural inner response), it can be the response of the deeper spirit working without conscious intent from the magician, or it can be old or current magical work triggering.

If the reading is about a place or structure and the Loadsharer card appears, depending on the question it could mean that the fate of this place is important and someone is upholding it energetically, or that the land itself is load-sharing for the wider area.

If the card falls in a 'past' position it is stating that the dynamic is now passing away and your energy should release soon. If this card falls in a withheld position, it is a warning to not take on burdens at this time, or it can be read as a negative: 'no, there is no load-sharing happening'.

If the card falls in the inner worlds position in a layout, the subject of the reading is potentially load-sharing for an important fate event that has not yet happened. Their energy is helping in the formation of that fate pattern to protect it and keep it balanced. In such cases the load-sharing can go on for months, and rarely, years. But when the event or series of events finally happen in the physical world, the burden suddenly lifts, and the person feels strong and full of energy. Another way of reading this card in this position, again depending on the question and subject matter of the reading, is that inner beings are load-sharing for the person or place that the reading is about. This is not common but does happen.

If the Loadsharer card appears in the relationship position, the subject of the reading is likely load-sharing for a partner. That can be a relationship partner, or a close friend, or even an organisation or business that is a major part of their life.

The appearance of this card in the position of hearth/home usually points to load-sharing for a family member. For magicians, psychics and natural empaths, the card in this position can also indicate load-sharing for the soul of a child who is yet to be conceived. If a soul waiting to be conceived into life is a fateful soul, i.e., if their life will trigger major changes in the world, or if their path will be very fateful, then such formation of a child can take a lot of energy which can be drawn from people in the bloodline or from someone who is tightly connected to a parent of the child.

The most common load-sharing in non-magicians is for old people in the family or ones who are closely connected to the empath. The same is true with people who are dying. Death takes a great deal of inner energy and sometimes the inner vital force of the old or dying person is so low that they do not have the energy to die properly. In such cases people close to them who are empaths will find their vital force drained off as it goes to help the dying person.

Although load-sharing drains inner vital force as opposed to physical energy, the body reacts as though it is low on physical energy. This is a dynamic which becomes more and more apparent to magicians as they mature in their craft and work in the various different fields of magic. What impacts the inner spirit and inner energy of the person is processed through the physical body. It does not usually make the body ill as such, but it can certainly feel like it, and at times it can aggravate an already present illness or condition.

In mundane readings, this card can also represent non-energetic load-sharing, such as helping a person with a physically or mentally demanding job they need to do such as moving house, caring for children, doing office work, or literally carrying heavy loads for them.

Sharing a burden, upholding others, caretaking, holding a magical working, protecting someone, helping, hard work, enabling someone.

22 Dead End

Meaning

This is one of the simple cards in the deck that has nothing beyond the surface meaning. It is a dead end.

In magic and in life we can often find ourselves in a situation where there is no way forward, even if we wait for that path to open up. Rather than being a temporary barrier or respite, the dead end is where there is nothing beyond: there is no fate path for the person to continue in that situation. Dead ends, however, can teach us as much as they block us. In magic, as in life, we can be sucked in by 'glamour' and promises of wonderful things, or we can go off exploring and find at times that the turns we have ended up in dead ends.

This is part of a learning process that teaches us to pay closer attention, to look at the layout of the land, to look beyond the surface of a glittery or tempting presentation, or to step back from a loud and expensive marketing extravaganza. It is also part of the learning process to learn to listen to that quiet and subtle inner voice of our deeper selves when it is whispering 'no'.

When we first start walking the path of magic, particularly in the early stages of our exploration and seeking, we have few if any reference points as to whether what we are exploring truly is magic, or is a fantasy dressed up as magic to separate us from our money, or is simply an expression of someone else's madness. There are also times when a magical path or system may be legitimate, but it has no way forward for us as individuals. This could be because of our own unique fate path and where it needs to lead us, or it could be that it is simply incompatible with aspects of our lives that we as yet cannot see.

A dead end cannot be hacked through or transformed: it simply is what it is, and there is no way forward. We simply have to retrace our steps, learn from the experience, and continue on our way in a different direction.

Divination

When this card appears in a reading, look closely at where it falls in the layout. If it falls in the short-term future, whatever your plans and the question is about, it is a dead end and it is pointless continuing. If, however, it falls in the long-term future, then the path forward for now probably has some benefit if a favourable card falls in the near future position, but in the long term it will come to a dead end. In such cases it is often worth doing further readings to look at options of different approaches or actions that will change that long term outcome, or to see whether it is worth continuing forward to allow other ways forward to open up when they are ready. But the plans and intentions of your current fate pattern will only work in the short term, not the long term.

If the card falls in a past position, then the blockages and dead ends that you faced, regarding whatever the question is about, have fallen away.

When this card falls in an 'endure' position, it is a prompt to wait and not make changes. Whatever is necessary for you to move forward will take time to unfold, and you will need to get through a period of stasis and frustration by being patient and paying attention to the small signals that fate can present to you for the eventual better way forward.

This card falling in the first position, which signifies the subject of the reading, indicates that the person is blocked, and is probably also either unhealthy or living an unhealthy life that is not going to take them into old age unless they make radical changes. It is not an end of fate; rather it is a dead end that can lead to an end of fate if the person does not make the necessary changes to their life.

If it falls in the relationship position, then the card is saying that relationships *at this time* are a dead end and if the person is not currently in a relationship, then they are unlikely to be able to change that soon. Often such a block is there for good reason, and that reason often becomes clearer as the person's fate unfolds: their focus and time is often needed for something that is far more important.

The same is true for magical interactions with beings. If the reading is about contacted magical work, and this card falls in the relationship position, then the contact is either not there (and the person is talking to their own mind), or it is not an interaction that can lead anywhere useful. Rather, it is more likely at some point to shut down the magician. This card in this position can also indicate where a person may have been magically shut down.

When the reading is about a place or a building, it indicates that the place has no future or has been magically sealed shut, or that it has energetically died. If the reading is about a choice of building for a magical space or a living space, and this card is in a prominent place, then such a place would not be good for purpose, no matter how wonderful it looks.

This card can also be interpreted in simple yes/no questions as a no. It is a negative, empty, stop card.

KEYS

No way ahead, blocked, dead end, empty, no, end, stop.

23 Four Creatures

Meaning

Arba'at El,[1] The Four Divine Creatures, is an ancient mystery that speaks of drawing closer to the Divine, or to put it another way, it speaks of coming into true focus of the Universal Divine within and all around you.

Traditionally, the four are divine guardians and are described in Abrahamic texts as angels: the *Hayyot*, or Cherubim. In magic the creatures are most often depicted as a part of the Chariot in most tarot decks. In some tarot decks they appear as beings on the Wheel of Fortune, and they also appear in Biblical visionary texts. They are also found in some fifteenth and sixteenth century grimoire texts, and the mention of these beings or their name in such texts can indicate magical workings around the theme of ascending to heaven paradise.

However, they are not exclusively a part of the Chariot but are independent of the Chariot while also being an integral part of it. Without the Four Creatures, the Chariot does not trigger.

These angelic beings do not guard from misfortune; rather they guard the fate of those on a path of deep divine, mystical, or magical awakening. As the person walks their fate path, one by one over time the creatures make themselves known through dreams and visions.

Their mystery cannot be explained in text, and the encounters with the creatures cannot be retold. Their mystery is learned through encounters (usually with one creature at a time) and by truly recognising the Divine human within you at a very deep level. When that awareness and understanding unfolds, then the magician or mystic sees what was always there, hidden in plain sight. This becomes your own knowledge over your lifetime that cannot be retold, simply because there are no words to express that knowledge.

Divination

The overall meaning of this card in magical divination points to an evolutionary step within the magician. The meaning of the card is 'that which is sacred within

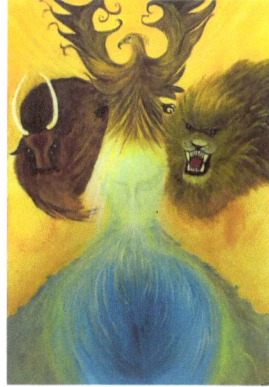

---

[1] In Hebrew, *Arba'at* ארבעת means four. *El* אל means 'God' in a generic sense and is a word found in a variety of Semitic languages. The combination of *Arba'at* and *El* was sometimes used in 15th and 16th century magical texts to quietly suggest the *Hayyot*.

humanity'. Every human has the potential to move closer to the Divine universal conscious power within and around them, but the development of that potential rests solely upon the footsteps, actions, and choices of the person on their journey through their life.

When this card appears in a magical reading it can indicate a next step upon the path of inner evolution, or a profound and life-changing inner experience, however fleeting it may be. It is the card of the developing one, the mystical magician who reaches for what is sacred all around them, and who strives to protect and be protected, and to serve and be served. A person who has a fate path of becoming a 'developing one' is likely to have dream or visionary encounters with the four creatures, sometimes from youth onward.

This card can also indicate a magical dynamic whereby the visionary is guarded by the Four and is 'carried in the Chariot'[1] to an inner threshold that would normally be beyond their reach. This cannot be magically triggered or forced by the magician, and to attempt such would be folly indeed, as the impact upon the mind and or body of the magician in the long term could be terrible. Instead, it is a spontaneous lifting of the spirit in a way that is a natural progression.

If the reading is about a place or event, then it can indicate that powerful Divine fate patterns are connected to that place or event and should not be interfered with.

If the card falls into a withheld position in the layout, it means that whatever the reading is about, there is nothing Divine or evolutionary about the subject of the reading.

If the card falls in a position of 'endurance', then the reading is telling you to be strong, to hold fast in the face of whatever struggles you are going through, as it is forming part of a path that will take you deeper and further into the Mysteries: the dynamic of the four creatures is somehow connected with the struggles you are going through.

In a mundane reading, this card can appear when the subject person of the reading is on the cusp of a path that triggers spiritual evolution. It can also appear in mundane readings for someone where they have or are about to have a fleeting experience that opens their eyes to the more profound and hidden aspects of our existence. This can be a religious revelation, or a discovery that there are indeed inner worlds, beings that cannot be seen, continued existence after death, etc.

In simple mundane readings, i.e., looking for a lost object, or how to approach an everyday issue, the message of this card can be to look up, or to take control of your own destiny and not be dictated to by others.

Keys

Angelic protection, evolving, spiritual revelation, profound life changing spiritual experience, be active in your own destiny, recognize your own self-worth.

---

[1] i.e. taken in vision.

Extra

Heaven' and the 'Garden' are all around us unseen, not of the physical. Wheels within wheels are sometimes still and silent, and sometimes alive and moving. They rise from the spirit of the land to create a bridge, or they slumber, waiting.

The four are three

The two become one

Seek not out the things that are too hard for thee, neither search the things that are above thy strength. But what is commanded thee, think thereupon with reverence; for it is not needful for thee to see with thine eyes the things that are in secret.

— Hokhmat ben Sira[1] (born approx. 170 BCE)

24 Chariot

Meaning

The Chariot is not an object or standalone vehicle; rather it is an energetic power pattern that transports. In western culture we view that power pattern as angelic: the Chariot is an aspect of the angel and comes forth from the angel. The 'horse' of the Chariot is visionary vocabulary for a power that is of nature and the land, a power that can transport human consciousness from one realm to another.

When you put the angel and the horse together in terms of visionary meaning, you have a power that is of the Divine consciousness of the land and also the stars planets, and that can carry the spirit of living humans from one realm to another. This motif of a white horse transporting the human in vision is a common theme that can be found in a variety of different cultures and religions, from Bronze Age Britain right across the northern hemisphere to the Far East.[2] In some other cultures this power appears as a barque, or as a chariot pulled by three horses, or simply as a white horse or unicorn.

---

[1] Schlechter and Taylor, 1899.

[2] The Bach Ma Temple in Hanoi Vietnam: Bach Ma means white horse. Uchaishravas in Hindu mythology is a seven headed white horse spirit.

In terms of magic, the two tales that stand out the most for me about a horse-drawn chariot that comes from an angel and carries a visionary into the heavenly realms are the tale of Elijah carried to heaven on a chariot of fire and horses,[1] and the tale of *Al Buraq*,[2] the bright horse that carries the Prophet Muhammad and is accompanied by the angel Gabriel on the Night Journey to Haram al Sharif in Jerusalem where he briefly visits heaven.[3]

The Chariot is a power that bridges the person to realms in vision that they could not reach alone. The reach of this angelic expression is from the depths of the earth to the heights of the stars, from the Underworld to the Heavens. If you read the Report of Anas bin Malik in the Sunnah,[4] and if you read some of the many traditional tales of faeries and land spirits in Europe, then you will spot the similarities in actions and behaviour of the chariot horse. This, and our own direct experience from magical visionary practice, tells us that all the spirits which we have categorized into boxes, i.e., angels, land spirits, faery beings etc, are not completely separate from each other but are all interconnected.

In traditional tarot and in Kabbalah, the chariot is intimately linked with the Four Holy Creatures.[5] However, while this relationship is close, they are magically and mystically two distinct units of power that sometimes come together to create the Chariot of Ascent.

DIVINATION

When the Chariot appears in a reading, it is pointing to major forward movement in terms of magical or mystical evolution. Sometimes the path of an evolutionary step is triggered by a vision that comes not from your own instigation, but from the powers and spirits around you. It indicates help, an uplift, Divine assistance that acts as a catalyst for your development on the path of the magician or mystic.

In magical readings it can also indicate the need for a visionary approach to something or can indicate that the visionary work being done or which is needed is deep and powerful. In such a case, if the work proposed is conducive to fate and is absolutely necessary, then it is possible an aspect of the Four Creatures will draw near and facilitate an extending of the reach of the visionary work.

Sometimes it can indicate a need for you to travel somewhere, either physically or in vision in order to have an experience, or to provide magical service to a place on the land, or a person or to spirits. Its core message is one of movement, inner or physical, and movement that will be assisted if necessary.

Sometimes the horse can appear regularly in the visions and dreams of the magician. In these cases it acts as an inner contact being that will carry you from

---

[1] *2Kings* 2:11.

[2] *Al Buraq*: literal meaning is the one of lightning brightness.

[3] *Quran* Surah Al Isra + Surah wal Miraj (part 1 and 2 of the Night Journey) and *The report of Anas bin Malik*: Sunnah (English) vol5, bk58, Hadith 227.

[4] *The report of Anas bin Malik*: Sunnah (English) vol5, bk58, Hadith 227.

[5] The Four Creatures card in this deck.

realm to realm until you are able to access those realms for yourself. One of my very first magical contacts as a young magician was a white horse that took me places in vision. Once I was more experienced and stronger magically, that contact faded off as it was no longer necessary.

In mundane readings the Chariot can indicate a car or vehicle, and/or travel. It can also indicate moving, for example moving house or moving to a new country. Occasionally, depending on the question and subject matter of the reading, it can indicate the need to physically move around, such as walking, dance, etc.

Keys

Visionary journey, evolution, forward action, travel between realms, travel, spirit creature that transports, travel, ascent, angelic bridge, moving, affirmative response, yes.

Extra

The following is a bit long for this section, but it is important magically. The story of Night Journey and ascent[1] (al-'Isrā' wal-Mi'rāj) of the Prophet Muhammed is a fascinating story to read as it contains so much that magicians and mystics would recognize, and it is a good illustration of the power we know as the 'Chariot' expressing in a very different way. It may also be interesting to note that the word Mi'rāj (mirage) which denotes a vision, is an Arabic word for ladder. Something that facilitates ascent, which is a theme within various ancient and classical cultures: the Ladder of Ascent.

Al-'Isrā'

The Prophet sat in meditation at the Ka'ba holy sanctuary in Mecca, and his heart was full of sadness. He had endured a year of sorrow with the death of his wife Khadijah, and of his beloved uncle. As he sat in silence, the angel Gabriel (Jibril) appeared to him. The angel opened the chest of the Prophet and washed his heart with Zamzam water, and then poured into his chest a golden gift of wisdom and faith. He then presented the Prophet with a white horse called Al-Buraq,[2] bigger than a donkey and smaller than a mule. Its stride was as long as the eye could reach. The horse was bright and shimmered with light and had the face of a woman.

The angel told the Prophet to mount the horse, and off they went to Jerusalem travelling at great speed upon the wonderous creature. The horse alighted at the 'furthest place of prayer' from Ka'ba, at the

---

[1] *Quran* Surah Al Isra + Surah wal Miraj (part 1 and 2 of the Night Journey).

[2] *Al-Buraq* from the Arabic word *barq* which means to sparkle or emitting lightning. Al-Buraq is a spirit horse, sometimes described as 'an angel horse'.

Masjid al Aqsa, the temple mount in Jerusalem. The Prophet tethered Al-Buraq and stepped into the sacred place with the angel. He prayed in this special place of Prophets and was tested by the angel.[1]

Glory be to the One Who took His servant Muḥammad (pbuh) by night from the Sacred place of prayer to the Farthest sacred place of prayer whose surroundings We have blessed, so that We may show him some of Our signs. Indeed, He alone is the All-Hearing, All-Seeing.

– Noble Quran Surah Al-Isra 17:1

al-Miʿrāj

Once the angel had tested the Prophet, the angel lifted the Prophet from this sacred place and took him through the layers of heaven where he met many great prophets, and he witnessed the angels, until the angel Gabriel told the Prophet, "I can go no further, you must continue alone". The Prophet continued until he was in the presence of Allah; God most high. The prophet was given instructions to take back to the people.

He left the presence of Allah and was guided back to the sacred place by the angel. There al-Buraq was waiting patiently for him. Al-Buraq took the prophet back to Ka'ba, where he recounted his experiences and passed on the message from Allah to his people. Pray to me, many times a day, pray.[2]

---

[1] Sahih al-Bukhari,K. al-Salah, 'Bab Kayfa Furidat al-Salah fi al-Isra'. Sahih al-Bukhari is a hadith collection and a book of sunnah compiled by the Persian scholar Muḥammad ibn Ismāʿil al-Bukhāri around 846.

[2] Sahih al-Bukhari, K. Manaqib al: Ansar, 'Bab al-Mi'raj

25 LEADERSHIP

MEANING

In today's world of greed, power and corruption, the true and ancient meaning of being a leader has fallen by the wayside in a lot of instances, be that a leader of a magical group, a team of workers, a town, or a nation. The whole structure and path of a true leader is anchored by one simple equation: *protect the weak and limit the strong*. This equation is underpinned by integrity along with checks and balances on power. It also has deep magical roots in core fate patterns, and when a good leader emerges, regardless of how small or big their 'territory' is, operating within the core leadership fate pattern will affect all the people and sometimes also the land. Stability and balance in a group or society starts and ends with the leader, and the leader's behaviour and decisions trigger fate patterns to shift in particular ways. This is true not only of magical leadership but also of mundane leadership.

Serious and experienced magicians operate like 'leaders' simply by nature of their work, and because most adept magicians are lone practitioners. Magicians work with power to effect change. This is exactly what a leader does; hence the two operate from within the same template of fate. And magic, just like leadership, is full of sacrifice and complexities that need to be understood in order to operate effectively. And leadership, just like magic, is littered with big personalities that falsely promise easy answers to very difficult questions and situations.

By understanding the difficult complexities of leadership, the magician also learns the complexities of magic, and thus can operate far more effectively, just with less showmanship and glamour.

DIVINATION

On a mundane level when this card falls in a reading it is indicating either a leader or the need to take the lead on something. As always, where it falls in the layout, and what the subject matter of the question is, always determines its direct message. If the card falls, for example, in the near or distant future, then it indicates that the subject of the reading will become a leader of something in the future or will need to take the initiative.

It can also indicate communal safety and protection, as well as indicating the power of integrity. If the question of the reading is asking about safety, and this card appears, then it can indicate that you are indeed safe. If the question is about whether you need to protect something and this card appears, then it is saying 'yes, step up and protect'.

On a deeper magical level, this card can indicate the need for the magician to engage the leadership equation: *limit the strong, protect the weak*. For example, if the magician is conducting magical work out on the land, then it can indicate the need to approach the gardening or tending of the land in the same way. Cut back and keep in check plants etc. that are invasive or aggressive without killing them all off, and ensure that the more delicate but necessary plants have the light, food, and water that they need. This is a simple, mundane act, but when done by a magician with intent, it can have inner effects that ripple out across the land.

If the reader looks at where this card falls, then, within the context of the question, it can tell them a great deal about how they need to move forward or make choices. It is a card of stepping up, of taking responsibility, and also of ensuring that their own lives and practice are conducted in a way that balances the use of power with integrity.

If this card falls in a withheld position, then its message is pretty clear. Depending on the question it is indicating either not to take a leadership role in this, or that the subject of the reading is not a real leader.

If the reading is about a building or space, and this card appears in a positive position, then it is stating that the space or building has solid integrity and will protect those who live or work in it. If the card is in a withheld position, then it is saying that no matter how good the building looks, it has no integrity: its foundations or structures are weak, damaged, or unable to fulfil its role in the long term. It will not 'limit the strong' (i.e. it will not be secure or withstand a bad storm) and it will not 'protect the weak' (i.e. its structure is likely unstable, leaking, and poorly insulated).

If the question is looking at a person and the leadership card appears, then it is saying that this is a person of integrity who will step up to responsibility and is able to make difficult but necessary decisions. If it is in a withheld position, then it is saying that this person has none of those qualities. If it falls in the last position, then it is likely that the person was once a 'leadership' type of person, but that they no longer have those qualities.

Keys

Stability, leadership, integrity, responsibility, a leader or boss, protection, safety, initiative, stepping up.

Extra

The following is an extract from the *Maxims of Ptahhotep*,[1] a Middle Kingdom

---

[1] Extract from Maxims of Ptahhotep, Prisse Papyrus, columns five, line eight, to column six, line

Egyptian text purported to have been authored by Ptahhotep, Tjaty[1] to fifth dynasty king Djedkare Isesi (late 25th century BC). In the text of the Maxims, Ptahhotep, who is now old and wishes to retire, instructs his son Akhethetep in wisdoms and methods of leadership. If you read carefully and in context of the leadership equation, then you will see how it is being subtly applied in the advice on how to act. This is also good advice for dealing with difficult people in general.

> Do not be proud on account of your knowledge but discuss with the ignorant as with the wise. The limits of art cannot be delivered; there is no artist whose talent is fulfilled. Fine words are more sought after than greenstone, but can be found with the women at the grindstone.

> If you meet an opponent in his moment, a director of heart who is superior to you, bend your arms and bow; do not take up your heart against him, for he will not be swayed for you. You can belittle bad speaking by not clashing with him in his moment; it will mean he is called a fool, when your self-restraint has subdued his excess.

> If you meet an opponent in his moment, your equal, a man from your levels, silence is how you establish your superiority over him while he is bad mouthing greatly to the disgust of the assessors, and your name is the good one in the mind of the officials.

> If you meet an opponent in his moment who is a poor man, and not your equal, do not vent your heart on him by his wretchedness. Put him on land for him to oppose himself. Do not pour out your heart at the man facing you. The demolition of a wretched heart is a difficult matter. What you wish will be done; beat him with the hostility of the officials.

six. Now held at the Biblotheque Nationale de France.
[1]A Tjaty is a vizier

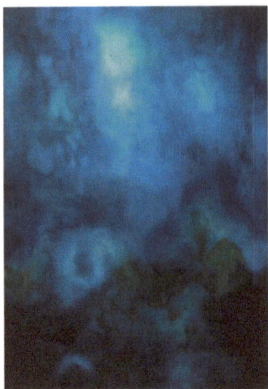

26 Hidden Knowledge

Within the void is everything.
Within the void is nothing.

Meaning

Hidden knowledge refers to an ancient magical dynamic where the deep 'waters' hold the most ancient and hidden knowledge (called the Nu in dynastic Egyptian religion). It is also referred to in the Tanakh as the 'watery abyss', a Divine inner body of water that all things come from and return to. Magicians sometimes know this as the Void, and as the incubator of great potential and learning.

The magical Hidden Knowledge is an elusive dynamic that slowly reveals itself as a sacred knowledge once we pluck up the courage to dive into its depths, to trust the sacredness of the path we walk, and to let go of our mortal fears. Reaching into Hidden Knowledge is an act of courage, an act of faith, and a willingness to let go of what we think we know. Its knowledge cannot be accessed through sheer intellect, rather it speaks to our soul: it is a knowledge that cannot be put into words.

It is the power of natural spiritual and psychic depth that is obscured by illusions created by its ever-changing quality that is hard to grasp; it is seemingly gentle and yet has the power to destroy mountains. It allows us fleeting glimpses of its power, yet vanishes when we focus our gaze upon it.

It corresponds with Da'at on the Kabbalistic Tree of Life, and with the power of Neptune: that which is obscured but has great depth of meaning. Hidden Knowledge is the dynamic of magical mystical knowledge that sleeps undisturbed in the depths until someone awakens it by reaching deeply into the Mysteries.

Divination

The appearance of this card in a reading can indicate an unseen force or unseen actions dynamics details that are affecting the situation of the reading. It points to something you cannot see or do not know, but whatever it is, it is having a direct effect upon the subject of the reading. It is a neutral card, and its interpretation is heavily dependent upon the subject matter of the reading.

If the reading is a magical one or about your own magical practice, the appearance of this card indicates that you have drawn close to the 'Lake of Hidden Knowledge'. While you cannot yet drink of its waters with understanding, the power of hidden knowledge is in your orbit and is starting to connect with you. It is that which is unseen but is eventually reachable; it is knowledge that must be earned through your own evolution, fate, and maturity. It is guarded well against the eyes of the profane and the minds of the ignorant.

Depending on the question and the position in which this card falls in a layout, it can indicate that the magician is on the cusp of a major step of inner development, and that they are about to embark upon a fate cycle which will reveal some of the mysteries to the magician if they pay attention. It is only through direct experience that hidden knowledge surfaces, and when it does, it cannot be expressed to another person, simply because there are no sufficient words.

If it is a withheld position, that access is out of reach to the magician on the path they are currently walking.

It can also indicate a stepping into the unknown, or a phase of preparation from which you will eventually emerge. Its message is trust. Continue what you are doing in the best way you know how, in as balanced a way as you know how, and that which cannot be seen yet will slowly reveal itself to you as you evolve.

If the reading is about a mundane subject matter, this card points to a hidden or unseen element in the story. This card can often indicate that what is hidden can also have deep roots, that it is not a simple unseen element.

If the card is in a withheld negative position, this message is either 'there is no hidden element' or 'do not hide something, be open and truthful'. In mundane readings it can also indicate secrets.

In a reading about a place or building, it can either indicate unseen or hidden issues, or that there is a cave or hidden basement underneath, or underground unseen water.

In personal readings it can also indicate a period of depression, where a person dives into their depths and feels like they cannot see a way ahead. However, with this card the depths hold the seed of renewal. If a person is depressed and this card appears in a reading it is saying that the depression is a temporary state out of which can come great things. It is the emptiness that is paradoxically full of potential, it is the incubator of new learning.

KEYS

Unseen, secret, hidden, beyond understanding, hidden potential, unknown, depths, unseen water, incubation of great learning, despair before emerging, dark night of the soul.

27 Inner Desert

Meaning

The Inner Desert is a non-physical space or inner realm that sits between unbeing and being, with the universal consciousness Divine being on one side, and the inner pattern potential of all physical life on the other. Between the two is the Abyss.

Magicians access this place in vision, passing into a space where there is nothing living, no plants or trees, no creatures, etc. It presents to our minds as a total desert devoid of any sign of life. This is a space or 'condition' where the Divine universal consciousness forms the inner patterns of fate, life, death and physical being. The patterns and energies which form then pass out from the desert into physical existence. It is the 'cooking pot' for all life which first forms as an inner structure, then finally expresses itself as it leaves the desert and passes into physical being. What it is not is a psychological or spiritual place that is of an individual person: this is a common misunderstanding with some magicians.

It is also the place where we can, as magicians, observe tides of energy that flow from across the other side of the Abyss, come into focus, and form in the Inner Desert before expressing out in the physical world. Sometimes these tides of creation and destruction form, in our terms, over many years before they finally express out in our physical world. These tides, which are constantly forming and flowing, are things that the magician goes into the Inner Desert to observe. When we see a major destructive or creative tide build up in the Inner Desert, we know that in the near future, destruction or creation is going to express in our world. We can then prepare using divination to observe how it is going to express, and occasionally get a timeline for its 'outing' in our world.

This is also the space where the magician 'crosses the Abyss'. Once a magician's training has reached a certain level of skill and maturity, then the magician stands at the edge of the Abyss and looks out over the vast crack in this space to the realm beyond which is the threshold of the Divine. To step on the other side of the Abyss is to step into the most sacred of spaces, and to be able to do that the magician must first face the being that dwells and guards this space. This angelic being is of humanity and is also of the angelic Divine: it is a threshold being and their human aspect allows this being to both understand and commune with human magicians.

Often a magician will spend many months or even years visiting this being and standing in its presence before attempting to step out into the nothing in order to cross the Abyss. To enact the crossing of the Abyss, the magician cannot ask for help from the being, nor can they expect help. What saves the magician from falling down into the Abyss is their own development and evolution, their true, deep recognition of the Divinity within everything, and their willingness to trust fate, their own true heart, and the power of the Divine.

As a magician spends more time in vision in this space, they start to realize that although there is nothing growing in the desert, there are still structures. The inner patterns of ancient temples, and the inner pattern of all human knowledge which presents in vision as a vast ancient library. These are places where the magician goes to work and learn, and the inner structures act as an interface between the stored ancient knowledge, skills, and beings, and the magician.

DIVINATION

The card of the Inner Desert is a very complex card that speaks of inner visionary work, inner realms, Divine judgement, prophecy, and vast angelic patterns of existence. Teasing out an understanding of what this card is saying in a reading depends not only on the subject matter, the person, the question, and where the card falls, but it also depends on the level of magical understanding of the magician or of person who is doing the reading. Its meanings are many layered, and divination skill is needed to ascertain in magical readings what level or layer of power is speaking through the reading.

When it appears in magical readings it can be either prompting the magician that they need to work in vision, or, that inner angelic beings from this realm have some part to play in the situation the reading is about. If the card falls in the endurance position, then it is stating that such work would be very difficult indeed and may have a heavy impact on the magician. If it falls in an unravelling or falling away position, and the magician has been working in this space in vision, then it is saying that the work is unravelling the person. The power of this place and particularly the crossing of the Abyss can trigger a person to start to unravel in health or mind if they are not prepared and strong enough to endure the energetic burden of such an act.

The Inner Desert is the inner template of existence and the source of vast angelic patterns. Hence it must always be treated with the greatest of respect. When this card appears, regardless of the question or its position in the layout, do not forget that it represents something deeply powerful and sacred: a sacredness beyond religions or ideas which we cannot understand but which we can recognize and feel. And it is an *active* sacredness that has a direct impact on the physical world.

If the magician is looking for the right way to approach a magical issue or working and this card appears in a good position, then it is saying that inner visionary work would be the most effective. However, if it falls in a withheld or past position, then visionary work would not be the right approach at that time for that issue.

If the magician is looking at their long-term development and this card falls in a prominent or favourable position, then it describes the evolution of the magician moving beyond surface trifles and systems in magic, and potentially into a phase of development that takes (or will take) them closer to the root of all being.

When you look carefully at what this place signifies, you also begin to understand that another thing this card can indicate is Divine or inner judgement. This is not judgement based upon our own human ethics and morals, but about Divine judgement based on necessity, fate, and cause and effect. If the reading is about such deep issues and this card appears, then it can indicate such a dynamic is active in the subject matter, and the cards around it in their respective positions can indicate how that judgement will fall, and what the outcome for the subject matter of the reading would be.

In more mundane readings, but also in some magical readings, this card can also indicate a threshold that must not be crossed unless you fully understand the consequence of such an action, and that you are willing to take any damage to yourself that such an action could trigger, even the loss of life.

It can be a warning that you need to take things seriously and not step forward until you are absolutely sure your actions are true and right.

Keys

Abyss, Inner Desert, inner temples, powerful threshold, a warning to go no further, inner vision, prophecy, Divine judgement.

Extra

> Then the Most High, the Holy and Great One spake, and sent Uriel to the son of Lamech, and said to him: "Go to Noah and tell him in my name, hide thyself!" and reveal to him the end that is approaching: that the whole earth will be destroyed, and a deluge is about to come upon the whole earth, and will destroy all that is on it.

> And now instruct him that he may escape, and his seed may be preserved for all the generations of the world. And again the Lord said to Raphael: "Bind Azazel hand and foot, and cast him into the darkness: and make an opening in the desert, which is in Dudael, and cast him therein. And place upon him rough and jagged rocks, and cover him with darkness, and let him abide there for ever, and cover his face that he may not see light. And on the day of the great judgement, he shall be cast into the fire.

> — Book of the Secrets of Enoch, ch.10.[1]

---

[1] Charles, 1913.

28 Test

Meaning

The ultimate test in the mysteries is to have your balance tested: can you become the fulcrum? Like all tests in the magical mysteries, this is not a ceremony or ritual; the ceremonies and rituals surrounding such tests exist only to act as triggers for the testing. The ritual or vision is done, and the power then flows into the fate pattern of the human. The test itself comes in life, and it is not one event but a series of events that together make a whole. It is a testing that puts pressure on the body, the mind, the spirit, the emotional choices, the physical strength, and the ethics of the person—and it tests them to their limit. It is not a search for perfection or perfect balance, as that does not exist in a human; rather it is to test the resolve to develop, to evolve as closely to your own balance as is possible in the face of adversity.

The magician is also tested by the power of the planetary spirits, and by the solar spirit. Each power 'leans' on the person as they go through the various events and situations that test them. Difficult astrological transits can become 'hotspots' for some of the tests; hence the important for magicians to have at least a rudimentary understanding of astrological influence.

Our cultures and the dominant religions on our societies can have a marked influence on what we perceive as ethical and moral, and this can hobble the magician in many ways. What is tested is our ability to be the fulcrum, the understanding of light and dark, of creation and destruction. This can often run counter to a culture's morals or sense of what is 'right and wrong'.

In general, people feel that what potentially harms them is 'evil' and what makes them happy is 'good'. This is an undeveloped understanding of life and the world, and is heavily unbalanced. As a magician matures, they begin to realize just how complex life is and how what can be generally considered 'dark' or 'evil' is something necessary for the upholding of creation. Without destruction there is no creation. Similarly, what people in general can consider to be 'good' or 'holy' can often run counter to balance, and can even be very unhealthy or unbalanced.

The preconceptions of the magician are constantly challenged on the magical path, and often the magician will be plunged into situations where the reality behind such preconceptions is brought right to the fore. If the magician is willing to face that reality to the best of their own ability at that time, then they will slowly begin to recognize the difference between necessary if severe *destruction*, and unnecessary

85

chaos: wanton destruction, which is the true evil. The magician is also challenged to see the harsh reality behind what can appear good and wholesome, which, when the veneer is removed, is simply a cover for rotten greed, weakness, and selfishness. Nothing is ever truly straightforward, and the magician learns to slowly pull to the centre, to search for the fulcrum where concepts of both light and dark, good and bad, start to fall away as the magician searches for what is truly necessary for balance.

The more the magician begins to understand such complexities, the less they act magically from a place of decision and control, and the more they simply *are* magic, so that it can flow through them. The magician becomes a link in the chain, a part of the holism that is a vast network of energy, consciousness, and power.

The life-story of a magician should be a series of changes and developments, of gaining wisdom and insight, and of changing views and approaches. Each magician should cringe at the memory of what they were like a decade ago, as to do so means that they have evolved in knowledge, understanding, and self-awareness. Such a willingness to learn and evolve brings the magician a step closer to becoming the fulcrum.

Why is it necessary for magician to go through such testing? As the magician develops in their skill set, each set of skills brings them closer to being able to work with power, and this can make them dangerous or useful. Once a magician gets to a particular level of ability, that ability is tested by fate, not to see how clever they are, but to see how potentially dangerous they are to themselves, and to everything around them. If the magician fails that test, then they flatline at that level of skill and get no further. It is not some 'judgement' being that decides a 'failure' or 'pass'; rather it is the junctions and crossroads of the magician's own fate patterns. Act one way and one road will open while another closes; act another way and either more roads will open, or they will all shut down and leave you sitting blinking in the dark.

As the magician climbs higher and higher on the stairway to becoming the fulcrum, the division between the right action and the wrong one becomes ever thinner and harder to deal with. The magician may fail many times in that they know what they should do, but at times they are too exhausted, too frightened, or too overwhelmed to act. But if they know that, and they do not hide from it but recognize that it is a test that they are not able to deal with at that time, then it is not failure because they have come to know their limits at that time—and the overarching key of the magical Mysteries is *know thyself.* The magician will keep trying each time that situation presents until they succeed. That is as much of a good lesson of the fulcrum as any successful one. Knowing your own weakness and maintaining an awareness of it is all part of the path to balance. That is important for a magician, as the spirits and beings they may encounter in their work can attempt to take advantage of a weakness in a hostile or dangerous situation. The more the magician works on their weaknesses, the less vulnerable they become to manipulation or attack.

DIVINATION

When this card appears in a reading, it is talking about a test of some kind. Whatever the reading is about, if this card appears then something within the situation or the fate pattern of the subject of the reading is about to go through a situation that will test their honesty, integrity, or strength.

Where it falls in a reading can give the reader a clue as to what in the life situation will be the vehicle for this testing. If it falls in the first significator position of a reading, then it can indicate the testing will come through a difficult situation with the body. If the card falls in the crossed relationship position of the subject, then either it will come through relationships (not just emotional ones, but who or whatever the person is strongly invested in at that time), or, it can be saying, your biggest interaction at this time is with the Test, in which case it will manifest through most if not all aspects of your life at that time. In this position, it is also a very 'now' timing: it is here, and you are in the midst of it.

If the Test falls in the position of the current fate pattern of the situation, then it can indicate that the testing will manifest through the fate cycle that you are currently going through, i.e., it will not manifest through a single event, but over a period of time. If the card falls in an inner world position, then the test will be a magical or spiritual inner one, and your actions and intent will be tested through various magical or spiritual situations that affect your inner and mundane life.

If it falls in the position of hearth/home, then the test will come through family, work, everyday life situations.

These situations of testing can be dramatic, or they can be mundane or subtle. It could be faced as a test of your magical, spiritual or ethical convictions, or your willingness to help someone in need. It can be as simple as seeing someone drop money and going after to them to give it back, or as complex as a crisis of faith or self-worth.

In mundane readings this card can also take on slightly different meanings, such as indicating law, courtrooms, exams, sports trials, interviews, or other situations where your ability, thought processes, truthfulness, and integrity are tested.

If this card appears in a mundane reading, then not only can it indicate being tested, but it can also warn that any deliberate untruth will be found out. Whatever the testing situation is, the weight of truth and the exposure of truth is the driving force behind the situation.

Honesty and integrity are the wisest choices to make if this card appears, as a great deal of power is hidden behind the test, and untruth will be exposed, along with the exposure of ability, knowledge and skill, or the lack thereof.

This card can also indicate a person who is ethical, a judge, or is a person who steps up to important challenges.

In mundane matters of health, it can be a prompt to get medical tests or to get your health checked out, particularly if it falls in the first position in a reading.

Keys

Being tested, law, integrity, truthfulness, crossroads of fate, challenge, exam.

Extra

The following is a series of extracts from the fifth hour in the Egyptian *Book of Gates*.[1]

> Twelve figures: Presences of humans in the Duat

> The accompanying text reads:

>> Their having spoken Truth upon Earth;
>> Their having been dedicated to the forms of the god.

> Says to them Re:

>> Valour to your Presences, Breath for your nose.

>> Cuttings are yours from the Marsh of Rushes, For indeed you are those
>> who are Righteous.

>> Your bases are yours at the corner-place[2]
>> The ordaining words of those in whom I am are there.

>> Their extension is bread,
>> Their scale-pans are hallowed vessels, Their cold refreshment is water.

>> Now, putting forth what is theirs on Earth
>> Means being a Peaceful One of their daily bread.

---

[1] McCarthy, Sheppard, and Littlejohn, 2022.
[56] 'This means 'Magistrate's Court'.

29 WISDOM

MEANING

In magic we equate wisdom with knowledge, knowledge with books, and books with systems of thought and actions. While that can be true to some extent, it is not the whole story. Study brings information, but that is not necessarily turned into knowledge, and knowledge does not automatically lead to wisdom.

In the picture, an old woman touches the side of her tiny house that is nestled in the forest, and whispers to it. The house is also a goddess, and an inner light shines out of the house that brings life and light to the immediate area beyond, which is darkness and winter. The wisdom in the old woman is that she understands her home is sacred and that she lives within the vessel of the goddess.

Wisdom, particularly in magic, comes from direct personal life experience and how we adapt to those experiences. If we learn from the bad experiences as well as the good, then the book-learning of magic will take on a whole new level. We start to recognize our own triumphs and failures in the mythical tales, and we start to truly understand magical power dynamics. And then, upon looking even more closely at the myths, we see the telling of strange experiences that we recognize as our own unique magical experiences. We start to see the patterns and threads of magic and fate as they weave around us. We see them not in an intellectual way from studying texts, but as a deep recognition from our own profound magical experiences.

The older you get, and the longer you have swum in the deep waters of magic, the more you realize that it is not systematic or predictable, and it has no cultural, religious, or theoretical boundaries. Truly deep magic flows like water. It is powerful, unpredictable, and you cannot grasp it with your hands.

The old woman in the image has reached that stage. She does not 'do' magic; she *lives* magic. She has cast aside religious systems and recognizes that everything is a vessel for Divine power. The trees, the creatures, the land and the dwelling itself are all vessels that Divine power flows into and inhabits, just as her own body is a vessel that the Divine can flow into. She has no need of great things because she has the greatest of all wealth: she lives within the body of the Divine, surrounded by the beauty of the Divine. The Divine is not worshipped; rather it is loved and lived within.

God is not male nor female. God is not of this land or some other land. God is not like a human, and does not live in a temple to be visited like a grandparent.

The Divine is all around you and within you: that is pure magical wisdom. That awakening takes the mature, experienced magician full circle. When we are children, we look at the world in simple, naïve terms. When we grow up, we become clever and sophisticated. When we grow old into magical wisdom, we turn full circle into seeing the world around us with that naivety and wonder of the child. But we never really reach the state of wisdom like a destination; rather it is constantly evolving process: we grow wiser with each passing year.

And the cat in the painting is called Odda, because the sun shines out of his ass.[1]

Divination

This card denotes an evolution of understanding, and its meaning is the same for both mundane and magical readings. It can indicate that you are on the right path, or that you have learned or are about to learn something in a deep and abiding way.

Depending on the question of the reading, it can point towards advising you that you are getting too far into the theoretical aspects of your practice or thought if it falls in a layout position that indicates what you need to do to move forward. It points to simplicity, to having an awareness of your surroundings, and of connecting with nature as a way of living. It can point to the need to shift how you live, and how you interact with everything around you.

If the reading is about a building or patch of land, then it can denote a special space, or a place of dwelling where humans and nature were in harmony for a while.

It can also denote old age, or 'when you are older' or in terms of time: the longer-term future. This card can also act as an affirmative: 'yes, that would be a wise choice'.

Keys

Simplicity, wisdom, evolving, wise choice, home, older, or when you are older, in the long-term future, divine protection, sacred enclosure, contentedness, harmony, peace, happiness.

---

[1] Odda the Elderman of Devon (Odda, whose sun shines out of his ass) from the British BBC TV series *The Last Kingdom* (2015).

30 Phanos

And the light shineth in darkness;
and the darkness comprehended it
not.[1]

Meaning

Phanos is a Greek word meaning a light, lantern, or flame torch: anything that lights the darkness. It is a word that also appears in many other Mediterranean and near eastern cultures, as *Fanus* (Persian and Arabic) or *Fanos*.

The magical meaning of this painting is the light that exists beyond the physical world, an inner light that is conscious, that is eternal. When it flows and weaves through time and fate, it expresses in all living things. It is the light that shines in the darkness.

For magicians, this light becomes our beacon in the darkness. Our maturing, our personal evolution adds to this light to strengthen it, hence in magic it is the harvest of our achievements and actions that becomes our lantern. This is the lantern of the Hermit in the traditional tarot. The core of our growth and evolution that adds to that light also adds to the light within everything and everyone around us: one adds to the many, as the light truly flows through everything.

We start to understand how our own changes trigger change around us, how our own magical actions have ripple effects far beyond what we could have foreseen. This light is not passive or static: it is a constantly changing energy, a powerful interaction between two people, or a person and a creature. A leap forward in our understanding changes the 'frequency' of the light for all living things in that moment. Every evolution of mind and soul that we achieve becomes accessible to all others as those achievements form an aspect of the Light. This in turn connects light to magical inner structures such as the Inner Library. It is at that moment of awareness that we really begin to understand how magic works and why.

When we are at a complete loss as to how to keep going or move forward, it is the lantern that guides us, not by telling us what to do, but by subtly illuminating the way ahead. Help from the lantern does not come from any external being, but from within ourselves. Everything we learn, everything we achieve and discover, becomes our own inner evolution which adds to this light. Hence when all other avenues have been exhausted, the magician turns within, and seeks solace and guidance in

---

[1] KJV *John* 1:5.

that eternal light within.

DIVINATION

When this card turns up in a magical reading, it highlights that, whatever the reading is about, an aspect of that situation is connected to your deep inner evolution. If it is a bad situation, then the card is saying, 'have faith in yourself and you alone'.

If the reading is about a magical way forward, then maybe you are questioning the path you are on or the work you are doing. If this light appears, then that way, for now, is the right one. However, if it appears in a past or withheld position, then the path you are on no longer holds benefit for you as an individual. It is not a judgement of the path; it is just not right for you at this time.

This card can be very confusing at times, as it can appear in a positive light in a difficult or negative situation—and this is where it becomes your lantern to guide you through the difficulty. The position that it lands in tells you the aspect of your life or magical work where that light is growing, and where your focus needs to be in finding a solution.

The core message of this card is that even when things can look terrible, the appearance of this light prompts you to look within, to be truthful with yourself, and to trust yourself: you have the answer within you. You are your own light that will guide you in the darkness. It can also indicate a time when a decision must come from you alone and not be influenced by others: it is saying that for this solution it is not wise to seek the counsel of others.

Depending on the subject matter of the reading, a simple message from this card can be to 'keep the lights on'. If there is some spirit or disturbance in the home, then sometimes leaving the lights on all night for a couple of days can back it off temporarily while a better solution is found. It can also be a prompt to keep a safe candle burning at night during difficult times. For magicians who are looking for a way to approach a magical working, this card points to light being a major element in the work: candles lit in certain directions, for example.

Its main message is to trust your own light above and beyond all others.

KEYS

Trust in yourself, light is needed, a flame, the centre, inside, yes, sacred light, lamp.

EXTRA

> *Gratia non tollit naturam, sed perficit.*[1]

The concepts of the Divine light as a consciousness that connects everything and thus holds all knowledge and experiences, is something that Thomas Aquinas[2]

---

[1] Grace does not destroy nature, but perfects it.
[2] Thomas Aquinas (1225-1274): an Italian theologian and philosopher.

attempted to express through the lens of Christianity in his work *Questiones Disputatae de Veritate*. He coined a phase 'the light of agent intellect', and presented the idea that this light, the illumination of knowledge (that is and is from God) is present in its completeness from the very beginning of one's life. When you lift the lens of Christianity off his writing, what surfaces from underneath is often quite remarkable.

> The soul forms in itself likenesses of things inasmuch as, through the light of agent intellect, forms abstracted from sensible objects are made actually intelligible, so as to be received in the possible intellect. And so, in a way, all knowledge is imparted to us at the start, in the light of agent intellect, mediated by the universal concepts that are cognized at once by the light of agent intellect. Through these concepts, as through universal principles, we make judgments about other things, and in these universal concepts we have a prior cognition of those others. In this connection there is truth in the view that the things we learn, we already had knowledge of.
>
> — *De Veritate* 10.6c

31 Akh

Meaning

The ancient Egyptian word *Akh* means both bright one and magically effective one. For more information on the Egyptian concept, see below in the last section of this card. The Akh is the inner spirit or soul of the human that has transformed into brightness. Not every dead soul becomes an Akh, and not every Akh is dead. I chose to use the Egyptian term for this painting, as the Egyptian concept of the Akh is the closest I have found to that describes what magicians over the centuries have seen and experienced. But the rest of this description is very much about the Akh from a magical practical experience perspective and not an Egyptian one.

The Akh is a description of the quality of a soul, not a name for a soul itself. Through magical training and then practice the magician can evolve if that practice is balanced. In Egypt they used the term Ma'at for this, which was also personified as a goddess of balance and truth. The same is true for some of those who follow a mystical path within their religion that is a path of truth and balance (as opposed to a religious 'truth').

Some forms of magical practice trigger experiences and self-awareness that bring the magician into a fuller understanding of themselves and of the world around them. They learn to interact with many different forms of beings, and through that interaction they learn about balance and imbalance, chaos and order, and the complex interweaving of all lifeforms in the vast web of fate.

These experiences and connections also create the conditions for the magician to develop within their own fate pattern to become the best that they are capable of becoming in their own lifetimes. It is through the actions, experiences and learning in life lives that the eternal soul becomes complete within itself. The challenges of the soul in death are also the challenges of the soul in life, as everything, in truth, happens at the same time. As you are in life, so you shall be in death and in rebirth, be that rebirth into physical form or not.

It is pertinent to point out that the modern understanding of the soul's evolution has become wrapped up in religious dogma and cultural programming. Most religions, particularly Abrahamic ones, have stitched in social and cultural morals into the concept of the soul's evolution. You can only become a 'saintly' one if you adhere to the particular morals and ethics of the religion, and of the country or culture that you live in. Nothing could be further from the truth.

If you cast all the religious baggage to one side, then what you are left with as a framework for the development of the soul is truth, necessity, and self-gnosis. How people get to those stages is individual to them, but it is a lone path of discovery. The magical path is one that accelerates the learning and development process, and accelerates and strengthens the fate paths and patterns around the magician. But here is the key: working on yourself does not evolve your pattern or soul. Rather, transforming everything around you does. Through the act of magical service in necessity to the universe, you become transformed. Why? Because you are in truth an integral part of everything around you. In magical dynamics the action of development is *outward*, not *inward*. Think of the connectedness of light described in the card Phanos. The Akh is where the light of the lantern becomes so developed that the person themselves *becomes* the lantern.

What is also important with the Akh is knowledge. Knowledge acquired through learning, combined with practical experience, develops the mind—and the mind is the interface between your spirit and everything else. Information is not the same as knowledge, and that is important to understand. We can all get magical books and read them, but that is just the accumulation of information, not knowledge. Knowledge is where the information is drawn in and used as part of the foundation for direct experiences, and those personal direct experiences then open out the knowledge of the magician. The magician is then able to see what is of truth and value in the information, and what is garbled or written in ignorance. The recognition of truth or value in information comes not from opinion, but from direct experience.

The Akh is the most balanced potential possible for you as an eternal soul, and also as a living being: it is where you are complete.

DIVINATION

The appearance of the Akh card is about the best potential, the highest level of development, and the greatest truth. Of course, its interpretation depends upon your question, the layout you use and the position in the layout where it falls. But when it appears it is saying, 'this is truth, this is good, you are developing towards your brightness, and you are evolving'.

If the reading is about a place or a building, then it is saying that there is something special there, or that the building is balanced, is clean, tuned, and nourishes those who seek shelter under its roof. It can also sometimes indicate that the building has become enlivened and has its own 'spirit' which is good.

If the reading is about a potential magical act, then it is saying that this action or ritual vision is balanced and is something that will move you forward a step in your evolution.

The Akh can also indicate the presence of an inner adept, an inner contact, an inner saint, or a Justified One.[1] The main thing to remember if this card is indicating an inner contact around you or in your work, is that the Akh is always a *human* soul, no matter how they present. It is the soul of a human who is in their brightness.

KEYS

Evolved, evolving, bright, truth of a person, self-knowledge, positive, the right path, clean and balanced, higher consciousness, servant of the Divine, Divine place, saint, enlightened soul.

EXTRA

Dynastic Egypt

The word Akh, transliterated as *3ḫ* or *Ax*, literally means bright one,[2] someone effective in their magic. Today we would call such a person a truly developed magical adept.[3] It also took on the meaning of 'Blessed dead', a transfigured one, or a risen

---

[1] Justified One: a term used in Dynastic Egyptian texts to indicate a soul who has been tested to the highest levels in the trials of the dead as they pass through the Duat Underworld, and found to be of truth. Justified was the term also used on the tombs or stelas of some priests (male or female) or high ranking officials to indicate that they 'lived to the laws of Ma'at.' Like all things, it was abused and used as a status term.

[2] i.e. they shine energetically: their truth shines out of them.

[3] Adept is a term often misused in magic today and can often mean just that a person has passed certain exams and initiations in a particular magical system. As such it is not an indication of their inner, magical or soul development. A true adept is one who is literally adept at magic and thus can operate within any magical system, and that through their development to adept skills they have evolved to know themselves. It is not a title, it is a quality and level of true magical knowledge.

one.

The hieroglyph for Akh, 𓅜 , depicts a crested ibis, which is a major clue to the meaning of the word. The ibis is the creature of Djehuty,[1] the god of knowledge and wisdom, one who knows the mathematics of the universe, who is the writer of all sciences, philosophies, and sacred texts. He was also the utterer of Ma'at, and lord of civilization.

In Egyptian funeral texts, the soul of the dead person undergoes a series of tests in the Underworld (the Duat) and is challenged by many strange and terrifying beings. If the soul passes all of these challenges successfully, then they rise with the morning sun and take their place among the stars. Here is an example of this concept from the Egyptian Old Kingdom Pyramid texts:[2]

Utterance 245[3]

(...) May you open your place in heaven amongst the stars of heaven! You are indeed the unique star, the comrade of Hu. May you look down on Osiris, when he gives orders to the spirits! You stand high up, far from him. You are not of them, you shall not be of them.

---

[1] Later known as Thoth.
[2] First attested inside the pyramid of the 5th dynasty Egyptian king Unas (mid-24th century BCE).
[3] Pyramid of Unas: passage to the sarcophagus chamber, south wall (inscribed west to east).

IV. Structures

32 FOUNDATION STONE

MEANING

The Foundation Stone is a concept in magic and ancient classical religions that denotes the beginning of something new and powerful. In the building of ancient and classical temples, the Foundation Stone was the first laid stone under which was often placed deity statues, or a brick of gold, or precious amulets. Sometimes incantations or prayers would be carved into the stone, as it was considered to be the anchor of the spiritual into the physical. These ancient rites continued in various forms in the early Christian world and were integrated into Masonic rites.[1]

It is also connected to our ancestors and the land. Many animist religions and belief systems regard the land as their mother, as the land beneath their feet gives life and protection as well as housing their ancestors. In some ancient cultures the Mother, considered the land, would be revered in the form of a stone, often a black stone.

The Cybele or *Matar Kubeleya*[2] was a Phrygian goddess who was worshipped at rock-cut mountain shrines and as a black meteoric stone. Such was her reputation of power that Rome asked for her help. During the second Punic war[3] Rome requested that Cybele be brought to Rome to protect the city and assist in what was a disastrous situation. She was brought to Rome in the form of the Black Stone.[4] Today we see remnants of this connection between the land and the Mother in nations which call their territory the Motherland.

In magic, the Foundation Stone is the Divine element of earth that upholds us and is the magical aspect of the building of a magical temple. It is also our anchor,

---

[1] Speth, 1893.

[2] Inscription from a rock cut shrine; 'Mountain Mother' in Phrygian, 6th century BCE (Beekes, 2010: s.v. "Κυβέλη").

[3] 218-201 BCE.

[4] Summers (1996: 363–364) describes this as "a rather bizarre looking statue with a stone for a face." Prudentius describes the stone as small and encased in silver.

sometimes known as an 'anchor stone': a carefully chosen or auspiciously found rock that is consecrated and worked with as a source of strength, protection and learning.

It teaches the magician that the land under our feet, like everything in the physical world around us, including ourselves, is a vessel for that which is Divine. When the Divine is consciously awakened in magic, the anchor stone becomes a vessel for Divine power to flow through. In turn, this brings together the magician and nature in a cooperative relationship, where in ritual, vision, and everyday life the magician is constantly aware of the power all around them. This power is worked with magically for mutual benefit, not for exploitation.

> I am the rock which emerges out of chaos.
> I am the rock upon which you stand
> The rock which bore you
> The rock which upholds you
> The rock that will provide your tomb.
> Within me is your Mother
> Within me is the memory of all things
> Within me is you.

Divination

The Foundation Stone in divination points to our bodies, or to the land upon which we stand. It can indicate the founding of something that will grow and evolve, such as a magical path, a company, a building, a school or system of learning, or a temple. It can also indicate the long-term health of our bodies. The Foundation Stone is the anchor from which the rest of the construct can develop without drifting into fragmentation or collapsing. The wise man builds on rock, not sand.

In both magical and mundane readings this card indicates stability, putting down roots, or building something solid from a good foundation. It can indicate that a training or education choice is a good one that will give the person a solid foundation for the rest of their lives.

In magical readings, depending upon the question and subject matter, it indicates that a path you are stepping on will give you a good foundation. Similarly, in magical work, it can indicate that a long working that you are reading about will form a good foundation for something.

If the card is in a withheld position, then it indicates that whatever you are reading about has no stability and will likely not last well. If the reading is about health and it lands in a withheld position, then it indicates that the foundation of the health is at risk and needs to be attended to, usually by a change in habits and how you look after your body.

If this card falls in a recent past or long term past position, then whatever you are reading about has an old but solid foundation in place. This can be useful to know if you are forming something, as this card in this position indicates there is no need to build a foundation: it is already there.

In readings it can also point to passive protection, inasmuch as the 'ground' you stand on is solid enough that you can focus on the issues ahead. Similarly in health readings, in good positions it indicates that whatever is wrong with the body, its core foundational health and structure is fine.

Keys

Foundation, core, body, land, anchor, first stage completed, solidity, stability, passive protection, shelter, mother.

Extra

There is a wonderful physical representation of the Foundation Stone as the anchor in the Tennessee Capitol State Building in the USA. It was built by architect and freemason[1] William Strickland. Strickland was apprenticed by Benjamin H Latrobe[2], and he became known for Gothic Revival and Greek Classical styles of architecture. He also designed and built the downtown Presbyterian church in Nashville, which inside is an astonishing church themed around the temple of Karnak in Egypt.

He became ill while he was working on the Tennessee Capitol State Building, and he died before its completion. Before his death, he requested that he be buried in the northeast corner of the building. This was dutifully carried out, and the wall now bears a plaque marking his crypt.

The northeast corner of a building is traditionally where the cornerstone would be placed: the most important stone in the construction of a building. It is the first stone to be set and had to be cut and laid with absolute precision, since it dictated the proper alignment of the rest of the building. In history, the cornerstone was often laid to astronomical positions to bring harmony and balance to a building, and in some cultures, offerings or saints relics were placed inside the cornerstone[3].

In Freemasonry, the Initiate is placed in the northeast corner of the lodge as a figurative Foundation Stone, to signify the unity and bridging of darkness/death[4] and light/life[5]. Strickland's request to be buried in the northeast corner of the building demonstrates his esoteric knowledge and his spiritual commitment to his work: he is literally the Foundation Stone of the Capitol building.

---

[1] Brother William Strickland Freemason of the Columbia Lodge no 91 Philadelphia USA

[2] Benjamin Latrobe (1764-1829), born in Moravian settlement in Pudsey, Yorkshire, England. He became known as the father of architecture in the USA. Freemason with the Jerusalem lodge no54 Richmond Virginia.

[3] Cornerstones were often hollowed out to contain relics, offerings, or more recently historical documents.

[4] North is the direction of Death and darkness in western ritual patterns.

[5] East is the direction of new life and light in western ritual patterns.

33 EAST GATE

The four gates are a purely magical dynamic and are not tied to the topography of the land, unlike the Pagan thresholds that relate directly to physical nature. Nor are they tied to the hemispheres. They are a pattern of access, and they bridge the flow of power between the inner worlds and the physical world. The four gates are the focal point of the directions and are a magical pattern that forms a foundational 'structure' that the magic can sit upon.

MEANING

The East Gate is the energy of formation and is also a threshold for the magical dynamics of air utterance. It is an 'incoming' direction: most magical patterns (not all) are 'conceived' by the magician at the eastern threshold before being brought into the centre of the directions for full formation before being released. The eastern threshold is one that when crossed in vision leads to realms and contacts that are rooted in knowledge, the word, civilization, and structure.

For example, when the magician needs to work with a deity that is rooted in knowledge, utterance, learning, measurement, and the building of structures, the magician would ritually anchor their working in the direction of east, and the main part of their ritual working would be at the East Gate's threshold. If the magician works with altars, then then the east altar would be their main focus for such work. If the magician needs to work in vision, then they would 'step through' the East Gate in vision, with their mental focus tuned to the deity, and would work with visionary constructs such as an inner temple, or a structure called the Inner Library.

DIVINATION

The appearance of the East Gate in a reading tells of a new opening, new learning, or the work of utterance and ritual. It is a direction of opportunities, the birth of new ideas and concepts, and the direction of learning.

If the card appears in a distant past position, then whatever the subject matter of the reading is, an aspect of the access point, knowledge, or action of what is being read about is in deep stasis in the past and it is unlikely that it could be recovered. That knowledge has been lost and is sleeping deeply in the past. However, if the card appears in a recent past position, then the knowledge or access to whatever is being read about has fallen into dormancy, but it can still be recovered. The recent past, like the near future, are both aspects of time that can be accessed magically to observe, learn, or 'shift' a dynamic or fate path.

If the card appears in a near future position, then it is saying that a new opportunity, or a new creation, or a new life is on the horizon[1] and whatever is being read about is leading towards that. If the card falls in an endurance position, then the new creation or opportunity will be difficult to get going or would need a lot of work to bring it into fruition, but it will be successful, though it will be a difficult 'birth'.

In mundane readings, depending on the question, this card can indicate the direction of east (if, for example, a reading is being done to locate something or someone). It can also indicate new learning, a new life, and something 'incoming', as it is a card and direction of something coming into the picture. It is already forming and is likely something already in the fate pattern or which has even manifested but has not yet been fully realized or seen.

This card's appearance can also be a prompt to learn new things, as the east is a direction of learning and of newness. Sometimes embarking on a new round of learning opens up stagnant fate patterns and 'stuck' lives. It is a positive card that can also be a 'yes' indicator in simple questions.

Keys

Beginnings, formation, newness, learning, expansion, new potentials, new knowledge, the power of invention, possible, yes.

Extra

The following is an extract from the extensive magical training course, Quareia.[2] In Quareia Apprentice module seven, lesson one,[3] the student is taught about the use of elements and directions in magical work. The following is an extract of the text focussing on the threshold of the east and the element of air:

> The element of air that flows from the east is also the element that works with the formation of time. The power that flows through the east, the power of uttering into existence, sets the stage for time to flow through a magical pattern. In the east, time has no past or future; rather it is in the process of formation; the use of the utterance, the power of the limiter, and the element of air come together to create a threshold which enables time to trigger into a pattern or substance.
>
> Magic takes advantage of this: the magician creates a magical pattern

---

[1] Often depicted in religious texts as 'a star in the east': meaning a 'bright one' or Akh is being born.
[2] www.quareia.com Quareia is a free, open-access training in magic.
[3] McCarthy, 2017a.

using the power of air (utterance, sigils, etc.) and the power of limitation (sword). These two powers create a vessel (pattern), and a lowering of energetic frequency (limiter) that together create a magical act that has time within its pattern.

As the pattern magic is completed, it begins its journey into the south, where time becomes the future. East is the cooking pot that cooks a road that time can step onto. This road is a two-way street: it runs into both the future (south) and the past (north). Which way it goes depends on the pattern created and the focussed intent behind the pattern.

34 SOUTH GATE

MEANING

The threshold of the South Gate is the threshold of future time, and of the element of fire. Its image is more formed than the East Gate, as the south is where formation comes into its full expression and potential as its energies open out to future possibilities. The figures in the painting represent inner contacts, both living and dead, who serve as upholders of fate patterns as they flow through time, and who sometimes assist humans in learning and development. This dynamic of assistance directly connected to time and fate is a dynamic that also emerges in humanity through magical actions; magicians who work in service to facilitate those who struggle against the tide of time in order to bring something to the land, nature or humanity for the future.

The South Gate is a threshold of the flow of time into the future and is a position where magic that has been formed is released into the flow of time. The energy of the southern threshold is one of coming into full fruition, where potential is realized and is fully active.

The energy of the south is volatile and can easily become uncontrollable in magic: it is a fire element. When contained and properly tended it bears wonderful 'fruits'; however if it is left unchecked it can unfold in a most chaotic and at times dangerous way.

DIVINATION

When this card appears in a magical reading it points to something that is full of energy and can be unpredictable, something that has the potential for far-reaching effects and that also has the potential to last well into the future. Whereas the East Gate is *forming potential*, the South Gate is that *potential realized* and fully formed. It is a highly active card that tells of something that could be good or bad depending upon how it is approached.

If this card appears in a reading, then look at the position where it has landed, as that will give you clues about what aspect of the question it is speaking about. If that part of story is approached with care, with discipline and with enough strength to control its fiery volatility, then whatever it is can be great indeed. If however it is approached in an *ad hoc* or lazy fashion, or without due attention, then it could quickly unravel and will have the potential to become destructive.

If this card appears in a layout, then keep its overall 'temperament' in mind regardless of the reading's subject matter. One of its key meanings is 'the future', so if, for example, it falls in the position of hearth/home, then it will indicate the potential of moving house or performing some renewal or renovation within the home that could vastly improve it. Either way, it must be approached properly, with attention to detail, otherwise the results will not last the tests of time.

In a magical reading, if this card appears in a near or distant future position, then its meaning is strengthened considerably: it indicates a strong future fate potential within the subject matter of the reading. The magician will need to ensure that they are ready for what is coming, be it good or bad. It is not a card of passivity but of action. Whatever you put into the situation in terms of action, effort, and focus, will be well rewarded when this card appears.

If this card falls in the near past position, then it is stating that the seeds for the future of the subject matter lie in past events that potentially have a direct bearing on the future of the subject. Here the situation must be looked at carefully to ensure that the future expression does not carry baggage from the past. It can also be a warning not to repeat past mistakes, or it can be speaking of the need to draw experience from the past to influence the future. Which of these opposing ideas applies in a reading is highly dependent upon the question and the subject matter of the reading.

Depending on the question, this card can also indicate the direction of south, and/or the element of fire or of heat.

KEYS

South, future, fire, creative fire, volatile energy, yes, positive.

Extra

The following is an extract from the extensive magical training course, Quareia.[1] In Quareia Apprentice module seven, lesson one,[2] the student is taught about the use of elements and directions in magical work. The following is an extract of the text focussing on the threshold of the south and the element of fire:

> Once the magical pattern is fully formed, it immediately becomes an 'action.' Magic always does something. In order for it to do something, it has to include the element of time. The magical pattern is the trigger, and time is the road delivery service that the magic travels within in order to do its job. That time can be past or future. The south is the threshold for the future, and most magic is aimed at the future.
>
> When we think of the future, we often think of years ahead. But in fact the future can be five minutes from now...or five million years from now. Any magic done to influence 'now' will fail miserably, as in essence there is no now; there is only future and past. So when the magic is aimed at the future, it switches its energetic directional flow to the south.
>
> The power that flows through the south is the power of energy (fire) that fuels the future, and direction (eg. wand or staff, chessboard). It is a direction that marries future time to a set event. But here it gets interesting. When the pattern moves to the south, the events the magic are meant to trigger do not simply become 'locked in time'; it is not quite so simple as that. The nearer to our time the magic is set to unfold, the more locked into an event it becomes. The further into the future the magic is set to unfold, the more potential there is for a shifting and changing dynamic that can be complicated to predict. The magic will still unfold as it is supposed to, but its setting, placement, and outcome may be different from what was originally envisioned.
>
> For example, a tightly constructed bit of conditional magic aimed at tomorrow will very likely go as planned. But a similarly constructed bit of magic aimed at next year will likely morph into variants of the same pattern. The further away the magic is aimed, the more possibility it has to shift and change its boundaries, as it will continuously intersect with various time patterns along the way.

---

[1] www.quareia.com Quareia is a free, open-access training in magic.
[2] McCarthy, 2017a.

35 WEST GATE

MEANING

The West Gate is direction of outputting: a threshold of composting, harvesting, and of things falling away from the physical world. Energy and magical patterns 'come into' the physical world via the east threshold, unfold their action in the south, and leave via the west when the patterns have done their job and are now fragmenting or breaking down. It is a threshold that leads to death, or to the end of something. Its element is water. When magicians need an energy that gives a magical pattern an 'end date' and embeds into that pattern a recycling and composting dynamic, the west direction gate is where, in the ritual pattern, they work. It is a very fluid energy, hence its connection to water: like mist, its energy can seep, or it can 'tidal wave'.

It is also the directional gate that magicians can use to work with the newly dead: the West Gate is a threshold whereby the magician can work in vision, ritual, or utterance to commune with the newly dead and guide them through their death process.

DIVINATION

When the West Gate card appears in a reading, it is pointing to the way out for something, or showing that something is leaving or preparing to leave. When this card lands in a recent past or a 'falling away' position in a layout it strengthens that message in relation to the subject matter of the reading.

For example, if the question is something like, 'should I continue on this current magical path or current magical working,' and this card falls in a 'falling away' position, then it is saying that the continued path is starting to fragment and has no future for you. If you look at the card that falls in the long-term future position, then it can indicate the other path is preparing to open up for you. If that position also has a 'closed down' or blocking card, then whatever you are asking about definitely has no future for you and it would be best to not waste any more time in the current path you are walking.

Traditionally in magic the West Gate is the threshold of death and mortality. Thus the West Gate card can appear if someone who has recently died is trying to contact you or connect with you: the West Gate is a threshold between the living and the newly dead, and its power flows through both worlds. Hence communion with the dead is highlighted with this card.

In certain instances, it can also indicate when a person is drawing close to death. If they are chronically ill or dying, then this card will appear when they are close to the transition from life to death. If this card appears in the reading of a healthy person and there are dangerous cards around this one in the layout, then there is a potential of death on the horizon. By using divination, the risk factor can be ascertained and avoided by looking at how to make a change that shifts the fate pattern.

Overall, if you are looking at the future of something and this card appears, then either an aspect of the situation or the overall situation itself will not last and is already starting to fall apart. If this card falls in an answer position to a question, then the answer is 'it is breaking down, leaving, composting or not viable'. As such it can also indicate old age or ageing.

Keys

Leaving, coming to an end, very recent past, slowing down, ageing, direction of west, probably not, no longer viable.

Extra

The following is an extract from the extensive magical training course, Quareia[1]. In Quareia Apprentice module seven, lesson one,[2] the student is taught about the use of elements and directions in magical work. The following is an extract of the text focussing on the threshold of the west and the element of water:

> As soon as magic crosses into the south, it starts to slow down. Just like everything that releases onto the road of time, its speed starts to decline: death is inherently woven into the birth of everything, and from the perspective of time, this means that from the moment time connects with the magical pattern, the pattern begins to slow down.
>
> Once something gets to a very slow, almost-stopped phase, then comes the point of decay and finally death. This is where the west comes in. Once the magic sent into the south has done its job and it has slowed right down, it starts moving towards the west threshold. In the west, we say that the pattern is still moving in time (passing into the past) because at this stage, even though the pattern is completed, it still has influence over the future. Think about how past events in your life still influence you: these are past events that are in the west. They are fully formed and completed, yet still having an effect on your life and time.

---

[1] www.quareia.com Quareia is a free, open-access training in magic.
[2] McCarthy, 2017a.

As the event pattern moves deeper into the magical west, its influence on the future fades until eventually it has no influence at all. Time stops moving into the 'future,' and the west is the terminal where time is turned to go into the past. When a magician needs to dismantle magical patterns, the magician works with the power of the west. Once the power influence has completely finished, the pattern is broken up and passes into the north, which is the distant past.

36 NORTH GATE

MEANING

The North Gate threshold is a place of caves, the Underworld, and the long dead. Everything that once had a physical existence or was energetically tied to a physical place, structure or person eventually is absorbed by the land and eventually becomes rock deep below the surface of the land.

The north is the past, from where something (usually) will not return. It is a threshold that magicians work with to access the Underworld, and to contact long-dead ancestors or ancient beings.

The well in the painting is a depiction of a dynamic which often shows up in magical vision when entering the shallows of the Underworld, and that dynamic is water: water is often (not always) the threshold between the entrance and the depths of the Underworld. This is depicted in some cultures' mythologies as a cave with a pool of dark water into which the magician dives. In the structure depicted in the painting, the magician would dive into the water and swim down into the depths, to emerge in the Underworld. In some cultural mythos there are lakes and rivers in the Underworld: basically, because that is what you find when you explore the Underworld for yourself in vision. Even magicians whose cultures do not have that pattern of water in the Underworld will discover it for themselves in vision at some point.

For the magician, working in the north is akin to being an archaeologist, as the most ancient things are found deep in the land, sleeping in the rock, and eventually becoming rock.

DIVINATION

In magical divination, the North Gate is a card of something long dead, something that has gone and will not return. It can also indicate the entrance to the Underworld.

For example, if a magician is asking the question, 'what would be the best magical approach to the work I want to embark on?" and the North Gate card landed in a prominent position, then it is advising that either working on the threshold of the Underworld or anchoring the work on that threshold would be the best approach. That would essentially mean visionary work, and potentially also bone work. It could also indicate a need for ancestral work, particularly if it appears in a reading that also has the ancestor card in a good position.

If the magician is looking to identify the source of an issue, such as in the exorcism of a person or place or dealing with a magical attack or a malign influence, and this card appears as the answer, then it is saying that whatever is causing the problem is not from the surface living world, nor from the stars, but is of the Underworld or the realm of death.

In divination this card can also indicate the direction of north, or it can also indicate a burial ground. It can also indicate long dead ancestors or the influence of such.

In mundane readings, it can indicate that something is long gone and will not return, or that it is something that has no useful place in your life.

Keys

North, ancestors, ancient, burial ground, access to the Underworld, beings from the threshold of the Underworld, past, gone, no.

Extra

The following is an extract from the extensive magical training course, Quareia[1]. In Quareia Apprentice module seven, lesson one[2], the student is taught about the use of elements and directions in magical work. The following is an extract of the text focussing on the threshold of the north and the element of earth:

> The direction of north, stone, and the past; hence the direction of ancestors. The north is where all the composted magic (and everything else) is buried. When time moves over the magical threshold of the west it ceases action in the future and begins to form in a way that we recognize as 'past.'
>
> What we tend to think of as 'past' in our lives is actually in the west. Those memories and events are still in their fully formed state and still have influence. It is only when a pattern of fate time no longer has any influence at all that it finally passes into the north.

[1] www.quareia.com Quareia is a free, open-access training in magic.
[2] McCarthy, 2017a.

108

North is the home of the patterns which no longer have any action or influence in life: think of dinosaurs as an extreme example. True magical past means that the event no longer has any bearing on the future at all.

37 PROFANE PLACE

MEANING

People think of profanity as foul language or people only partially dressed, or actions that go against a particular norm in a religion. However true magical profanity is deep injustice to fellow humans, creatures, and to the environment around us. The word 'profane' comes from the Greek word *phanós*, meaning light or lantern. *Profanus* in Latin means outside the sacred, or 'before the temple'. Profane is the darkness.

Interestingly, in early Christianity, particularly when the Christian Romans attempted to convert the Germanic tribes, the names of the old Pagan gods were used as swearwords in order to 'profane' the Pagan sacred. Hence even today, we use the word profanity when describing swearing. That has taken the meaning a long way from its roots of 'outside the light' (beyond what is balanced).

This is a card that portrays the greed, selfishness, and indifference to everything except that which inconveniences the self. It is a card of oppression of others for gain, a card of harvesting all resources in order to gain wealth far beyond necessity. And necessity is the key, or the lack of it, when looking at the meaning of profanity. In today's world of climate issues and fossil fuels, we are becoming aware that using oil, gas and coal are 'profaning' the natural world. However, particularly in cold countries, where there is no alternative for an individual, they must burn or use whatever they can in order to stay warm and survive, and it has always been this way for human survival. But there is a difference between a choice made from survival necessity, and a choice made from greed. When greed wins, it becomes profane.

When a magician steps into more serious magic, they work with and become involved with many non-physical forces, beings, energies, and intelligences. How we are in the physical world directly influences how such forces and beings perceive us, because what we do, what we think, and how we behave in the everyday world is imprinted on our inner energies like a book. We cannot shield our true selves from such beings, and what they pick up from us directly influences how they will react to us.

When a magician is still lifting themselves slowly from such ignorance and is trying to learn to be more of a part of the holism of life, that is also signalled to inner beings, and they pick up on us as what I call 'stupid but saveable': at least we are trying. And as such, many beings will not only interact with us, but they will over time step in and begin to work with us to guide and passively teach. It is not about being a saint or being perfect; it is about *trying*, by building awareness for how choices and actions affect everything else around you. Inner beings and powers respond in kind: what you are and what you do defines how you are treated by them.

The same is true of a place. If a place is heavily polluted and is full of oppressed people or animals, then inner beings will not come anywhere near it, unless it is to answer a call for help from a non-profane person who is trapped. The only beings likely to be regularly present in such a place are parasites and beings that break up and destroy things, as a place of rot needs scavenger beings and choppers (destructive beings) to break everything down. And where there is rot, there are always parasites. When you are trying to get your head around a magical and inner dynamic, always look around you in the physical world, as the dynamics run on the same tracks. Go into a woodland and look at a fallen log that is rotting down: if you break a piece off, then you will see that it is full of insects busily breaking it down.

This brings into focus a dynamic in magic that is an important one to learn, which is that just as a living human or animal perceives dirty water, excrement, and overcrowding as threats, so inner beings perceive emotions and energy residue from actions such as extreme greed, hate, selfishness, corruption, and violence or oppression, as dangerous contaminants.

One major warning of this card is: *do not try to change someone*. If someone is steeped in their profanity then walk away, as they can only change by themselves. Do not entangle yourself in the profanity of others. Do not be a rescuer: profanity is a choice.

Divination

When this card appears in a reading, it speaks about something that is greedy, rotten, very imbalanced, toxic, or with the potential to be so. When the reading is about a situation, this card indicates that there is no 'light' or wisdom there, and that greed, selfishness, or ego is the hidden agenda. If this card appears in a reading about your work or choices, then it is prompting you to look carefully and truthfully at your real reasons for doing something. Often we try to hide from our own truth: this allows profanity to grow.

The Profane card speaks of something or someone that is rotten, a possible contaminant, or something that is deeply corrupted. If the reading is about a place or a building, then the place has no goodness: it is not stable and is unhealthy. This card can also indicate hidden contaminants in a building or patch of land. It can also indicate heavily industrialized cities or areas, usually where there is a lot of pollution and poverty.

If the card falls in an endurance position, then it may be pointing to the need to work hard at overcoming something that is corrupt or rotten. Or, if the reading is about the magician and their magical path, then it can indicate the need to work on their own behaviours, choices and actions. If the reading is about a magical group, building, or place, and it falls in the endurance position, then it is saying that for the group, place, or building to flourish, first the profanity or rottenness needs to be dealt with—and it will not be easy. The endurance position is always one of 'this will be tough but with work you will succeed'. In such readings, bear in mind that the card's aspect will depend on your exact question. There may be other ways to approach the situation that would be better or easier, and the way to find that is to look at the problem with a different 'plan of attack'.

If this card falls in the first position that signifies the subject of the reading, or the body of the person, then it indicates that there is something wrong with the person that is self-inflicted and that will likely kill them eventually. Profanity, in terms of this card, is always a choice, and this card as a person indicator can either be saying that they are a 'profane' person, or that their body is rotten from misuse. In the first position, or when it appears in a health reading, this card can also indicate that there is toxicity going on. This could be caused by treatments, or contaminants in the food and water, etc. The clear message with this card, though, is always one of choice, which means that whatever it shows it can be changed by choice. It can be an indicator of a need to change medications or diet, for example. If a person is undergoing chemotherapy for cancer, then this card will likely appear in the person's readings until the treatment has finished. Then the person can engage in cleaning their body up. Sometimes profanity is needed to survive.

This card can also appear for a person, place, or event that superficially looks just fine, but energetically is rotten to the core. This card tells you what is behind the veneer. However, when the reading is about a person, you must tread carefully with how you interpret it. For example, a body that is slowly degenerating under the weight of toxic medicines that are nevertheless keeping them alive can appear as profane in a reading, since they are 'choosing' the poison in order to survive for a while longer. That is not 'bad'; that is survival.

With a difficult card like this, while sometimes it does indeed point to something obvious, you nevertheless have to be careful not to judge, as the situations with people in particular can be complex and can hide deep suffering that can project or appear as 'profane'.

This card has two overall meanings. One is a picture of degeneration, greed, and oppression: problems relating to behaviour and choices. The other picture is of a degeneration that relates to illness, age, or defeat, and that requires compassion.

This card can also indicate physical pollution, contaminants, toxicity, and depending upon the question and subject matter, it can also indicate poison. In health readings it can also indicate something that is very imbalanced or that is becoming toxic.

KEYS

Degenerate, greed, pollution, toxic, threat, oppression, selfishness, bad, no, poison.

38 HEARTH

MEANING

The Hearth is a stage on the magical journey where the magician withdraws to their mundane family life to rest from the strains of magic and to regenerate. It is also the time of focus on family, mundane life, and attending to the basic needs of shelter, food, companionship, and warmth. The image shows the immediate family unit by the hearth, along with the ghost of a dead ancestor watching over the baby.

Often after major work of development in magic, it is necessary to withdraw back to the hearth not only for rest, but also not to forget the importance of home and family, regardless of what that family consists of, whether it is a conventional family, an unconventional family, or a home full of animals or spirits. The mundane hearth is the anchor that keeps the magician a part of the mundane world: this is important. It doesn't matter if the hearth is in the midst of a community and extended family, or if it is a home that is remote from people and the magician lives at home alone with cats and dogs.

The mundane stresses and demands of home life keep the magician tied into everyday life. This is important for their mental wellbeing, and it also stops them drifting too far into the wilds of magic, as without an anchor it is easy for a magician to lose track of the real world. Magic ultimately flows through the mundane world and anchors it in the fate patterns of those whom it touches.

The ghostly ancestor in the painting indicates how ancestral spirits, be they blood ancestors or ancestors of the land, draw close to a balanced home and can act as guardians for the people who live there. The two bluebirds represent the animal kingdom around the home: again, if the home of a magician is balanced and kept properly, and the magician is walking a good path through magic that is in harmony with nature, animal (particularly bird) spirits will often draw close and act as guardians, early warning systems, and as family members.

Sometimes the hearth is a stage in magical development whereby a magician who has worked and served is guided through fate to a home that will become theirs. If it is necessary for the future work of the magician to have a stable home base, then even after maybe decades of moving from one place to another, none of which ever felt like home, the magician will be guided and enabled to settle into a home that has the rootedness of the hearth. In such cases, it is often a tradeoff. The magician is expected to live up to the 'rules' of the hearth in return for its stability. This means if there is a garden, it must be tended: not as a fancy, regular garden, but one that is welcoming of nature (no pesticides herbicides, growing plants for the insects and bees, etc.). And the magician must make connections and friends with the spirits, land beings, and ancestors that flow through that land.

This card is also about bloodlines and blood connections, nations, and communities: the families and generations, and the non-human family members such as animals, spirits, and ancestors.

In older age, the magician begins to realize that the home where they live can become infused with the consciousness of a spirit or deity. Just as there are personal daimons, there is also a spirit or deity of the house. This is not saying 'there is a guardian spirit in your house'; rather it is saying, 'your house is a vessel that houses a great spirit', just as your body houses your spirit.

DIVINATION

This card is an indicator of home, family, and community. Depending upon the question and where it falls in a layout, it can indicate the need to rest and spend time in the home, or to be mundane for a while: i.e. no magical work! It can also indicate empathic connections with family members, and sometimes it can indicate a pregnancy depending upon the question.

If this card falls in a difficult position, then it can indicate issues with the home, family, or community. These issues can be mundane, magical, or both. If the layout you are using has a position for the home/hearth and a difficult card falls in that position, and the Hearth card also appears in the layout, and if the question is magical, then it can indicate magical disturbance in the place where you live. Such a disturbance may come from an object you have brought into the house, or a shrine or working space that is getting out of balance. It can also indicate that the balance and protections of the space have been breached and need attending to.

If the reading is about the wellbeing health of the magician, and this card falls in a difficult position, then it can indicate an issue with the reproductive organs, a hormone imbalance, or a health problem that runs in the family. It can also indicate that something in the house is affecting the energy of the magician, which in turn is making them sick or tired. Depending upon the cards around it and the outcome, this could be a minor but difficult issue, and it would be wise to keep an eye on health readings for a while. It can also sometimes indicate that your family is driving you nuts!

When this card falls in the endurance position in a layout, it is indicating that your home life or family is creating a burden that must be endured, but which will resolve with time and effort. If the person that the reading is about is an empath, then it can indicate that they are carrying an energetic burden that is connected to a family member, or a place that is traditionally their home or homeland.

Overall, this card is one of refuge, rest, rejuvenation, connection, and tribe.

For magicians, home, families, and community are often a blessing and a curse at the same time. Learning to find the right balance is a huge part of the magician's evolution as they walk their magical path.

Keys

Home, family, safety, nourishment, rest, spirit and nature family, house, children, goddess of the hearth.

Extra

Here is a hymn to Hestia, a Greek goddess whose name means 'the hearth' and Hermes is also included. It is a good exercise to think magically about why Hermes is also included in this hymn of the hearth.

> Hestia, in the high dwellings of all, both deathless gods and men who walk on earth, you have gained an everlasting abode and highest honour: glorious is your portion and your right. For without you mortals hold no banquet. Where one does not duly pour sweet wine in offering to Hestia both first and last. And you, slayer of Argus (an epithet to Hermes), Son of Zeus and Maia, the messenger of the blessed gods, bearer of the goldenrod, the giver of good, be favourable and help us, you and Hestia, the worshipful and dear. Come and dwell in this glorious house in friendship together; for you two, well knowing the noble actions of men, aid on their wisdom and their strength. Hail, Daughter of Cronos, and you also, Hermes, bearer of the goldenrod! Now I will remember you and another song also — Hesiod, *Hymn to Hestia.*[1]

---

[1] Hesiod, 1914.

39 Obscure Path

Meaning

This is a simple card with a straightforward meaning: 'your path ahead is obscured'. Be cautious, as the deep forest can house many predators and dangers.

This card appears when the situation or way ahead is not as clear as it may seem: dangers lie ahead and caution is needed. In magic and the magical life, there are more dangers and pitfalls than in a mundane life, so a magician needs to learn to be watchful and to pay attention.

There are also times in a magician's life when the way ahead is deliberately obscured in order to slow you down, especially when choices you make at that point in your life may be counterproductive to your overall fate. Things become obscured from your sight or perception to limit your decision-making process. This can happen particularly with divination: sometimes finding out too much in advance would limit us, so the reading basically tells us little or nothing. For example, if you are looking for a way ahead, a solution, or are weighing up an action and use a reading to get clarity and this card appears, it is pushing you back on yourself to use your own instincts and judgement.

This card also indicates a magical dynamic of passive protection. Sometimes the magician needs to be obscured for their protection: the 'mists' descend around you, and you cannot be seen, either physically, through inner vision, or through divination. The mists protect and obscure you until the way ahead is safe.

Divination

This card is a card of warning, telling you there are things ahead that you had better not see...or that had better not see you. It can also indicate that you do not as yet have all the facts in a situation, and that you should therefore wait before making a decision, as things will come to light soon enough.

For example, if you are doing a reading to look at a future outcome and this card falls in either the near or distant future, then it is saying 'there are unseen elements operating in your fate path, and if you could see them, then it is likely you would make the wrong decision'. In such a case tread carefully, pay attention to what is around you, and seek your own counsel, as the answer lies deep within you.

If as a magician you are looking for advice on how to approach a magical problem

and this card appears, then it is telling you to 'go undercover', or to fade into the background and not make yourself visible. It can also be a warning to stop divination, as doing readings can sometimes make you visible from an inner perspective. If there are destructive energy tides lapping around you, then being seen would make you vulnerable.

It is sometimes difficult to decide whether this card is telling you to stop looking or to go undercover. But basically, the way ahead is the same: bide your time, stay undercover, do no divination for a while, and make your own decisions while also treading very carefully and not making big decisions or taking major actions. 'Tread water' is a good mantra when this card appears.

Keys

Hidden element, trust your instincts, tread water, wait, no, stay hidden.

40 Inner Library

Meaning

The image of this card is not what people would expect for a library: a painting of trees with roots that hang down into an abyss. The trees are densely packed, and through them you can see a hint of land and sky. Poetically, trees have their roots in the Underworld and their leaves in the sky. They are a bridge between the Underworld and overworld, yet they dwell on the surface world.

The imagery also moves us away from the idea that knowledge comes only from books. The true library of magical knowledge is all around you in nature, and in the stars, planets, and the Underworld. Books are ways for one magician to pass the knowledge they gained into the future to act as a guide for future generations, but they are not the true source of that original knowledge. Practice and experience are the deep wells from where we draw knowledge, which must be paired with understanding.

This card is also the indicator of what in magic is sometimes called the Inner Library. This is an inner state that presents as a place where all knowledge that has ever been learned and ever will be learned is accessible. This brings me back to a quote from Thomas Aquinas: 'In this connection there is truth in the view that the things we learn, we already had knowledge of.'[1]

---

[1] *De Veritate* 10.6c.

Magicians can access this place or state using visionary magical structures in order to interact with it. The 'books' and 'scrolls' that we find there are the accumulated experiences and knowledge of people who lived and died; the 'books' are aspects of lives lived which have survived the death of the physical body and have been 'stored' in a timeless state.

Another dynamic indicated by this card is this: sometimes, when someone dies, their knowledge on a core subject can be jettisoned, and the nearest available living person or vessel who is attuned to that same stream can 'pick it up'—often without realising it. They experience it as a sudden leap forward in their understanding of a subject or skill: it is as though they were 'downloaded' with a major update to their skillsets. That is another aspect of the magical dynamic of the Inner Library.

So keep all of this in mind when this card appears. Work on loosening your ideas of where knowledge comes from, and where it goes.

Divination

When this card appears in a reading, it is pointing to knowledge beyond information. It can be a prompt to widen out your learning, or to deepen your learning through practical application. This is not a card of the 'armchair' magician; rather it is a card of a magician moving out of their comfort zone in practice, and of the magician loosening their sense of boundary, place, and consciousness. It can also be a card of magical learning that can come from nature.

Like most cards, this one needs reading in the context of the question, the situation, and whereabouts it appears in a reading. But its core meaning is 'true learning'. If the card lands in an inner realm position, then it is stating that the learning comes from deep inner sources, such as the Inner Library or inner contacts. If the card falls in the position of hearth/home, then the learning will more likely come from 'person to person' within your 'tribe': your magical group or family.

It also emphasizes the need for learning when it appears in a reading: one of its messages can be 'you need to learn more first'.

If you are involved in education or training already, then one of the messages of this card can be to look beyond for *real* learning. That means don't just study the minimum necessary, but expand your learning outwards, especially where it crosses into different disciplines and areas of knowledge. The modern world of education (just like modern magic) is very good at focused specialization, and pretty bad at a wider base of knowledge.

If you are making a choice on where to study, or what magical group to join, or what system to delve into, then this card can identify the place where you will learn best. So you can begin to see how the meaning of this card very much depends on the situation you are looking at in divination.

If this card is in a withheld position then it is a clear indication that whatever you are looking at, or whatever choices you are making, will not result in real learning: knowledge is withheld.

The overall message of this card is deep learning, the acquisition of knowledge through experience, ancient knowledge, and knowledge that is passed from person to person and generation to generation.

Keys

Deep learning, acquiring knowledge, connecting to the Mysteries, learning from nature, profound education, a place of higher learning.

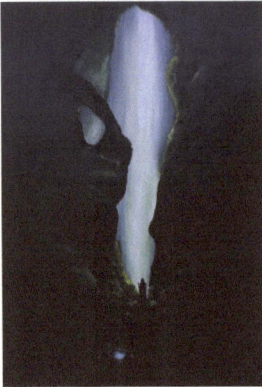

41 Sanctuary

Meaning

In magical terms, sanctuary is a space that removes the visibility of the magician. It protects and enables them to have rest, and to build up their energy reserves after a period of dangerous or intense work. It can also give them some respite in the midst of a long, ongoing magical attack. Even the healthiest, strongest magician at some point needs rest and regeneration if they are continually having to work magically, and as a magician ages, that need becomes more frequent.

There are few places indeed where a magician can go that would render them invisible to inner forces, hostile magical attacks, or temporarily shield them from the weight of working magical patterns that are constantly triggering. Some of those areas include consecrated sacred spaces like an old church or cathedral, a well-balanced temple compound, a river isthmus, or an underground cave. Not all religious places are properly consecrated or magically energetically balanced, so deciding if a religious space is workable depends on the knowledge and skill of the magician. The religion itself is not important: what is important is that the place is tuned, balanced, and has a sacred presence.

Some nature places also have the ability to block or divert energies that could be difficult for magicians. Caves are the very best at blocking everything out: the sheer cover of tons of rocks is often enough to block out everything. In my days of magical heavy lifting, I always knew where the nearest caves were that I could access. Even if they were a two-hour drive away, when my energy was stretched to its limits through prolonged or difficult magical work, I would go and visit a cave for a day. By the end of the day, my energy reserves would be restored enough that I could go back and carry on my work. If the cave has water running through it, then all the better. The one thing I would be cautious of is the nature of the cave.

If it was a cave with burials and stories of 'hags' or ghosts, then I would steer clear of those caves as they would not offer respite: they would be more likely to become jobs. Commercially opened caves are usually the best, as they are lit and used to people being there.

Rivers can also be a good sanctuary, and being on an isthmus is best of all. An isthmus is where the river loops back on itself enough that the land within the loop is almost an island. Running water can be a good block of difficult or hostile energy.

The weirdest 'one day sanctuary' was something I stumbled across by accident. It was a period where I was under a serious and prolonged magical attack by a competent group of magicians (I always piss people off) and the energy it took to constantly fend it off was exhausting. I had to go and get some cheap supplies, and the nearest place was like a 'superstore' that was vast, noisy, and full of people. I realized after being in the space for five minutes that the constant 'cheese-grater' feeling of the attack on me had stopped. The place had a café, so I got some food and a drink, and spent some time there. Even though the place was energetically grubby, it was peaceful among the noise: it was so chaotic that no coherent magical pattern could penetrate it. So that café became my planning office: I could work there among the noise to design and preconstruct the basics of an underlying magical pattern to shut out the attack and drain its energy off. By working there, the magicians could not use divination to track what I was doing, as I was hidden behind a wall of chaotic energy and noise.

Real magical sanctuary can be found in the weirdest of places, and sometimes not found where you would most expect it to be. Experimenting and paying attention is how you find a sanctuary near you where you can go if you need to.

DIVINATION

This card is very simple in its message: 'sanctuary'. It indicates a need to withdraw to a safe place and rest so that you can recharge. How you apply the meaning of this card depends on what the question is about, and where it falls in the layout.

If you are looking at a building or space and the sanctuary card is in a central or positive position, then it indicates that this is a place where you can find sanctuary, or that this place is energetically peaceful. If you are using divination to choose a ritual space, then this card would indicate that you have found a good spot.

If you are ill or struggling with a heavy life, work, or magical burden, and the sanctuary card appears, then it can be a warning to you that you are pushing things a bit too far for your mind or body to cope with, and that you need to rest, withdraw to a safe or quiet place, and recharge.

This card can also appear if you need to withdraw undercover, not because of weakness or illness, but for safety. It can point to the need to step back quietly, to stay silent and invisible, and to allow whatever is coming at you to pass by without seeing you. For example, when the spring inner tide of death flows through the land, if it is a strong one, then you do not want to be caught up by it, since it doesn't just kill the weak, but it can also sicken the healthy or drain your energy resources. Withdraw, and go magically silent. Also, blood your doorframe[1] as a decoy: this tells the inner tide that death has already visited, so there is nothing more to do. This is a very old magical method still used to this day in some Near and Middle Eastern places, and particularly by some North African Bedouin tribes.

In mundane readings this card can have a variety of meanings depending upon their question and subject matter. It can indicate the need to withdraw for a while and rest, or the need to heal by resting.

It can also indicate the need to go silent and invisible, particularly if the question is about how to approach a conflict or difficult situation. It can indicate the need for a temporary breathing space in which you can step back and recharge your batteries so that you are fully ready to take on the challenge. Such withdrawing and silence or waiting can also be useful in that it gives you some advice regarding timing. Hence this card's message can sometimes be 'not yet': this often happens when astrological or fate events are not yet quite in place for a good outcome.

With mundane matters, this card can also be a prompt to find a safe place. This can come up when a major storm or destructive event is coming over the horizon but has not yet been seen. This is strengthened considerably when this card appears with cards of destruction, danger, etc. It is telling you not to try and ride it out, but to get somewhere safe.

If the question is about the safety or balance of a place or person and this card is prominently placed in the reading, then the answer is 'yes, this place or person is safe'.

KEYS

Withdraw, need to recharge, go invisible, seek shelter, place of safety, place of sanctuary, stay hidden, not yet.

---

[1] Appears in Exodus Old Testament. Was and still is a magical method of decoy, using lambs' blood.

42 Nature

Meaning

One of the biggest mistakes that magicians make is to ignore nature in terms of their magic. They may enjoy hiking or walking in nature, but they do not connect with it as an integral part of their work: they have little or no interactive relationship with their environment. And yet nature, which is all around you even in a city, is one of the greatest sources of power, contact, and assistance in magic.

Magic and its expression in ancient religions was deeply rooted in nature, even if that religion was temple-based. For example, in ancient Egypt, and also Mesopotamia, the gods themselves were expressions of the natural forces that were in the land. The wind, the rivers, the rain, the storms, the sun, the moon, the land, the animals...all of these were recognized as inherent powers that could be magically harnessed or cooperated with as part of the existence of the people.

The relationship between the magician and nature is one of cooperation. You don't bite the hand that feeds you; rather you nurture and protect it. In turn, the spirits and beings within nature nurture and protect you. And they are certainly a force to be reckoned with: mythology around the world is packed with tales and warnings of the powers within nature from the tiniest being to the biggest rock. Mythology is the oral history of how to live in the community of nature.

Everything is conscious, everything has power, and some of that power is dangerous to us. Working magically with nature is not a pretty, gentle, or whimsical act: that idea is programmed into the western mind after decades of emotional feel-good movies. Working magically with nature is tough, and dangerous at times, but it is powerful, and when you learn to make friends with the spirits, rocks, forest, desert, mountains, and caves, it opens up a whole other layer of magic that many magicians are totally unaware of. However, one word of warning: nature in general does not like humans, at all, and never has done. It was a shock for me to realize this through my magical work and divination over the years. What I did find is that making individual friends in nature does help, but the actual land (mountains, caves, deserts etc.) basically hates humanity in general with a vengeance and always has done. So making friends and working within nature requires treading a fine line with caution and patience.

This card is to advise and teach you that even in a city or a desert, there is a vast force of nature all around you. The first step is simply to recognize it: the rocks and earth under the city are still there, the weeds grow through cracks, the wind blows around the buildings, and rivers run close or under cities. Don't fall for the modern idea that nature is only 'out there': it is not, it is everywhere. Recognize that, then start to talk to it.

Once that relationship is established, then these forces, spirits, beings and powers can be worked with magically in cooperation. This is not a new idea: it is an ancient one, and one that Paracelsus,[1] for example, understood in his own way.

As magicians we draw power from the land that we stand on. The magician is the power of five[2] and the land that we stand on is the magical power of four[3]: without that connection to the land upon which we stand, we are without foundation, and so our magic will have no roots or base.

DIVINATION

If this card appears in a reading, then it is indicating that either you need to connect and work with nature magically, or that the local land or land beings where you live need help or connection. If you are looking for the best way to solve a magical problem or how to approach a magical working and this card appears, then the answer is in nature and in working with one or more of the powers of nature (i.e. the elements in their natural state of wind, fire, water, or rock earth, or with a storm, or with caves, etc.).

Another message of this card to the magician is one of *knowing oneself*. It can point to a need to work on the understanding that you are truly energetically connected to everything around you, and that everything you do magically and mundanely has a direct energetic effect on your surroundings and the people, beings, and creatures around you. Opening out that awareness not intellectually, but in true understanding, will lead you on a path of care and attention to the effects your actions have not only on what is around you, but also upon yourself. What you do magically to others, or to your surroundings, also happens to you at some point in your fate path, not as a punishment or reward, but simply because you are both inherently the same collective being.

If this card falls in a negative or withheld position in a magical reading then it can sometimes point to the more dangerous side of nature, such as storms, earthquakes, predators, etc. Then it is often a prompt to get out of the way of something, i.e. to withdraw from nature for a while.

In mundane readings this card's appearance can be a prompt to get outside more, or to tend to your garden, feed the birds, etc. Walking out in nature whenever

---

[1] Philippus Aureolus Theophrastus Bombastus von Hohenheim (1493-1541). Swiss alchemist, theologian and magician.

[2] The magical number for the human, which is why the magical sign for a human is the pentacle: the five-pointed star.

[3] The magical number for the land, outlining the four directions or four horizons. This is depicted as an equal-armed cross: the body of the land.

possible is good for your inner and outer health, even if it is a short visit.

If this card appears in a health reading then it can indicate allergies triggered by pollen, seeds, fur, etc.

Another message of this card can be, 'it's ok, its natural and a part of nature'.

Keys

Land power, nature power, commune with nature, natural elemental force, natural.

43 Underworld

Meaning

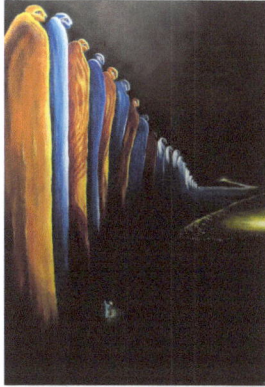

From a magical perspective, the Underworld is a complex and many-layered 'place' or state. It is a place where our spirits and minds encounter challenge, change, and transformation, both in life and in death. It is not 'hell' as some religions assume, but it can be if not approached properly. For magicians, the Underworld is one of the first training grounds for the spirit and mind, as first we learn to go 'down' before we go anywhere else.

The Underworld is a place of storage, where that which no longer belongs in the living world either rests if it is conscious, or decays and ossifies if it is not. Its layers include ancient ancestral consciousnesses, ancient deity powers, vast beings that are destructive to the world of the living, and dangerous powers that are 'locked up' or reside deep in the Underworld to prevent their powers unleashing chaos in the living world.

It is also a place where the living and the dead confront their own 'demons': it is a place where we cannot hide from ourselves, and the transformative aspect of the Underworld is a place of confrontation and 'winnowing'.[1]

As magicians, it is a part of our training ground and continues to be so throughout our lives. In ancient Egypt where magic was an inherent part of the religion, this aspect of the Underworld was strongly understood. For Egyptians, life was one big training ground in preparation for death and entering the Underworld. Successful passage through the Underworld enabled the soul of the person to rise as a spirit into their eternal 'real' life.

Playing at being a 'dark dangerous Underworld magician' never ends well:

---

[1] Winnowing: a harvesting method for separating chaff from the grain.

suicide, madness, cancer, or your life falling apart around you are the slow, eventual unfolding results of trying to play imaginary games with the powers of the Underworld. The Underworld is a place that can be very dangerous or very educational, depending upon how you approach it and your level of self-awareness and maturity.

In this painting, a living magician walks through the darkness of the Underworld holding up their Phanos, their lantern, which is lit by the wisdom of their soul. The ancient Titan deities watch silently as the human passes by. In the distance is a trail of light, as other souls both living and dead, journey through the Underworld towards the dawn.

The Underworld powers are such that when some of them surface in our world they seek what is rotting, unbalanced, weak or cracked. Their power can intensify that imbalance. Hence working in the Underworld as a magician teaches the magician to get themselves into balance and maturity so that they can navigate through the deeper layers of powers safely and without incident. Direct experience is always the best teacher, and the young magician learns to navigate this place and power in small but considered steps, first paddling in the shallows of the Underworld, and then venturing beyond.

DIVINATION

The meaning of this card in a reading depends heavily on the question posed and the position in the layout where it lands. For the most part it is a card of warning, and the dangers it represents are such that they can be avoided with the right choices and actions.

The positive side of this card is when it appears as a prompt to the magician to work in the Underworld. For example, if the magician is using divination to discern the best next step for their learning and development and the Underworld card appears, then it is prompting the magician to work in the Underworld in vision, and to learn the various layers of consciousness in that place.

It can also appear in readings when 'Underworld'-type energies or dynamics are around you or are a threat. Underworld beings or powers are often worked with in magic, and if this card falls in a positive position in a reading about magical work, particularly in the inner worlds or relationship positions, then it can be a prompt to work with such powers.

If the reading is about potential magical threat and this card appears, particularly if negative cards are around it, then it states that an element of the threat is of the 'flavour' of the Underworld. This would indicate the beings that chop, compost, or challenge your weaknesses. In more extreme circumstances it can indicate the rise of the serpent power of chaos which, when it rises from the Underworld, infects everyone who interacts with it. In turn, that person becomes a vessel for that chaos.

It can also appear in readings when a group of people, or a communal space, has become heavily infested with rotting energy, parasites, and hostile beings. As such, you can see how this card is a major one for exorcists to keep an eye out for in readings. Whenever this card appears, a good clean-up is needed.

What protects the magician from such powers is staying ritually clean, keeping as balanced as possible, and being just in your actions. That in turn 'seals up the cracks' in ourselves so that we can work safely with Underworld powers and beings.

If this card appears in a magical reading along with cards that indicate ancestors, age, wisdom etc., then it can indicate one of the powerful Underworld goddesses who can be worked with. Working in vision in a balanced way with such powers can slowly bring much maturity to the magician. But it is pertinent to point out that such work will trigger any weakness in your personality so that you can spot it and deal with it. If you are prepared for such, then it is not a problem: the lantern lights the way through the darkness.

In mundane readings, this card can indicate difficult or destructive times, or elements of the story that are rotten. Look at the other cards that surround it and also look at the short-term and long-term outcomes of the reading: this will give you an idea of how long, short, or difficult the influence may be.

It can also be a warning in a mundane reading when looking at people or situations that they are underhand, rotten, and not to be trusted.

In a health reading it can indicate suffering or an infection getting out of control.

Keys

Potential danger, imbalance, rot, darkness, realm of the dead, work in the Underworld, facing self, being tested.

44 Sacred Place

Meaning

I chose to paint natural features rather than a temple or church as a sacred place, because many people have forgotten that there are also natural places and natural features that are sacred as well as constructed temples, churches, etc. This is very important for magicians to understand, since locating a sacred place where one can find inner sanctuary, cleansing, or rebalancing is part of staying healthy and safe. It is also a good place to 'talk to the gods': a natural or properly constructed sacred space is a place where there is far less interference in the communion between a magician and the Divine ones, regardless of how we perceive or depict them (as one god, many gods, nature, the universe, etc.).

There are various places in every land where certain features come together in a particular way that creates an inner harmony (just as there are places with certain features that create a powerful but at times disturbing place). And there are various religious buildings that are built to specific harmonies which create an inner harmony, just as there are religious buildings that are not. Norman-style cathedrals were built (and often decorated) to look like forests, and some Byzantine cathedrals were built to look like vast circular caves.

Truly sacred places are nothing to do with religions, even though they can be a religious space. A sacred place is simply somewhere that the Divine power can flow through in a more focused and present way. And that can be through nature or through man-made buildings. So be careful never to let any negative opinion about a religion cloud your judgement regarding a sacred space.

Divination

This card can be interpreted in different ways according to what the question is and where it falls in a reading. If you are looking at a place to see if it is balanced or truly sacred, then this card will indicate this. In a negative position, it points to it not being sacred or balanced. It can be used for natural places, buildings, and magical temples. It can also indicate the sacredness of an inner place where magicians go in vision: again, if it falls in a negative or withheld position then it indicates that it is not a balanced or sacred place, which can be a warning to magicians that it is potentially unbalanced or parasited.

This card can also indicate the magical 'cleanness' of a place. This can be particularly useful if the job in hand is one of exorcism or clearing a place or area. If you suspect that a home, building, space, area, etc. may be haunted, parasited or possessed, and this card appears, then the answer is no, it is probably not. This place is energetically clean and balanced, and something else will likely be going on with that space or the person experiencing the disturbance.

It can also indicate if a place is a good place to start a magical space or a working space out in nature. If you are doing readings to find the right room, building, or outside space for magical working and this card appears as an answer to a place, then you have won the lottery. This place would be perfect for you to work in, as it is clean, balanced, and has the right alignments for power to flow through it. However, if you do identify such a location and choose to work magically there, then you must upkeep it properly: the work you do there should be balanced magically, and the space treated respectfully. Doing unbalanced, vicious, or stupid magic in such a space can trigger a huge backlash on the magician, particularly if it is a nature space.

If this card comes up in a reading about your home, then it can indicate that the inner vessel of the house has attracted a deity or Divine spirit that has moved in and become the 'house spirit'.

This card can also indicate a safe place. If you are in a crisis and are doing readings to look at whether a place is safe or not for you, then this card can indicate that that place is indeed safe, and that you will be protected there.

If the reading is about a person and this card comes up in the position that indicates that person, then the person in question is far more than they seem: their body is a sacred place, which means their spirit which is housed in the body is a very special one. They are an Akh (bright one) in life, or they are a soul carrying out a Divine path or fate, or they are a holy person. They may not appear so on the surface, and they may not even have a balanced life, but their soul is working in service through the physical life they were given.

In mundane readings, this card can indicate a good and solid building, a healthy patch of land, a special place, a nature power spot, or a place of protection. If this card appears in a reading with the Sanctuary card, then they will strengthen each other. Look at the positions in the layout where the two cards land: that will tell you how and where the inner powers are flowing to make this such a special place.

It can also indicate a person who is a good priest, a spiritual person, or simply a really good human.

KEYS

Holy place, sacred space, place of Divine presence, clean, balanced, safe place, special person, nature power spot.

EXTRA

Here are two Old Testament extracts[1] which talk about sacred ground. Note that the characters in both stories are instructed to take their shoes off, not just because they are in the presence of God or an angel, but also because they are standing on sacred ground. It is the land itself that is sacred, not just the presence.

> And it came to pass, when Joshua was by Jericho, that he lifted up his eyes and looked, and, behold, there stood a man over against him with his sword drawn in his hand; and Joshua went unto him, and said unto him: 'Art thou for us, or for our adversaries?'
>
> And he said: 'Nay, but I am captain of the host of the LORD; I am now come.' And Joshua fell on his face to the earth, and bowed down, and said unto him: 'What saith my lord unto his servant?'
>
> And the captain of the LORD'S host said unto Joshua: 'Put off thy shoe from off thy foot; for the place whereon thou standest is holy.' And Joshua did so
>
> — Joshua 5: 13-15
>
> And the angel of the LORD appeared unto him in a flame of fire out

---

[1] JPS *Hebrew English Bible*, 1917 edition.

of the midst of a bush; and he looked, and behold, the bush burned with fire, and the bush was not consumed.

And Moses said: 'I will turn aside now, and see this great sight, why the bush is not burnt.

And when the LORD saw that he turned aside to see, God called unto him out of the midst of the bush, and said: 'Moses, Moses.' And he said: 'Here am I.

And He said: 'Draw not nigh hither; put off thy shoes from off thy feet, for the place whereon thou standest is holy ground.'

— Exodus 3:2-5

45 WIND SPIRITS

MEANING

The image represents the magical communion between elemental beings and the magician. In this representation, the female magician is communing with the consciousness of a storm, the beings of air that ride the storms and which also *are* the mind of the storm.

The storms and wind, along with other elemental powers in nature are conscious and at times are willing to commune with the magician. They wish to be recognized as sentient powers and respected as such. That communion and respect in the face of such raw power builds relationships between the conscious aspects of the elemental forces and the magician. A consequence of that relationship is a working partnership between those forces and the magician, both in a purely magical sense, but also in a sense of cooperation in how we live. By building relationships with such powers, we come to understand their actions better, and can learn to either get out of the way when they are 'doing their thing' or to facilitate them.

Storms clean, pin (though lightning), and clear what needs clearing. Their wind can fill our 'inner lungs' with utterance that is then written down. The wind can be worked with magically for magical utterance and writing, for gauging the health of the land, for moving power from 'a to b', and for learning how to live with the vast elemental powers that surround us, in the best way we can as humans. I have worked with this force for many years, and it has taught me so much.

A wise magician communes with everything in nature that is around them and learns to build a working and cooperative relationship with every aspect of nature. Working with the wind spirits and storms is probably the hardest to do simply because finding the conscious spirits within a storm can be difficult at times. That difficulty comes from within us and our preconceptions: it is far easier to create a filter in the imagination to 'see' a spirit in a river, a rock, or a fire, but not so much with the wind. But persistence usually wins out. Going out and talking (uttering) to the wind, acknowledging the majestic power of a storm and so forth will eventually get you noticed, and a wind spirit will draw closer to 'check you out'.

Empaths, natural psychics, and magicians can often feel the 'mood' of a storm. If it is angry then a magician can go out into the storm and talk to it. Sometimes that can be enough to shift the mood and consequent fury of a storm. But communication always first starts with 'feeling into the wind storm' to see what it feels like, and then taking it from there. However, if lines of communication do open, remember you are a tiny ant in the face of a vast power, so don't try to act tough or 'command' anything, as you are likely to get squished. Simply be polite and offer the voice of friendship and respect.

DIVINATION

The appearance of this card in a reading indicates that there is a conscious force of nature around you that wants communion, or suggests that you need to connect with the elemental nature surroundings. That connection is not passive, i.e., just going for walks in nature; rather it points to an active participation in the inner life of nature around you, even if you are in a city.

The reason a reading would be prompting you to do this is either so that you can learn, gain skills and build working partnerships with nature powers around you, or because there is a need for your connection with the consciousness of a nature force. Wind blows through cities, skies are above you, grass grows through cracks, water runs under cities, storms visit no matter where you are. These are all things that have an inner consciousness: it is up to you whether you choose to open the door to commune with them. Once that link is established, then that mutual working relationship can take the magician down the road of working with storms, working with land powers, and learning to utter with the wind. These actions in turn strengthen the magician and give them many skills they could not find by doing rituals in a closed building. Power is all around you all the time, and the appearance of this card is prompting you to tap into that power.

Occasionally this card can appear in a reading, depending on the question and subject matter, to warn that a powerful or destructive storm is coming. The warning can either be for you to get out of its way, or to communicate with it. Sometimes this can pacify a storm in a given small area: it can effectively nudge the destructive aspect of the storm away from where you are located.

This card can also indicate that a spirit is trying to communicate with you: the appearance of this card is a bit like a telephone ringing.

In mundane readings, this card can indicate the need to listen or to communicate with someone or something, or that someone is trying to get in touch with you. It is about verbal, in-person communication as opposed to text or email.

It can also indicate in a mundane reading that the person the reading is about has a natural inner ability to commune with spirits and needs to develop it. The best way to do that is to start talking to everything. Eventually something will start talking back, either through the mind or the person's dreams.

If the reading is about a place or building, then it can indicate that the place has a spirit that resides within it or around it. Such a spirit as indicated by this card is not a ghost, parasite, etc., but is an elemental spirit that is either inherent to the land there or has embedded itself within a building. They are of no real harm, but communication with such a spirit would be useful for both the human and the spirit. It can occasionally indicate that an elemental spirit has become trapped somewhere and needs releasing. That can happen if a rock is brought in from outside, or if the house has a well inside it.

For further reading on working with elemental and nature consciousness, see my book *Magic of the North Gate*.[1]

KEYS

Storm, nature communication, wind, utterance, elemental consciousness, working relationship, element of air, weather working, need to talk to someone or listen.

EXTRA

I painted this image over the second week of February 2022 in the UK. On the day after I started the painting, on Feb 14th, storm Dudley hit the UK, quickly followed within twenty-four hours by storm Eunice, which in turn was followed quickly by storm Franklyn. The first two storms created what is known as a 'sting jet': an explosive cyclogenesis which created absolute havoc across the isles of Britain and left a trail of death and destruction in its wake. I had to paint this through constant power outs, seventy mile an hour winds, lightning, and flooding.

I didn't know when I first started painting it that three storms (I was aware of one from the weather report) were lined up in quick succession, nor was I aware of their seriousness or power, but by the end of the week it became clear why three beings instead of one had to be painted.

On day two I went outside and communed with the storm. It was curious, excited, and happy to cause destruction as it was doing its job of cleaning and clearing. It was also happy to have conversation with a human, to be recognized and respected. I told the storm it was beautiful, because it was, and I asked the storm if it wanted anything. Its reply was 'you'. I was rattled by that, as I was not willing to die in the midst of a storm just because it wanted a friend. Then I realized

---

[1] (McCarthy, 2020a)

the painting I was doing had no human in it: it was suggesting I paint their portrait with a human in it. So, I put in a woman. The image was not of me, but I realized the storm had not meant me as an individual, it wanted humans to commune with it, to be a part of its dance.

46 FIRESTORM

MEANING

Firestorm is a fairly simple card in that it represents the element of fire, and particularly where an energetic or physical fire has grown too strong and is tipping out of control.

In magic, the energy of fire is worked with as a gateway, a focus, and an anchor point for some magical patterns. Practically this involves working with candle flames and small controlled fires. The inner energy of fire is also worked with alongside other elements as a building block in the construction of magical patterns.

This card can also represent the 'fire' of certain energies in our bodies which also flow around us in the natural world. We call it 'fire' when it rises in our bodies as it can trigger heat, fever, and a sensation of burning. We also use the term 'inner fire' when magicians observe a destructive tide of energy that is about to release, or has released, upon the world, when that tide appears to us in vision as 'fiery' or as a firestorm.

Such a fiery destructive energy (not all destructive energies are fire-based) can act in a similar way to a wild forest fire: it can creep underground unseen until it explodes, or it can skip across the top of the trees while unseen on the ground. A person doesn't realize fire is all around them until it suddenly explodes and by then they are trapped. Inner fire when out of control can act in the same way; when an inner fire storm or tide of inner fire erupts into the physical world, it brings natural disasters, war, and pandemics: all are events that we would term as 'fiery'. Hence magicians are trained to pay attention to what is happening around them, as often there are small signs that show when there is an inner fire storm coming.

DIVINATION

When Firestorm appears in a reading, unless the question is something like, 'what is the best main element to use in x magical working?' (The answer would be fire) it can indicate that there is too much fire in something. That can be literal fire, or inner fire energy.

This card can appear where there is a natural inner energy buildup that is becoming destructive. If the reading is about a building, for example, and this card appears, then it would be wise to check the electrics or gas lines, and to ensure that you have a fire extinguisher in the building. If the reading is about an event, then it can indicate either that there is possibly going to be a fire, or, that there could be a violent emotional fight or an overreaction to something.

The strength of the warning of this card depends upon the context of the reading: it can indicate anything from a bad argument and loss of temper to a house fire, or a fever, or an inner energy buildup that will trigger a war in the physical world. So always read this card in context. If the reading is about something simple like, 'is this the right building for a magical temple or my next accommodation' and this card appears in the reading in an active position, then the answer would be no. It would be likely that either the building is imbalanced energetically and living there would cause a lot of temper outbursts, or that it will have a fire at some point. Also be aware that if you subsequently choose not to move to or work in that place, then the fire may not happen as the fate of a place or building is often inextricably linked to the fate of the people who live there.

Sometimes that 'fire event' fate is embedded solely in the structure, so whoever lives there would suffer it. But with magicians, often we bring stronger fate triggers with us wherever we go, and you need to keep that in mind when doing such readings. Sometimes magicians will 'feel' the inner energy of fire build up in a place or thing; I once tested a car for a friend and told them not to buy it as the 'pattern' of a crash and fire was embedded in the car. They bought it anyway, and a few months later had a crash where the car set on fire. Thankfully my friend got out ok. The more you work with inner energies, the more you will start to feel them building up in something.

If your reading is about your magical work and Firestorm appears in an inner position, then it is warning that a fiery destructive energy is building up and unless you change something in your life, it will likely manifest itself in some form. Sometimes these inner buildups are specific to us and our fate, and sometimes it is an inner tide that is building up and will break across a society. This becomes apparent if this card keeps appearing in an inner position regardless of who or what you are doing a reading about. In such a case, it is wise to plan ahead for difficult times.

In mundane readings, depending on the question and subject matter of the reading, it can indicate a fire, a bad argument, an aggressive out-of-control person, a violent act, or violent temper. What exactly this card is pointing to can be ascertained from doing subsequent readings with focused questions.

Keys

Element of fire, anger, fever, inflammation, out of control fire, rage, burning, destruction through fire, war, violent personality.

47 Water of Life

Meaning

Those who drink of the waters of life, water their souls. The water is not of the short physical life; rather it is the watering of the spirit that existed before birth and that continues after death.

When we walk a magical path, at first we are enamoured by the rituals and magical acts that enable us to take control of aspects of our lives. As we move further along the magical path, we start to realize that magic is a door that opens out onto many vistas that are not visible to the mundane. As we walk through that door another one presents itself, and the further we walk, the more we realize just how complex, beautiful, and astonishing the world is, both in its physical form and its inner one.

We delve deeper and deeper into magic and ourselves, and then realize that we know nothing. We thirst for that which we cannot name and cannot see. No religion, no magical system, no mystical path quenches that thirst, but we continue to search, not knowing exactly what it is we are looking for.

Then slowly, drip by drip, our inner visionary, magical, and dream experiences start to wet our parched lips. Through those experiences we gain insight, flashes of revelation, and occasionally 'downloads' of knowledge that is beyond words or books: it is the conscious Divine gently revealing itself through everything. If we pay attention to that experience and allow it to change us as we integrate it, then that is the nourishment of the Water of Life.

It is the water of soul healing, of soul awakening, and the water of miracles. It is the Divine power of healing that flows through physical water in the form of cold springs, and through the inner water that we cannot find; rather it finds us.

Divination

This is a card of healing of the soul: it appears when we have cried out in the darkness and our cries have been heard.

When this card appears in a magical reading, it speaks of inner healing, and the refreshment of the soul through awakening to the deep mysteries. It is a card that indicates something is on the right path, something is resolving, something that has been endured for as long as possible is now on the cusp of healing.

As magicians we often come from a story of wandering through the mundane

133

world feeling like we do not belong, that there is no one with whom we can find fellowship. That solitude is borne as a burden until one day we really cannot bear that burden any longer. When this card appears, it is the drink of water as you emerge out of the desert. Its message is: 'you are not alone, here, drink of Divine water and awaken to the magic around you'.

It is a card of deep love. Not the love of relationships, but the deep love of being part of the consciousness that is all around you in all living things. The card is saying, as a voice from the inner and outer planet you stand on, *you are loved*.

In magical readings about magical work, if this card appears it is a prompt either to use consecrated water as part of that working or to work with water magically in a healing renewal capacity (such as magically prepared water subsequently poured into rivers or lakes to trigger renewal healing).

It can indicate coming back into balance or healing after a long illness, or it can indicate a healing of the emotions and the lifting of a depression.

KEYS

Soul nourishment, sacred healing, physical healing, Divine love, regeneration, working with water energy.

EXTRA

Ab-i-Hayat,[1] the water or fountain of life, is said to spring from the Divine name of Allah *Al Hayy* which means 'the Living'. It symbolizes Divine Knowledge, and it is said in the Islamic Hadith that the one who drinks the Water of Life finds eternal life through *Al Hayy*.

This is illustrated in the stories of Al Khidr, the green prophet, a contemporary of Moses who was said to have taught Moses. Al Khidr is described as One who drank of the Waters of Life and still appears to teach the holy ones in the Great Mysteries. He is still in this world, and he has insight of the heart which is god-given knowledge from Allah's presence. He is called the green prophet because where he treads, the land turns green.[2]

If you study the mythos of the Dynastic Egyptian religion, then you can see the source of, or at least an inspiration for, this later myth, in the story of Osiris: the green-faced god of regeneration. He is the god that died, descended into the Underworld, was renewed with the rising of the sun, and brought greenery and crops to the land on his renewal. His deeper mysteries talk of the regeneration of the soul after death, and the mysteries of the soul's evolution. One of the reoccurring themes in the funerary texts which illustrate the mysteries of death and rebirth, and ultimately Divine immortality, is the theme of Divine waters that hold and dispense sacred knowledge: Cool Refreshment.

---

[1] Persian for 'water of life'.

[2] According to Imam al Bukhari (810-870 CE), a Persian scholar, in his Hadith *Sahih-al Bukhari*.

48 BALANCE

I am that which is straight and true.

My daughter is truth

My son is justice.

My voice is quiet

But listen well when I speak.

MEANING

The painting depicting Balance is an abstract
using colour. On one side of the painting is blue, and on the other side is red: red
is a long wave band which peaks around 560-580 nm, and blue is a short wave band
that peaks around 400-440 nm.[1]

The two colours of red and blue are at either end of the visible spectrum, with
a bolt of white painted down the middle. The pure white is a thin line. Absolute
balance is fragile and fleeting, but its influence 'bleeds' into whatever is around it.
The white paint 'bleeds' into the two colours, changing them, influencing them,
but the absolute colour in their strongest expression is pushed to the edges. The
balance not only goes to the edges, like the pans of a balancing scale, they are also
in vertical opposition. This illustrates from a magical perspective how the power of
the fulcrum maintains the balance of oppositions by constantly adapting, expanding,
and contracting in order to maintain stability: the light is neither good nor bad, it
simply expands or contracts to dilute or strengthen one power or the other.

In magic, balance is not a fixed point or dynamic: it is a constantly shifting
and evolving power that relies on counterbalance. Absolute balance is a fleeting
experience in magic and life, and for the most part the magician is constantly
adapting the working pattern and themselves to move towards or away from balance
depending on what they are trying to achieve. However, in that moment of absolute
balance the magician is in complete harmony with the powers around them. This
produces a moment of momentous insight or a step forward in their own internal
evolution.

DIVINATION

This card is counterbalanced by the Serpent of Chaos. The Serpent stands at one

---

[1]Nm stands for Nanometer: a unit of length used to specify the wavelength of electromagnetic
radiation near the visible part of the spectrum.

end of the story, and Balance is the conclusion of that story. And yet they are not apart from each other: they are constantly dancing around each other. That dance plays out in our lives and the lives of nations, landscapes, and every living thing. We are either collectively moving towards balance or moving away from it: we are rarely in full balance except for fleeting moments.

When this card appears in a reading depending on its position, it often denotes a period of imbalance coming to an end. It can also imply that while a person or situation is out of balance, there is an underlying movement towards balance that is playing out through opposing imbalances.

Imagine having a very fine set of scales but no matching weights: to balance the scales you have to try adding and removing small objects on the two scale pans until the scales stabilize. This can also play out in fate: various seemingly difficult and imbalanced situations can sometimes take us to where we need to be to stabilize the fate pattern for the future. But while you are going through the difficult situation, it can be hard to see that it is in fact taking you towards a better, more balanced condition. If you are in the midst of a long and difficult situation and this card appears, then it indicates you will get through as you are on a path towards balance.

The Balance card can be a prompt to you, advising you to seek the balance and truth in what you do: it's appearance in a reading is a strong indicator that by trying to achieve a balance in whatever the reading is about, you will be successful. And that means looking for truth and speaking truth, being evenhanded, and being willing to look at what is behind a situation. If you accept convenient lies then you will move further away from balance.

One of the biggest mysteries of balance is that you are the centre of your own fate. If you strive for truth and balance, then it will slowly affect everything and everyone around you in terms of fate, like the white bleeding into the colour.

This card's lesser and mundane meaning when it appears in a reading is resolution and coming back into balance from difficult situations. It is a positive card that states 'yes, this is the way', and it signals the end of a struggle with imbalance. It is balance that comes from effort and work, from trying and succeeding.

If the reading is about a place, then it indicates that the place is balanced and stable, but it may need a lot of work to keep it that way. Balance always takes constant work.

It is also a card of conclusion, where an outcome is balanced for everyone concerned.

KEYS

Truth, balance, effort, process, succeeded, resolution, the right path.

EXTRAS

Our bodies are constantly working hard to maintain a finely tuned balance in order to survive. This balance is called homeostasis. This is a word which encompasses multiple mechanisms used by our body to maintain our physiological needs and to ensure our system functions properly. This word describes many regulatory biological processes which allow our body to adapt to changes in the external or internal environment, whether that be temperature, light, altitude (as a few external examples) or acidity, glucose, and sodium concentrations (as a few internal examples).

The precise regulation of pH[1] within our blood is a simple example of how important it is that our bodies constantly work to maintain homeostatic balance. As we breath in and out, our bodies take in oxygen as we inhale and release carbon dioxide as we exhale. The balance of oxygen taken in needs to balance with the level of carbon dioxide that we exhale out, in order to maintain the correct homeostatic pH balance in our blood.[2] The correct homeostatic balance of pH in our bodies is primarily required in order to maintain the correct structure of our proteins. Slight changes in pH results in the unfolding of many proteins, thus loss of function and structure.

Inhaled oxygen diffuses from our lungs into the blood, binding to the iron-loaded haemoglobin protein contained in our red blood cells. The red blood cells then circulate the oxygen around our bodies, enabling our cells to take up the oxygen where it is used to make energy. The process of creating cellular energy (ATP) creates carbon dioxide as a waste product. Carbon dioxide diffuses from our cells into the blood, where it combines with water to create carbonic acid, which converts back to carbon dioxide before it is exhaled.

If too much carbonic acid forms, then the blood becomes too acidic. During exercise we create more energy to meet the demands our physical movements. This creates more carbon dioxide, which is why our breathing rate must increase in order to excrete the CO2, but also increase the amount of oxygen intake required to meet the increased demand for energy production.

Should our blood become too acidic, and our body is unable to correct the balance, then we will die. If we don't have enough carbonic acid in our blood, as is the case during hyperventilation, then our blood becomes too alkaline. This results in loss of consciousness, which typically restores a normal level of breathing.

---

[1] concentration of hydrogen ions in a solution which determines whether the solution is acidic or alkaline

[2] Approx. pH 7.35-pH 7.45.

V. Beings

49 Ancient One

Meaning

Her image is based around a neolithic statue from Çatalhöyük:[1] a seated goddess or matri-archal ancestor that was probably a prototype for the later goddess of the same region, Cybele. Cybele was the Anatolian Mother goddess who brought life or death, and who was the Divine expression of the land of Anatolia.[2]

The woman in the image is ancient. She is Divine either as a goddess or as a root ancestor, a mother of the people. She is powerful, frightening, and has dominion over the animals, as shown by the two wild felines under her control. She sits upon a stone throne in a cave before which is a deep pool of water: this is an old pattern that is found throughout the northern hemisphere's magic and myths, with many countries having their own version of this female power.

The hill is a sacred place; it is a burial mound that holds the chamber of an honoured ancestor, and the tree upon it guards the mound through time. Magically, this is a place we go to in vision to commune with the female Divine power within the land that is both goddess and ancient mother of the people. The water is 'cool refreshment', a life-giving water that cleanses and heals. She guards the entrance to the Underworld, and once you have been accepted by her and cleansed by bathing in the waters, she may allow you to carefully navigate the stone pillar steps that run aside her, that lead into the Underworld.

Divination

When this card appears in a reading it can indicate an ancient ancestor either as

---

[1] A very large Neolithic and Chalcolithic proto-city settlement in southern Anatolia (modern day Turkey), which existed from approximately 7500 BC to 6400 BC, and flourished around 7000 BC.

[2] Anatolia is modern day Turkey (Anadolu). Interestingly the Turkish word for Mother, is Ana, though the root of the name Anatolia is Greek: Ἀνατολή (Anatolé) means 'the East'.

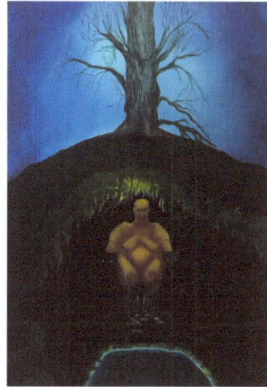

an influence in the reading's subject matter, or as an actual active presence in the surroundings or work of the magician.

It can also indicate a land or Underworld goddess, or an ancient female power. If the question is about a patch of land, then it can also indicate an unexcavated burial mound, an ancient burial, or that this female land power is very present in the land or place that the reading is about.

Its appearance in a reading can also indicate the need to work with more ancient ancestors, or, depending upon where the card falls in the layout in relation to the question, it can point to the need for caution. Ancestors are not the loving feather-wearing protectors that appear in movies or in books. Ancestral contacts can be powerful, dangerous, vengeful, and can wish to try to 'relive their lives' by influencing ours. If you are working with or considering working with an ancestral contact, then caution is always the best way to proceed.

In a magical reading this card indicates a powerful female goddess or spirit who can easily destroy you if you do not tread carefully, but who will protect or help you if she accepts you. She is the consciousness of the land, but in a form that you can commune and work with.

If the magician is looking for the right approach to a working and this card comes up, then it can indicate the magical entrance to the Underworld, i.e., suggesting that you work in the shallows of the Underworld once you have been accepted by the goddess in the cave.

In mundane readings this card can indicate an older powerful or matriarchal type of woman who is not to be messed with. It is also a card that can indicate menopause or post-menopause in health readings.

This card, by nature of its power, can also indicate a good harvest, the bounty that comes from the land that feeds you. If the reading is about the health of a patch of land, then this card tells you that the land is strong and healthy.

Keys

Ancestor, goddess of the land, ancient, burial mound, harvest fruits of labor, older woman, menopause, matriarch, mother, entrance to the Underworld, female genetic line.

50 Companions

Meaning

Animals, birds and insects play a major part in our mundane and magical lives, and they are an important feature of a magical life in so many different ways. How we treat creatures has a direct bearing on how inner beings will treat us.

In magic and religion, we as humans often expect a lot of beings like angels. We want them to look out for us, to guard us, to help us and so forth, and yet we don't in turn extend that help to the creatures around us.

It can be as simple as not killing a bug but putting it outside or in the right place for it, or feeding a stray animal who is starving, or feeding birds, or moving a harmless snake or turtle off the road and to a place of safety. This is not to say that you do not defend yourself against a threatening animal: this is not about cartoon fantasy feelgood approaches, but it is about being a decent human being.

Actions such as defending, protecting, moving a creature to safety, feeding and giving shelter, all embed themselves in your inner pattern. When you then need help, or feeding, or moving to safety, that pattern signals to inner beings that also behave like that: you are treated as you have treated others. It creates a loop of behaviour that brings change all around you.

Sometimes creatures come to live with the magician and become more than pets. In fact, the concept of what a 'pet' is starts to change for the magician as they work more and more with creatures: they become more like co-workers and companions. They stay in the relationship with the magician because they choose to, and they work alongside the magician in so many different ways, and are treated as intelligent, sentient beings by the magician. Cats are a very interesting creature to work with, as they spend a lot of time in the inner worlds, and when a magician works in vision, often a cat will come along with them as a guard and early warning system.

Similarly wild birds over time start to recognize when a magician is living in their territory and is looking out for them. It can take a long time, but slowly a trust builds up and the birds know they can come to the magician for healing, food or shelter in times of difficulty, and in return they will act as an early warning system for the magician. I have 'friends' in the rook, crow and raven families who live in my territory (or I live in theirs) and they will warn me of bad storms coming, or they will draw near when I am in difficulty, or when they are in difficulty.

When a magician is doing ancestral work, or land faery-based work, animals will

sometimes come along for the ride in vision, and a 'language' of behaviour, sounds, and actions will communicate information to the magician if they pay attention. Sometimes it is directly to the magician, and sometimes it is in response to a certain energy pattern that is around. When a certain energy pattern builds or locks in place, it creates an energetic environment that can influence how creatures behave; hence animal signals and behaviours are often parts of mythic stories. Learning to observe this is very useful to the magician as it can be used as augury, or as signals. I live in a wild place called Dartmoor, and when I wander off across the moor, I watch what the creatures are doing. When I spot certain behaviours, I follow that animal or bird, and am often led to a remote stone circle or ancient burial place that would connect well with whatever magical work I am doing.

That merging and interacting with the rest of nature is a foundational core of magic that has almost been lost in the rush for grand rituals in fancy outfits done behind closed doors. Out in nature is where magic can often be found, but to work that way we first need to gain the respect of the living things around us. As humans we do not have a good reputation in that regard, but that can be remedied by an individual magician by being respectful, being helpful, and being a compassionate friend to everything that doesn't want to eat your face off.

Divination

If this card appears in a magical reading, then it indicates that the world of animals and creatures has a bearing on what you are looking at. It can be a prompt to start working with animals, spiders, birds, insects etc., both in vision and in your physical life. It can also be a prompt to start observing nature around you, even in a city: there are birds, insects, rodents, and various mammals that wander around cities, and it is good to be aware of what lives in your territory. By observing and paying attention, you start to understand how they change behaviours over the seasons and how they respond to coming future events, and by learning such signals they become early warning systems for you.

If the reading is about magical work, then it can indicate that a creature is key to your work or an important part of it. You may need to research a little to see if there are past writings about this. Or it can be an indication to work with an animal that lives with you. That can mean, for example, if you work in vision, first go in the vision to the room where the animal is, and then continue your vision work, and observe what happens. Or it could mean that having them in your working space may be useful.

This card, depending on the subject of the reading and where it falls in the layout, can be a prompt to rescue or take in an animal as a companion and to approach it as an equal relationship: you provide food and shelter, and the creature will slowly (or sometimes quickly) work with and for you in your magical work. If you are an energy empath or have thin inner boundaries, then you may find over time that the boundaries between you and the creature start to merge, and you can think at each other, you can feel what they feel, and they become a part of your magical working life. That can be a doorway of progression for the magician to begin to truly understand that all living beings are all heavily interlinked and that on an energetic level we are constantly interacting with each other. That in turn evolves the magicians understanding of how their magic works, what it can do and how it can unfold in the physical world.

This card can also appear as a prompt to the person to simply be aware of nature around them no matter where they live and work, and not to lock themselves away from the wild places and creatures around them.

In mundane readings it can indicate a pet that you have, or that one is coming to you that will be important for you, or it can be a prompt that you need an animal living with you. If the card appears in an inner world position, then a spirit creature is watching over you or has moved in with you. For years after one of my many cats died, he would turn up when I was in really difficult times, and just lay at the end of the bed for the night.

KEYS

Working creature companion, tend to creatures, augury, an important animal or bird, an animal is the key.

51 SECRET COMMONWEALTH

MEANING

The Secret Commonwealth is an illustration of the many living spirit beings that inhabit nature. Where there is nature, no matter how little, there you find living beings that inhabit that landscape. These beings have no physical body, but their conscious presence is an integral part of the land. For example, you can come across a land being that lives in a particular tree, but also the tree has its own consciousness, as do the many physical creatures that take shelter in that tree. Everything around you in nature is alive and conscious, and as a magician, all you need to learn to do is talk to them, respect them, and keep a healthy level of caution around them.

In 1691 in Britain, the Reverend Robert Kirk, who was an Episcopalian minister in Aberfoyle, Scotland, wrote a manuscript called *The Secret Commonwealth of Elves Fauns and Faeries*. The book was a record of the stories collected from local people who lived in the wild land around Aberfoyle, and the stories were about the beings

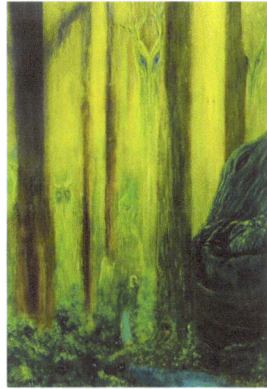

the locals had encountered over generations in the hills and forests around them. Hence I called this card Secret Commonwealth, which at the time for Kirk meant 'community of common good'.

It is easy to slip into romanticism when considering the beings of the land which some call faeries, but that would be a big mistake. The beings that inhabit the land are powerful. They can be fierce, and they do not live to the same sorts of rules as humans do. And in the last hundred and fifty years in particular, humanity has behaved appallingly badly towards a lot of the natural landscape as we seek minerals, wood, coal, etc., while dumping our trash and poisons all around them. That has created a great deal of hostility in the land being communities, and sometimes that hostility spills into dangerous violence. It is important to bear that in mind when you seek to walk among these beings. They can be funny and kind, and they can be vicious and a physical danger to you.

We call them many different things according to what culture we come from, and the names terms we use are often inadequate or confusing. But when you step back and stop trying to decide whether it is a faery being, or a land dragon, or jinn, or a tree spirit, or a water demon, and simply term them as 'land beings' i.e., spirit beings that emerge out of the natural landscape around us, then we start to gain a better understanding as a result of direct experience.

For the magician, working with land beings regardless of what you call them is an important part of magic, as they are all around you in the landscape and will pick up on your magic. Learning to work properly with them in cooperation and mutual respect is not only the right thing to do, but it is the safest thing to do for a magician.

Faery or land beings can be drawn in by the energy your magic creates, like moths to a flame. Sometimes your magic can clash with their community, and sometimes when you walk out on the land in vision, you will bump into one or more of them, and sometimes they will be curious and draw close to you. A magician is never 'switched off' magically: once a person steps beyond the basics of magic, their energy takes on a signature of magic that other beings, animals, and sometimes people can pick up on. Because of this, it is important to be first aware that the land is filled with different types of non-corporeal beings, and then learn how to navigate within and around that 'commonwealth'.

Just bear in mind the harsh learned hostility that such beings have for humans in general, and that as a part of the species that caused so much suffering, you will have to earn their respect. That can be done simply by starting to feed birds and creatures (remember how it changes your pattern?), as our buildings, pretty but sterile gardens, and our infrastructure has damaged a lot of food forage areas. Speak to everything: the trees, the rocks, the water, the rain, the wind, and pay attention to what happens around you. Where you can help, do so by picking up trash, or helping an injured bird, or not putting pesticides and herbicides on any land you have, and being respectful of the living consciousness around you. That will get you noticed as much as your magic, and the combination of a human with a magical energetic signature who also is respectful and helpful will help towards making friends.

In terms of magical practice, be aware of everything you do magically, and think about whether such practice is oppressive, rejecting, or manipulative towards these beings, whether intentionally so or not.

DIVINATION

When this card appears it is talking about inner beings that emerge out of nature, beings that are sometimes called faeries. Like animals, land beings are attracted to magical energies and can affect our magical energies to quite a large extent, yet they are most often ignored in western magic. When this card appears in a reading, it can be speaking of one or more spirits or beings that live on and within the landscape and that are somehow relevant to the reading. Depending upon what the subject matter of the reading is about, and where it lands in the layout, it can either point to a being that is drawing close to what you are doing and could be a threat or a help, or one that is simply curious.

Land beings are not cute, nor are they harmless. They are just like wild animals in that they can be harmless or annoying, friendly or curious, and they can be very dangerous depending upon how much you have pissed them off. They do not operate to human rules of what is right and wrong—and that is a really important message of this card in a reading. Usually, land beings appear in magical readings when the magical work has drawn them near, and one has entered the house space and probably gotten stuck. This happens most often in springtime when growth energies are high. Young ones venture in because something has attracted them, and they can't get back out or are terrified. The remedy for such is to remember that a stone (no smaller than half your fist) can be a vehicle for them. Use readings, inner senses or inner vision to figure out where they are, put the stone there, and in your mind and with your voice tell them to get into the stone so you can free them. Leave the stone for an hour or so, then take it outside and put it safely on the ground.

If this card is indicating a land being in your reading, then remember that integrity on the part of the human is very important in dealings with such beings, but also it is important to tread very carefully and never make an agreement or deal that you truly cannot keep. And never agree to something unless you are totally clear about what you are agreeing to. Most problems with land beings working with magicians come about by a magician agreeing to something in a vague way and then backtracking once they realize what is involved. The breaking of an agreement is considered a terrible thing to a land being, and they will take revenge for such behaviour.

In both magical and mundane readings, this card can also indicate qualities or dynamics rather than beings: it can indicate that it is *not* this, but is *like* this. It can indicate something or someone that does not operate within the norm in terms of social rules, or rights and wrongs. Their ethos is very much their own and it could be at odds with yours, yet not appear so on the surface. It is a card where the quality of unpredictability, brilliance, danger, hostility, help, a warped sense of humour, and emotional turbulence is strongly suggested.

If the reading is about an action or a choice and this card appears, then pay attention to where in the layout it falls, as it can indicate a volatility and unpredictability that could either be an asset or a hinderance in what you are trying to achieve. Either way, be prepared for unexpected demands that are costly, a sudden loss of availability, or a sudden successful breakthrough.

What is also inherent in this card is that its effects rely strongly on the type of person you are, not what you project or would like to be. Weaknesses and negative aspects of a personality are likely to be amplified under the influence of this card, just as strengths and positive aspects of a personality will likely endear you to the power that flows through this card. Its message, regardless of the situation, is to be the best person you can be in this situation, as that will favour the outcome for you. If you bring out your less wonderful side, then the situation could go very badly for you in the long term.

Overall, this is literally the 'wild card' that indicates unpredictability, strangeness, and a need for absolute integrity.

Keys

Land being, faery, nature spirit, unpredictable person or situation, make no promises, strangeness, a need for integrity in the face of unfairness.

52 Threshold Guardians

Meaning

Threshold Guardians is a term sometimes used in magic to denote spirits that prevent the magician from treading into visionary or ritual territory that would be harmful for both the magician and the spirits beyond the threshold. The deeper into inner spirit territory you go, the more likely you are to bump up against these guardians. The thresholds are not fixed for the most part, but are ever-changing according to what current energies are flowing where, what state the magician is in, and what is happening in the fate patterns of the magician and the land upon which they stand. When an inner place or state should not be breached, then the guardians are triggered.

These guardians can either appear in vision to the magician, or the magician will simply feel their presence. If the magician carries on with what they are doing, then the guardians will strike with a warning shot. If the magician is working in vision, then they will be bumped out of vision suddenly and without warning. If the magician is working in ritual or in other externalized ways, then the magician will suddenly find that they cannot remember what they are doing, things will break, fail, and the magician may start feeling nauseous or very uncomfortable. This is the result of the guardians triggering.

The guardians can also trigger in dreams; magicians often work in their sleep without realising, and if their spirit consciousness reaches into areas where it shouldn't, then they will be kicked out of the dream and out of sleep.

In vision they can appear in any form or none, hence the basic painting: they have eyes to see and they observe, but there are no discernible features. They are so ancient that they are not dressed by our conscious imagination (which is our filter in vision), and they do not communicate. They watch, and they push away. When I have come across them in my magical work, they always feel as if they are on autopilot: there seems to be no active consciousness or communication, there is no negotiating with them, and they do not move from their threshold. They appear to be purely functional and are very good at what they do. One push from one of these beings can physically injure you, and it certainly shakes you up.

In the deck, this card indicates the presence of these threshold beings and a threshold that must not or cannot be crossed.

DIVINATION

When this card appears in a reading, its message is simple and clear: you or the subject of the reading cannot go forward within the current choice being made. This card is a hard barrier that cannot be pushed beyond, and if the person tries, they are likely to get hurt or their circumstances will unravel badly.

It is also a protective card depending upon the question of the reading and where it falls in the layout. For example, if the reading is about the safety and security of a person, and this card falls either in the near future position or in a positive position, then it is saying that either in their short-term future, or in the area of life that the card lands in with regards to the layout position, they are safe and protected and nothing can get past that barrier. So, if the reading is about someone who is under a magical attack, for instance, and this card lands in the near future, then it means that they are safe for now. If it lands in an inner world position, then all incoming magic is being blocked from reaching the person. If it lands in the position of home/hearth, then the attack cannot breach their home security.

When the question is about the near future of someone's life and it lands in the near future, their way forward is blocked. If that is the case and the layout you are using has a long-term future position, then look to see what lands there. If the card that falls in the long-term future is a good or active one, then the block will release when the time is right, and the block is likely there to protect them. A good example would be for this card to appear in the position of home/hearth or the near future in the event of a pandemic lockdown.

Sometimes magicians use readings to look at the viability of a specific magical working they are considering doing. If this card falls in any positive position, then it questions the viability of that method: the magician may have to rethink their approach and do readings to look at different options. But always remember that this barrier is fluid: it can change according to the conditions around a person. The barrier may be there because it is the wrong timing, or the wrong point in a fate pattern.

When it appears in a magical reading it is wise to step back and look at what is happening around the person, and also in the wider community. It could be a block that is there for safety reasons, or a block to slow the person down so that when they do the magical work the timing is perfect, or it can be that the magician is about to get sick and doesn't realize that their magical work could tip the sickness into something dangerous for them if they expend their energy on magic at that time. So never think of the appearance of this card as a judgement: it is not, it is purely a defence mechanism.

When thinking about this card, think about a brick wall that is too high and too dangerous to climb over. Such a wall can protect you, or such a wall can lock you out of a place. If you think about this in relation to the question, the subject matter, and the person that the reading is about, and also pay attention to where it falls in the layout, then it will give you a lot of information as to why that barrier is there, and what will unfold in the future if the chosen way ahead is not changed. Always look at the longer-term outcome when such a barrier presents: if it does not look good, then change your approach. If the outcome is good, then a long wait may be necessary.

If the reading is about someone who committed a crime and this card shows up in the near future, then it is likely that they will be caught and sent to prison: a barrier that cannot be escaped from.

Keys

Barrier, closed, no, stop, rethink, no way ahead, safety, guards.

53 Light Bearer

Meaning

The Light Bearer is an angelic power connected to the Kabbalistic concept of Chesed on the Tree of Life, which in literal translation terms means loving kindness. However, it is important for magicians not to project human emotions onto the Sefirot. Loving kindness means different things to different people, and the deep, profound understanding of this power can get lost in a mess of emotional wants.

The Tree of Life is, among other things, a map of Divine consciousness expressing itself into the physical world. The light that the Light Bearer carries is the light of *Ohr Ein Sof*: the limitless Divine light that shines through all things that exist as a result of this light. Its 'kindness' is that it brings light and life into the darkness and awakens those sleeping in the dark: it awakens and brings new beginnings. It is the light that is shining on the face of the person in the card 'Awakening': the light of the Divine in the darkness.

It is kept in check by the power of the Sefirot Gevurah, which is a limiting power. Limitless light ultimately destroys when physically manifest. In between those two powers on the Tree of Life is Tiferet, compassion, as in necessary balance: the fulcrum between the two extreme powers. But what does this mean in terms of divination, and specifically magical divination?

For magicians, this angelic being is in a constant act of creation, bringing the light of life into something and keeping the world going. It is not an angelic being that you can talk to, as it is too far removed from humanity. It is the being that carries the light and Word in order to bring light to the darkness, and utterance into existence: that is the magical key of understanding this power.

In magic, the magician works equally with creation and destruction, and acts as the fulcrum between the two. A magician that works only with 'the light' and works only for creation is a magician who is heavily imbalanced and most likely to bring destruction to what is around them, and to themselves. Similarly, a magician who works only with destruction will trigger an excess of creation. These core powers are heavily entwined, and they are constantly rebalancing themselves through the tension between light and dark, and creation and destruction: this is the natural cycle of life. The magical key to working with these powers is *necessity*: that which is necessary.

The appearance of the Light Bearer in vision or ritual is the appearance of great potential, of a newness through which the universal Divine power and consciousness can flow. That can sound heady and deeply mystical, but in practical terms it can be as simple as the birth of a new child, or the start of an idea that will one day expand into greatness that brings major change. It is like a pebble dropped into a pool of still water: its ripples can carry on for generations.

Divination

When this card appears in a reading, it heralds new potentials that are likely to go unrecognized at first. 'The light shines in the darkness and the darkness comprehended it not.'[1]

The new potentials indicated by this card are ones that can possibly bring major change, but when that potential first appears, it is so small, quiet, and seemingly normal that it can be easily overlooked. It is a potential that has a great deal of fate behind it and will eventually bring great good.

Suppose a person is in the process of starting university and they have second thoughts: if this card appears in their reading, then it is saying, 'go, you cannot as yet imagine where this is going to take you'. Eventually that person qualifies and ends up in the future being a legal champion for a nation of dispossessed people.

When this card appears in a magical reading, there are two things to be aware of. One is the gravity of this card; the other is the ego. The gravity of this card is such that it speaks of Divine fate, of a path, event or life that will be far more than it appears and can potentially change the world. When a magician spots that in a reading it is easy to be overcome with a sense of importance and to fall into the 'messiah syndrome' trap: this is a common trap in magic where you start thinking you are something great and special. To go down that road is stupid and dangerous. We are all small players in a vast play that we cannot even begin to comprehend. We as magicians are more like the postman, the school dinner lady, or the door attendant at a hotel. When we think we are doing great magical things, often we are simply one link in a long chain. So settle that ego down and get on with the work!

Magical workings can sometimes have a much greater reach than was planned, and when that reach is going to be ultimately creative and positive, this card can appear. Understanding just how magical actions can affect the wider fate of everything around us is a complicated thing to grasp, and while it doesn't happen with all magic, it happens often enough. When this card appears, it heralds such a reach. If you look at where the card falls in a layout, then it will tell you how or where that reach will play out.

In more mundane readings, this card can herald a new, positive beginning. When it appears, its message is 'stay with it, this will grow and be good'. When this card appears and the subject of the reading is in a difficult situation or depressed state, then it is saying, 'have hope, the light will shine again, and you will rise out

---

[1] KJV *John* 1:5

of this in a way that is much better for you'.

If the reading is about a place, then depending upon the question and where it falls in the layout, this card can indicate that either great things happened in this place, or that it is a place that can nurture great things. As such, if the reading is searching for a location (such as a missing person) this card can indicate a church, a mosque, a temple, a museum, or a sacred place.

For mundane readings, it is the torch in the darkness, and a peek at the good things to come that are hidden over the horizon.

For both mundane and magical readings, this card's baseline message is: 'be kind'. Kindness is the emotion that can bring a lot of power through into a situation. No matter how hostile the situation may seem, and no matter how much that kindness is derided or flung back, it will still trigger good change if this card has made an appearance in the situational reading.

Keys

A new dawn, the seed of greatness, a light in the darkness, kindness, great potential about to be realized.

54 Divine Servants

Meaning

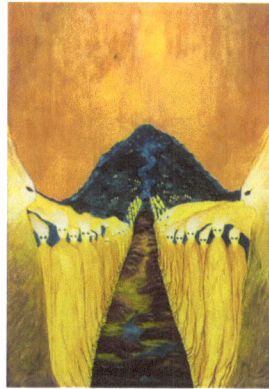

The Divine Servants are what some cultures would call angels. They are beings that are an expression of Divine Universal will, and their job is to maintain the order of fate, of Divine will, and its expression in the physical world. For the magician, this card's meaning is about angelic beings. I use the term Divine Servants for the card as the concept of angels has degenerated so much both in religion since around 300 BC, and as a consequence, in magic.

These beings are non-emotional, which means they are not vulnerable to the emotional manipulation of humans: their function is simply to ensure that something happens or does not happen. This can be very difficult for some people to understand if they have grown up in a Christianised culture where an angel is seen as someone who loves you no matter what. Tangling up emotion with necessary action is something that a magician needs to be very wary of, if it creeps into their narrative: such misunderstanding can destroy what could be a strong working relationship with these beings.

The Divine Servants card is specific to the angelic beings that work within the patterns of fate and power, which today in magic we view as the 'higher order' of angels. These beings do not work closely with humans, nor do they present to us in any form we would recognize as the typical Christian angel with two white wings, a nice white frock, and a kindly face. Rather, these beings can be terrifying to encounter; some can appear in vision to us in a vaguely human form, or in a form that is almost beyond our comprehension. They can sometimes appear as geometric shapes, or spinning wheels, or as structures. They are functional beings that do a specific job and are often unaware of us as individual human beings...just as we are often unaware of quite how many bugs we inadvertently crush as we walk through a forest.

The closer to humanity an angel is in its role or mode of action, the more humanlike it can appear in a vision or dream. The further away from humanity it is, the more it takes on a strange and more complex appearance in vision. All of these appearances are simple visual vocabularies that let we humans comprehend what we are looking at: we see an interface, not the actual being itself.

We magicians cross paths with these beings far more often than the average human would, and it is important for us to be able to recognize and work with them, regardless of what we call them or how we label them.

A Divine Servant is a being that is involved in the upkeeping of creation, stasis, or destruction. It is not a being that relates to the natural features of the world (like a deity of the wind or a mountain); rather it is a being that interfaces between the Universal Divine powers of creation and destruction, and the physical world of nature as well as the inner worlds. These beings are traditionally called servants, messengers, and thrones (upholders) because their actions uphold a fate pattern, and because when necessary, they do indeed communicate with the living in order to ensure a fated event happens or does not happen, or that through their messages, humanity evolves or devolves according to the pattern being upheld.

They are powers that can 'become' part of a sacred or inner structure: thresholds, gates, doorways, doors, walls, and altars.

As a magician, your tradition or system will have some form of visual and ritual interface for working with these beings. However, just remember that the dogmatic information around these beings (names, hours, functions, presentations, etc.) is often the result of generations of theory and dogma, not practice. A magician often has to unlearn a great deal before they can truly start to learn from direct experience.

DIVINATION

If this card appears in a reading, then it points to the presence or action of one of these beings in whatever the question is about. Such an appearance in a reading can indicate that within the subject matter of the reading, there is an active presence of these beings in the current fate pattern of the person, place, or thing.

If the reading is about a choice of magical action, then this card indicates that angelic beings and the structures they operate within are the best way forward. For example, if this card appeared for a question of 'what would the best magical approach be for this specific working or issue', then the answer is working with angelic structures, beings, and the fate paths they operate through, as opposed to working with Underworld beings, ancestors, land beings, etc.

Occasionally this card can become prominent in magical readings when an important and fateful part of your life is about to open up. In such cases this card will appear repeatedly, like a runway opening up. For the magician, this often means that a major part of your magical work is about to come to fruition in a way that will move you forward in an evolutionary step.

Whenever this card appears, it is always a time to step back and look very carefully at where you are going in life, and to be ready for a stage of maturing, evolution, and of being put to work by the Fates.

If the reading is about a building or place, then it can indicate that there is a consecrated or sacred space where humans at some point worked magically and within sacred patterns to construct a sacred temple, building, grove, etc. Occasionally, it can represent an active presence of these beings within a patch of land that is a natural energy focal point. Such places, with the presence of these beings, are naturally sacred grounds.

If the reading is about an object, then this can indicate that it is a consecrated or sacred object and should be treated carefully.

In mundane readings, the appearance of this card can indicate a powerful destiny, a sacred act, a sacred presence, or a time of important fate activity for the person the reading is about.

Keys

Angelic being, sacred place, important destiny, magical evolution.

Extra

When an angel presents to a human, we tend to think of it as a one-to-one communication, when in fact such an angelic being is part of a hive: the one angel you see is a collective of beings, who are in turn part of a bigger collective. Humanising angelic beings limits how the magician can work with them. Don't fall into that trap.

When you come across angelic beings guarding physical temples, it tells you quite a lot about that temple or tomb. It tells you that the magical powers worked with in its construction are ones that stretch into the inner powers of Divine creation and destruction, and that the sacred structure of the religion has deep, powerful roots: ones that reach beyond the Divinity in substance. That is to say the people priesthoods who shaped that religion worked with different realms and beings in vision and ritual, from the first spark of Divine impulse all the way down to the depths of the Underworld: they worked with completion.

— Josephine McCarthy[1]

55 ORACLE

MEANING

The word oracle comes from the Latin verb *orare* which means to speak. Traditionally an oracle is a person through whom the gods speak, often in the form of prophecy. But for magicians, it has a much wider meaning.

Magicians often work with various types of spirits from deities to land beings, ancestors, inner contacts, and also their own deepest eternal self. These spirit forms can often speak to and through the magician, not only to warn of future events, but also to teach, guide and advise.

Card divination is one of the ways that magicians can commune with spirits. Some magicians work well in vision and can gain communication with spirits in that way, others work with dreams, some work with contacted writing where the spirit speaks through the human and the human writes it down, often without fully understanding what they are writing. And many magicians use divination cards as a vocabulary and method of communication. Most magicians use a mix of all the above.

The skill for the magician is to know when their own conscious or subconscious mind is speaking, and when it is a spirit from outside of themselves. The ability to differentiate comes with practice. Along with that skill of knowing what is speaking to them, is the skill of knowing when whatever is talking to them is bullshitting them: this does happen, either to misinform, distract or lock down the magician, or simply because a being is amusing itself. It can also happen when a magician is being manipulated to behave a certain way by an energy parasite so that the being can feed off the magician. This is more common than a lot of people realize. The way to avoid that is experience, training, and a good, solid, well-balanced vocabulary: this can take the form of a divination deck that is magically balanced, or magical parameters in the mind of the magician. Generally, if it smells like bullshit, then it

---

[1]McCarthy, 2017b: Module 6 Lesson 1

likely is.

The image for this card is unnerving for some, but that is good, as true oracle spirits are not fluffy and friendly: they are powers that warn in the most forceful way possible. They are often deity powers that are expressions of land powers, hence the image depicts a nature setting with water, since water is often a key element in prophetic powers. This is why a lot of ancient oracle temples had springs within them or nearby. They can be hot or cold springs, but water that comes up from the Underworld is particularly strong in connection with oracles: water carries energetic information.

The oracle power can function in a variety of ways: this is good to keep in mind not only when doing readings, but also in magical practice. The one we all know is prophecy and divination. However, when it is important for knowledge to be sent into the future, an oracle spirit can draw near to a magician and 'teach' them or speak through them. The key sign that this is happening is the clarity, power, and uniqueness of what is coming from the oracle.

During the 1980s and 1990s there was a big New Age fashion for 'channelling'. People made vast sums of money by pretending to be the voice of a great spirit speaking through them. However, what came out of their mouths was usually pretty banal. Be nice, the end is nigh, we are all rainbow children, love everyone, etc. All very sweet, but not particularly ground-breaking. A true oracle spirit's words are never banal and obvious, but are stunning and often counter to the norm.

Working with oracles changes the adept magician over time, so that combined with the power of magical utterance, the words of the magician can trigger change: this can become a strange cycle whereby the oracle tells of a future situation and the magician by speaking that message actively triggers the change which brings about the future situation. This is something for magicians to think about and chew over.

DIVINATION

This card can have a variety of meanings in a reading depending on its subject matter. In magical readings, if you are looking for a solution or a choice of working methods and this card appears, it can be saying that you need to look further using divination as there is a possibility of complexities that you haven't spotted or thought of.

It can also be a magical prompt to write or speak. In the magical life of an adept, the expression and work of their magic can change from period to period. As each different path of magical work can produce specific strains on the mind and body, each working phase of a magician has a shelf life. When I stepped back from working as an exorcist as I was burned out. I did a reading basically asking, 'what next?' And the oracle was the outcome. I was to write, teach, and speak.

For magicians, this card can also be a prompt to make your own deck. A deck is *literally* an oracle, and sometimes a magician needs to make a deck that is specific to them so that each card, and each layout position, is clearly understood and works within the framework of the magician's life and work.

It can also be a prompt both in magical and mundane readings to speak out. In some situations we can waiver on whether to speak out or not, and if the question of the reading is about such a situation, then this card is saying, 'yes, speak, it is necessary'. Where it appears in a layout can indicate where that speaking needs to be aimed: for example if it falls in the relationship position, then either your partner or the person you work with is the one who needs to be told something. If it falls in the home/hearth, then it is family or your immediate community of friends or neighbours.

If it falls in an inner position, then this card is prompting you to address the inner worlds, deities, or spirits, or to allow them to speak through you. One word of warning, though. In many western cultures we like to make pacts and swear oaths, and that is often mirrored in our magical behaviour. This is not such a wise thing to do: an oath to a spirit that is broken, no matter what the situation, can be a really bad thing in magic. It is better simply to declare your intent and your wishes: tell them what you are planning to do and why, as opposed to promising on your life that you will do something. In general, beings that do not have bad intent will not ask you to swear an oath or pact.

In mundane readings this card can also mean 'communication', i.e., some communication is coming that can be important, or it can also be a prompt to send a letter or communication as part of a solution.

If this card falls in the dream position in a layout, then it can be an indication that a warning or important communication is trying to get through in your dreams. If that is the case, then keep detailed notes for the dreams you can remember for a while, and look back over them.

KEYS

A message, inner communication, a need for further divination, a prompt to write or speak, an important communication.

56 COLLEGE

MEANING

The College is an image that portrays the magical concept of inner contact. Inner contact is basically visionary, inner, or dream communication between yourself and a non-corporeal being. It is one of the cornerstones of magical practice and is a very old practice that that reaches back millennia in the history of humanity.

The meaning 'inner contact' is an umbrella term that can denote many things, such as a spirit, a deity, a land being, the spirit of a dead person, a once living master teacher, the consciousness of a tree or patch of land, an animal spirit, or even an energy parasite. It can also denote communication with a form of your own timeless deeper spirit consciousness. Magicians talk to everything, seen and unseen, and through the active communication with the inner and outer world around them, the magician learns to forge connections with their surroundings on all levels. This in turn brings the magician closer into the fate pattern and inner consciousness of the 'collective' of the world around them. It is through this interactive relationship that the magician learns, evolves, serves, and observes.

In the history of magic, various terms have been used refer to inner contacts, such as 'astral beings', inner plane teachers, 'higher adepts', saints, daimons, akhs, channelled spirits, ancestors, etc. The terminology is of no consequence, and the 'who' is of little consequence: what is important is whether or not the communication is of real use to the individual. Inner contact communication centres around learning, magical working, being warned, being assisted, or the passing on of knowledge that is in danger of dying out. It is a practice that has deep roots in some religions such as Tibetan Buddhism, and in many tribal cultures and practices. In some types of magical practice, both present and right back to late Neolithic times, learning is passed from magician[1] to magician by inner contacts.

Often parasitical beings that want an energy meal from you will 'dress up' as an inner contact and will essentially lie to you in order to connect with you. This is one of the learning curves of magical inner contact, and the ability to identify them is a skill that is learned through practice, mistakes, and experience. They are rarely

---

[1] I use the term magician as a 'catch-all' identity that includes priests, priestesses, shamans, healers, etc. Remember that in the known ancient world up to around the 6th century CE, magic was a part of the religious and cultural practice in many cultures. It was not considered something separate.

dangerous, but dealing with them can be exhausting.

Similarly, your own subconscious can take on the form of an inner contact. This in itself is not a problem so long as you recognize it as such: our own subconscious can be a deep well of learning for us to drink from, but it has to be done in full knowledge that this is what you are talking to. The subconscious externalizing itself in dreams and visions is common, particularly in the early days of visionary practice, and once it is recognized as such, it can be a valuable tool.

A basic rule is if the contact appears in your visions or dreams and presents itself in grandeur, with flowing robes, unpronounceable or special names, i.e. 'I am Melchizedek' and offers overblown but simplistic advice such as 'we need world peace' or 'you are a special saviour of mankind and I have come to help you', then it is likely that you are talking to a parasite or your own subconscious.

DIVINATION

The appearance of the College card denotes inner contact for learning. It can indicate that an inner contact (or inner collective such as the Inner Library) is in your orbit and is willing to offer guidance, or is working alongside you quietly, or is guiding you through your visions or dreams.

This card can help to differentiate what type of being it is you are talking to. Is it a parasite? Is it your own subconscious? Is it a land being? All of these different types of beings are identified in this deck to help you be clear about what it is you are talking to. So, if this card appears and you have been consciously working in vision with a being, you can be pretty (not 100%) sure it is a true inner contact. If you are still not sure what you are talking to, even if this card appears, then it can be identified by way of carefully thought-out questions and a suitable layout.

For magical readings, its appearance can be a prompt to learn to work with inner contacts, or to open out the magical conditions for such an interaction to occur. Such work is usually visionary work, as that is the easiest way to conduct such connection. Just always ensure that you are not 'overtaken' or bullied by an overzealous inner contact that has its own agenda. Sometimes the spirit of a dead adept can have its human reference points frozen in the time around which they died, so all of their prejudices can still be present.

If the reading is about a place or building, then it can indicate a 'spirit of place' i.e., a conscious and communicative spirit that resides in a specific place for a reason.

In a mundane sense, this card can indicate learning new skills or knowledge, or a place like a university or college. Its appearance in a mundane reading can be a prompt to take up the study of a subject, or to expand one's knowledge.

Depending upon the question of the reading and the subject matter, particularly in mundane readings, it can be a prompt to teach or support guide someone in their learning, or if you are retired and have specific skills, to volunteer teaching those skills to the next generation.

KEYS

Learning, vision contact, advice, spirit contact, learning dreams, collective knowledge, being a mentor, studying, learning new skills.

EXTRA

> Someone may wonder why I go about in private, giving advice and busying myself with the concerns of others, but do not venture to come forward in public and advise the state. I will tell you the reason of this. You have often heard me speak of an oracle or sign which comes to me, and is the divinity which Meletus ridicules in the indictment. This sign I have had ever since I was a child. The sign is a voice which comes to me and always forbids me to do something which I am going to do, but never commands me to do anything, and this is what stands in the way of my being a politician. And rightly, as I think. For I am certain, O men of Athens, that if I had engaged in politics, I should have perished long ago and done no good either to you or to myself. And don't be offended at my telling you the truth: for the truth is that no man who goes to war with you or any other multitude, honestly struggling against the commission of unrighteousness and wrong in the state, will save his life. He who will really fight for the right, if he would live even for a little while, must have a private station and not a public one.

— Plato, *Apology*[1]

---

[1] Plato's Apology is a Socratic dialogue of self-defence, which Socrates spoke at his trial in Athens in 399 BC, after which he was condemned to death. Plato was present at the trial.

57 GHOST

MEANING

This image depicts a ghost: a human who was recently alive but no longer is. It can also depict a person who has been dead for longer, in which case it indicates only this person themselves, and not any other being attached to them.[1]

As magicians we can postulate over what happens after death, we can look at ancient descriptions etc., and we can do visionary work into the realm of the dead. However, what we experience and perceive is from the perspective of the living, not the dead. And that is important to keep in mind when dealing with ghosts: we do not really understand what happens from their own perspective. However as active magicians, at some point we have direct and physical experiences of the newly dead that leave no doubt they are trying to communicate. The nature of a magician's training and subsequent work in inner and visionary methods enables them to communicate, give shelter, or move on a ghost.

Magicians who are working in a balanced way and are developing their spirit are far more visible to ghosts than other people are, so ghosts in distress can be more of an issue to working magicians than they are to non-magical people. But it is also important to be able to distinguish what 'type' of ghost a presence potentially is:

A recently dead person can be fully in their identity from the recent life, can come and go, and can communicate in one way or another depending on how magically active they were, or how naturally psychic they were. But sometimes what presents as a ghost is more of an energetic 'recording' of a moment in time. In this case, they will always appear in the same place, do the same thing, and do not interact with a living person. It is not actually the dead person that it is there: it is just an energetic loop or an 'echo', for want of a better word.

The recent dead can communicate in a variety of ways depending on how they could use their energy and mind while they were alive. I have had situations like all the lightbulbs blowing at once, which was my mother trying to tell me she was still alive after death...she was so excited to tell me, and electricity manipulation was the only way she could figure out how to get my attention. She then went and did the same to some of my siblings: an expensive form of communication! I have also had more focused interactions with the dead, such as them pushing or throwing

---

[1] Some long dead active ghosts are actually composites of the dead person and another type of being.

something across a room. Usually this is a specific thing (such as a phone: 'we need to talk') to get attention. A magician can then converse with the ghost through their mind or through divination, but it is not easy and can get frustrating for both sides.

Often the ghost of someone you know or are connected to wants to simply let you know they survived death, and at times, also help you, or warn you about something, or pass something along. And that brings up a weird aspect of the dead, and that is time. Time is something that governs our lives (our aging etc.), but to the dead time ceases, as it is connected to the physical world, not the inner, nonphysical world. I have had numerous situations where a newly dead person has turned up, we communicate, they may take refuge in my home for a couple of weeks or so until the funeral, and then they fade off. However, a couple of years later or sometimes longer, they turn up again to warn me of something or to try and turn my attention to something important. I struggled to understand that as a young magician, and eventually realized that to me, it was years since they died, but to them it was still a new experience, as they were newly dead. They could see my whole life at once, and as a newly dead person they wanted to be helpful in the danger spots they saw. When they have done what they need to do in order to let go and move away from their past life, they fade off deeper into the death process. For them there is no time; only process.

In terms of troublesome ghosts or long-term ghosts who cling to a place or person, that is a different situation again which can cause a variety of problems and have numerous different presentations. You need magical experience (practical, not reading books) to deal with it properly in a balanced way.

Anyone who is on a magical path in a serious way and is learning or working practically, and not just absorbing theory and magical dogma through reading books, is going to bump up against a ghost issue at some point.

As a divination card, this image can have a variety of meanings beyond dead people, and once you get used to the different layers of meaning, then you will start to understand patterns of magical expression of life and death, and how they interconnect with each other. We can learn a great deal from the various layers of meaning: each of them reflect different layers of magical understanding and help us grow as magicians.

DIVINATION

When this card appears in a reading it can have a variety of connected meanings. The most obvious one is that there is a ghost active around you or the situation you are looking at in a reading. This can be confirmed by using a straightforward yes/no layout, the best of which is the Tree of Life layout. You would simply ask, 'is this card in the reading telling me there is a dead person's spirit around me or the situation?'. Then you can use further such readings to ascertain if you know knew the person, or if they have been attracted to you for a particular reason. If you have good basic skills in divination, then you can use various layouts and focused questions to ask what it is they need, want, or are trying to convey to you.

One type of ghost, which is not common, is something the ancient Egyptians used to call 'hungry ghosts'. These are people who are dead, who often lived and died within a religion that is strong on burial, resurrection etc., so that when they die they feel they must stay in the living world and close to their body to wait for the 'end of days'.

Some such people are buried in consecrated ground: this essentially puts boundaries around them so that they cannot leave the burial ground. But others are not buried that way, and energetically they become 'hungry' for the energy of life. They can prey on the living, usually at night, drawing energy from them as they sleep. This connects to the concept of energy vampires, and often such a ghost was an energy vampire type of person in life as well as death. They need dealing with promptly, as they can do a lot of damage to the living. However, if the person they are feeding off of was connected to them in life and has fond memories of them, it can be hard to break that connection. Thankfully this does not happen often, but I have come across it enough times to be on the alert for it.

If the reading is about a building or space, then it could indicate that there is an active dead person clinging to that space, or that there is an echo connected to what was once someone who lived or worked in that space. In such a case, a ritual cleansing of the space and breaking up of the space will usually get rid of it (redecorating, changing the structure, or moving a lot of things around). If that does not work, then the echo can be attached to an object, and again you would have to narrow down what it is. That can be done by taking note of where the replay echo is active, and then looking around at the objects in the space. It can be a statue, painting, box, etc. Once you have identified potential suspects, you can then do readings for each object, or, if you are energetically sensitive enough, feel each one out. Or you could simply exorcize each object until it stops.

The ghost card appearing in a reading can also indicate something that is fading away but has not yet gone. This can appear in a health reading and mean a few different things. If the card is in a central position, then it could indicate that the energy of the person is weak and fading away, in which case whatever is wrong with them needs attending to quickly, as they are becoming a ghost of themselves. If the person is a magician, then it will be necessary to do readings to find out if the problem is purely physical, i.e., an illness, or if it is magical or energetic, in which case you would need to pinpoint what is causing the energy of the person to drain off so badly. It could be work they are doing, an object that is inhabited by a spirit that is draining them, a parasite, or something else.

This card in a reading can also indicate that something has lost its power and is breaking up: it has become a ghost of itself and is fading away. For instance, if there has been a lot of disturbing energy flying around from a magical or energetic situation and then this card turns up, it is saying that the energy is now fading off but has not completely gone, in which case ritual cleaning will normally get the residue out of the space or person. It can also indicate an 'echo' of magical working that needs dismantling and clearing away as it is causing problems.

In mundane as well as magical readings, regardless of the situation or person the reading is about, this card indicates that something should really not be there, that something is no longer itself and the fragmentation is likely to cause problems. It can indicate that something is a 'ghost of itself'. A mundane example would be a laptop that is about to die, or something that is no longer energised to do what it used to do or is supposed to do. Another mundane example would be a marriage that looks great from the outside but is actually at the point of collapse as it is no longer what it used to be: it is a ghost of whatever it previously was.

KEYS

Ghost, apparition, presence, something that is a ghost of what it once was, weakness, energetically almost empty, almost gone but not quite, last remnant of something.

EXTRA

Here is a short excerpt from an interesting tale of a ghost haunting encounter from Homer's Odyssey. The story of the death and haunting of Elpenor is spread across chapters 10 to 12.

> Odysseus sailed the River Ocean to the land of the Cimmerians and did the ritual libations and sacrifices that Circe had instructed him to do, so that the dead would appear. To the shock of Odysseus, the first dead to appear was Elpenor, a comrade who had recently died in an accident. He told Odysseus what had happened and that he had died in humiliation as a drunk, and was unburied, which had turned him into a wandering ghost. Elpenor wanted to go into death as a sailor with all the honour that comes with such and asked Odysseus to return, find his body and give it proper funeral rites. He did return to the island of Circe, found the body of Elpenor, and he along with his men built a funeral pyre for Elpenor's body along with his armour. Once the funeral pyre was burned, they built a mound over it and stuck an oar on top as an epitaph to him.

> Leave me not behind thee unwept and unburied as thou goest thence, and turn not away from me, lest haply I bring the wrath of the gods upon thee. Nay, burn me with my armour, all that is mine, and heap up a mound for me on the shore of the grey sea, in memory of an unhappy man, that men yet to be may learn of me. Fulfil this my prayer, and fix upon the mound my oar wherewith I rowed in life when I was among my comrades.[1]

---

[1] Homer, 1919: 72–78.

58 PARASITE

MEANING

Just as our bodies can pick up parasites like intestinal worms, ticks, fleas etc., so too can our energetic body, and what happens to the energetic body affects the physical health and vice versa. Minor or temporary infestations are usually shrugged off by the body's immune system, but sometimes they can cause use health issues. Major infestations of parasites in the body can cause untold damage to our physical and mental health, and the same is true for energetic parasites. Energy parasites are different types of inner beings who need to feed off the energy of a living physical being in order to survive.

The magician is far more vulnerable to energy parasites by nature of their work. The magician works with their mind and inner energy which is the main target for energetic parasites, as they feed on our vital force: the core energy of our spirit and body. Think of the magician as a forester who has to work in an overgrown environment full of ticks, leeches, and exposure to animal droppings which can carry tapeworm.

Magicians and priest magicians have been aware of this issue for thousands of years and have learned to adapt their work and way of living in order to keep most, if not all, parasites away from them. However, with the advent of Christianity a lot of those precautions and methods fell by the wayside, and the understanding of beings in general was lost in a sea of dogma. That has influenced magic in western Christianized countries for hundreds of years to the detriment of magicians. For example, a lot of the behaviour that people suppose is a demon is actually simply an energy parasite, and the understanding of that for magicians is often blocked by the overlay of emotive dogma and ignorance that has built up in western magic in Christianized societies.

Energetic parasites are attracted to energy, and energy is triggered and released by first the mind and emotions, and then the actions of the body. An intelligent parasite will manipulate the mind of the magician in order to get the magician to do things that will trigger a surge in energy that the parasite can feed off of. The same is true for non-magical people: all living physical beings are affected by such parasites, but the stakes are higher for a magician.

The one thing to remember as a magician is that the core energy that a parasite wants to trigger is emotion. It is through emotions and sensations that we energetically open up: fear, anger, hate, love, arousal, emotional highs, etc. This is why it is so important that when a magician is working, they put their emotions to one side and become very focused.

As a lot of magic works through the mind. This in turn triggers bodily reactions. It is their mind that the magician must therefore first come to know, and then learn to control. If you are aware of your triggers and aware of what you do with your mind when you are bored, lonely, frightened, in love, or any other emotive situation that produces strong emotional reactions, then you will discover your weak spots and can strengthen them.

Magical banishing does not work on parasites: this is the first lesson to learn. In fact in many cases, it can end up attracting them. This can be hard for a young magician to get their head around, as banishing is the basis of a lot of western magical systems. This loops back to what I was saying about Christianized dogma influencing magic. We don't banish lice; we kill them and clean off the eggs.

Basic magical and mental hygiene gets rid of parasites. Instead of erecting a magical boundary to stop them getting in, the magician disciplines their mind, body, and actions to keep them in relative balance so that there is no energetic food to attract them. And should a magician pick up a parasite while being around people who are heavily parasited, which can happen a lot, the magician takes a ritual bath: this cleans them off. If you are a magician and are not really aware of these beings, then it is worth reading up on them a lot more so that you have a good understanding. There is a lesson about parasites in the Quareia magical course.[1]

It is also worth thinking about the effect of chronic parasite infestation which can cause disease or can be attracted by a disease in the body or mind. As they munch on your energies, your body is getting less of the inner energy that it needs to stay healthy, which in turn can cause someone to become sick. A strong infestation in a person can also trigger a dormant mental illness or make a minor mental illness much worse. Parasites come hand in hand with disease: this is why it is so important to keep mentally clean as a magician, and also to learn how to clean these things off.

DIVINATION

When this card falls in a reading it indicates a parasite infestation unless it falls in a withheld position, which would be read as 'no parasites'. If the layout you are using has indicators for home and the parasite card falls in that position in a general reading, then it can indicate the presence of a parasite in the home, in a family member, or in both. That can happen if you bring something into the house that is infested, or if someone who is infested comes to your home. Think about their spread in terms of lice and fleas.

If the reading is about health and you are not using a specific health layout and parasite falls in the position of home/hearth, then it can indicate you are infested

[1]McCarthy, 2017a: Module 6 Lesson 4 (also available for free at www.quareia.com).

by nature of your sexual activity: the home position when the reading is about a person is often an indicator for the reproductive organs.

If you are using a health layout and the parasite card appears, then it can mean either a physical infestation such as worms or a viral illness (viruses use the body to reproduce and spread), a bacterial overgrowth, or an energetic parasite infestation. You can pinpoint which it is by how you phrase your question, e.g. 'do I have a physical parasite infestation or illness?' 'Do I have an energetic parasite infestation?' If it is an energy parasite, then where it falls in the health layout can tell you what let it in. Thoughts (head), sex (reproductive organs), inner worlds position (magical work), etc.

If you are reading about a magical working and the parasite card appears, then your magical work has picked up a parasite. Using pointed questions with readings, you can then ascertain what aspect of the work is infested and what drew it in. If the parasite card falls in a position that indicates the inner realm of magical work but the rest of the reading including the outcome is good, then one has been attracted to the work but it cannot penetrate through into the work.

This card can also appear in an inner realm position when a magical system has become parasited or the egregore has become infected, or when the egregore itself is a parasite (which can happen). If you are building up a magical working relationship with an inner being and at some point the parasite card appears in a reading, then it can indicate that the being you were working with has withdrawn for one reason or another and a parasite has stepped in and is masquerading as the being. This often happens if the magician lets emotions, wants, or needs seep into their work, if they start to project a sense of religious 'worship' onto the being, or if they attempt to get into an energetic sexual relationship with the being: any of these will trigger the withdrawal of the being and the arrival of a parasite.

Parasites are very good at cross-dressing: they can present a visionary image and a set of behaviours that mimic the beings we are trying to work with. The key is that the parasite wants something: it will tempt you by offering you something that you want, or it will flush you with an emotive 'high' in order to get you to open up energetically. By contrast, an inner being that is not a parasite is far more 'clinical' in its transactions. This can be hard for a human to understand, as we are essentially one large bundle of emotions, wants and needs (this is just part of our body chemistry that helps us physically survive). This goes back to the magician learning how their own mind and psychology works, and learning to spot where their weaknesses are.

If the reading is about a place or building, then it can indicate that the building is weakened, damaged, or infested with something physical (termites, wood rot, etc.) or energetic (energy parasites). If the reading is about a patch of land, then it can point to disease in the soil, or in the plants and trees that grow there.

In a mundane reading, this card can also indicate someone who is abusing your time or energy, or who is pretending that they are interested in you so that they can get something they want. To understand this card in a mundane sense, think of the term 'vampire' in terms of someone's behaviour: they are sucking you dry emotionally or financially.

This card can also appear when you are being financially manipulated, either by a person or a company. They are sucking you dry while smiling and pretending to be nice.

Lastly, this card can indicate a living person who is an energetic vampire: some people intentionally or unintentionally siphon off the energies of others. And while that can happen a lot at a low level in a normal way (e.g. our children), some people are extreme in their munching of other people's energy. Some do it through interactions at gatherings or within close relationships, and others do it in their sleep: their spirit wanders around at night and tries to find a sleeping person who has thin energetic boundaries. They will visit that person each night and siphon off their energy as they sleep. This is done unintentionally and is a classic situation with some vampiric old people who literally suck the life out of you. I suspect this is where the legends of vampires come from.

KEYS

Parasite, illness or disease, vampire, infestation, rotten, unhealthy.

EXTRA

Here is a short excerpt from an article in The Journal of Experimental Biology.[1] It is part of the introduction of an article titled: *How much energy should manipulative parasites leave to their hosts to ensure altered behaviours?* As you will see, the *modus operandi* for physical parasites is very much the same as energetic inner parasites. Most importantly, it is pertinent to note that physical parasites manipulate the behaviour of the host in order to get the food they need, just like an energetic parasite does.

> Parasites, by definition, are organisms that take advantage of their hosts. They do this in many ways, for example through the exploitation of their nutritional resources (e.g. haemolymph, lipid or tissues) **and by changing behaviours**. From a bio-energetic viewpoint, the host–parasite association can be seen as a perpetual conflict between the needs of the parasite and those of the host for growth, reproduction and survival. Although maximal exploitation of host resources could be advantageous for parasite fitness (e.g. increase in growth rate and or adult reproductive success), the negative consequences of this strategy could in fact be fatal for parasites if they lead to early host death. Therefore, parasites face competing demands for shared host resources and should evolve to manage this conflict by adopting the most

---

[1] Maure, Brodeur, Hughes, et al., 2013.

profitable trade-off between the benefits of resource consumption and the costs of reduced host viability.[1]

59 Choppers

Meaning

The painting represents a type of inner being that is of low consciousness, and usually is active where there is an energy of degeneration or destruction. A chopper is the inner equivalent of a woodlouse: an insect that scavenges on dead and dying matter, and occasionally on seedlings and small fruits like strawberries.

These beings are present in both the Underworld and the surface world most of the time; however their presence in the surface world (our physical world) is usually small unless there is a destructive tide of inner energy flowing through the world. Tides of inner energy of destruction and creation are constantly lapping across the world, and where there is an extended destructive tide manifesting in the surface world, the Choppers appear in larger numbers.

They target what is weak, dying, or rotting, and they chomp on the inner energy and inner patterns of whoever or whatever is their target. This speeds up the destructive process of an individual, a land area, or a community. They do not operate with emotion or intelligence, so they do not target something or someone intentionally: they just smell rot, which to them smells like dinner.

These beings feature in some of the Egyptian New Kingdom funerary texts, including the *Book of Gates*, as beings in the Duat[2] who carry sharp knives. They chop up that which is rotten or degenerate. Hence their name 'Choppers'.

They congregate where there is overgrowth that has become destructive: in other words, where there is too much stale and rotting life force or inner energy, too much accumulated inner or outer trash. The more accumulated stale energy there is, the more the Choppers will congregate. If a large number of them gather, then they can become a threat to the wellbeing of a person or place, or they can destroy magical patterns. Large gatherings of Choppers can also signal that there is a tasty 'dinner' to inner parasites: these will then be drawn into the surroundings, and they are a much bigger threat to a magician or their magical work.

---

[1] Poulin, 2007.
[2] Egyptian name for the Underworld.

DIVINATION

If these beings appear in a reading, then it indicates that something about the subject of the reading is badly out of balance. The most common situations for a magician that would draw in the Choppers is a badly cluttered working or living space that is unhealthy with a lot of stagnant energy. They are attracted to spaces that are full of hoarded belongings, or where old disused magical implements have not been disposed of and are sat collecting inner and outer dirt. The more that is hoarded or kept, the more stagnant inner energy is collected, which in turn attracts these beings.

The same can be true of magical inner patterns: old magical workings that have not been dismantled and disposed of, and which had no self-destruct timed end mechanism built into them but were just left drifting. They build up over time until they accumulate a lot of imbalanced and rotting inner energy, which in turn attracts these beings.

This card can also indicate a similar accumulation in the person or magician. If a magician does not keep themselves ritually clean and they 'hoard' inner energy by way of taking in energy by various magical means but never releasing or giving out, then they become energetically like a cupboard crammed with rotting mouldy belongings. This attracts Choppers which try to munch on the inner energy of the magician, and this in turn attracts inner energetic parasites who also muscle in for a meal.

So if this card appears in a reading, look around you and look at yourself. Is there inner or outer hoarding or clinging to things that are old, rotted or disused? If so, then it is time to clean them out. If the reading indicates that you or the person you are reading about is the target of the choppers, then it is time to ritually clean up your body and sort out how you maintain yourself.

Ensure that your magical workings have time limits on them, or have a completion built into the work, and keep your working space clean physically and ritually. Get rid of old magical implements that are not serving a purpose, but do not give them away: burn or bury them.

In a mundane reading, depending upon the subject matter and question of the reading, this card's appearance can indicate that something needs cutting away or getting rid of. It can appear in a reading where a necessary change, cleaning, or renewal has not happened, and things are getting stagnant to the point of being very unhealthy. It can indicate clinging to old or no longer used belongings, objects, places, or people where it has become unhealthy to do so. Here, the card's appearance should prompt you to cut away these things from your life before fate does it for you, which is usually unpleasant. Or it may indicate that such a process has already started: if the subsequent cards in the reading are good ones, then the process will have a good outcome for the person.

In a mundane reading this card can also indicate cutting ties, dismantling something, or physical surgery.

Keys

Rotting, breaking down, needs chopping back, cutting ties, clearing out, surgery, clearing deadwood.

Extra

There are numerous biological examples that exhibit-chopper like functions, even within our own bodies. By understanding the process in our bodies it becomes easier to understand the inner and energetic dynamic of these beings. For magicians, if you read the following two paragraphs carefully and in direct context of magical inner dynamics and beings, I think you will find it enlightening, as it is a direct parallel to magical inner processes:

Phagocytes, or cell eaters, are immune cells which serve an important role as part of our innate immune response. These cells consume and ingest any substances they perceive to be pathogens, foreign particles, debris, or cellular waste products. Once engulfed, substances are broken down by organelles called lysosomes. Lysosomes are not only found in phagocytes but in all cell types, where they act as recycling centres. Lysosomes not only breaking down pathogens and debris but also old cellular components to the molecular and atomic level. The remaining molecules can then be recycled by the cell for the production of new cellular building blocks.

Phagocytes also carry out autophagy (the eating of cells from our own biological system). Autophagy is a normal, healthy function within the body and is required to maintain a normal balance of healthy functioning cells through the removal of old, defunct, and unnecessary cells. An imbalance in the autophagy function of the innate immune system has been linked to multiple autoimmune diseases. Underactive phagocytosis can result in the ineffective clearance of dead cells and thus greatly increases the risk of the development of immune sensitivity to our own cellular components, increasing the potential to develop an autoimmune disorder. Overactive phagocytes have also been linked to autoimmune diseases where our phagocytes begin to target our healthy cells.

VI. Dynamics and Powers

60 PARTNERSHIP

MEANING

Partnership is a simple card that expresses connection, cooperation, agreement, and union between people, beings, the land etc. In western magic, for the longest time the idea of connection, particularly with beings and spirits was one of 'what is in it for me' or, 'you will do as I say'. That very much comes out of a Biblical attitude of 'everything is here to serve me, as humans are important'. That attitude also filtered into relationships between people, and particularly in the attitude from a man to his female partner. It is something that can be so entrenched in generations that it can at times be difficult to step back and see it for what it is.

The deeper understanding of relationships, and a person's view of them, is vitally important in magic, as it sets the tone for the sort of interactions that a magician is going to have with the beings, spirits, and powers around them. It also defines how a person or magician will interact with the world around them. As everyday humans, we do not think much about how we interact with people, places, or objects, but to a magician everything has an energy signature that is potentially interacted with, and that in turn defines how everything will interact with the magician.

It is equally important to think about balance. It is easy to think that a good relationship with anything should be 'nice' and gentle and kind: I call this sort of thinking the 'Disney realm', since there is no understanding of the harsh reality of the wider world and of nature. The fantasy of a loving world is very much the product of the New Age and privilege, just as much as the abusive and manipulative approach is the product of a religious culture and privilege.

When a person or magician works with divination, if they pay attention and ask the right questions, then they will start to learn about the hidden complexities of relationships. This in turn not only informs their everyday life, but also deeply informs their magical practice. A mature approach to any connection or relationship is vital in magic for long-term practice, and that, ultimately, is what this card is about.

Lastly and importantly, remember that a relationship in its depths is a stable, longer-term connection of energy between you the person and something else. It is the energetic connection that holds the power, and how we act on the surface in our day-to-day dealings defines whether that energetic connection will be fruitful or not.

DIVINATION

The partnership card can appear where there is a need to connect on equal terms with something, or the subject of the reading is already in connection with something or someone.

Depending upon where it falls in the reading, and what the question is about, it can indicate a love relationship, a partnership, an agreement, an energetic connection, a working relationship, and so forth.

Interestingly it can also indicate a relationship with something. When a layout has a relationship position, what lands in that position is whatever is having the most impact (for good or bad) on the person at that time. That could be medicine, food, the energy of the house they live in, a spirit that is drawing near, or it could be their partner.

If the reading is about a problem or difficulty and the partnership card appears in the reading, then read it in conjunction with the card that is in the relationship position: this will give you a wider understanding of the situation. Look at where the partnership card has landed to gain insight into what aspect of the problem is connected to a relationship.

For example, if the question is about something like 'why am I constantly exhausted in my magical work?', and the Loadsharer card appears in the relationship position, and the partnership card appears in the hearth/home position, then it is obvious what is going on. Such a reading is showing that someone in the family, either an elderly parent, a child, or the person's partner is drawing energy from the person. Most of the time such a situation is unconscious and not intended: this is just how some relationship energetic interconnections work at times, particularly if it involves someone who is sick, elderly, or very young. If a person is also carrying the energetic weight of magical work as well as being energetically drained by a person close to them, then it can totally exhaust someone to the point of collapse or illness.

If the question is a magical one and is about working with beings and this card falls in a favourable position, then it can indicate that the connection could develop into something longer-lasting that would be beneficial to both parties. If it falls in a withheld or difficult position then the connection will not happen, will not develop, or is not what it appears to be: a cross-dressing parasitical being may be pretending to be something it is not in order to connect with the magician.

In mundane readings, this card tells of relationships, partnerships, agreements, and potentially, contracts.

Keys

Energy connection, contract, relationship, union, friendship, connection, interacting, an influence, partnership.

61 Separation

Meaning

Separation is the ending of a connection, be that in a partnership, relationship, or of a way of life, or the ending of a habit. Its key is a connection that is severed. That connection can be with a place, a person, a thing, a substance, a being, or a path that someone is walking.

In the imagery of the card, a serpent rises and affects the energy around it. It hints that the serpent severs a cord of connection between a person and something that is hidden behind the energetic influence. It is hidden because it is no longer relevant and is no longer in the sphere of influence of the person.

Magically this card is very much about fate patterns and how the powers and beings that work within fate patterns add and subtract connections in those patterns. We often think we are in control of our fate at all times, while others think that we are purely driven by fate and really have no choice. I have found that it is not as straightforward as either of those options: it is far more complex than that. What I have found is that sometimes it is a mix of the two: we trigger something, a being or power acts, and things change...whereas other times a being triggers something, we act, and things change. In magic, it is wise to be aware of the complexity and layering of fate, time, and decisions, and to not get too hung up on control, or be too willing to fall into absolute submission, as both are unhealthy and too simplistic. But knowing that there are times that beings can be involved in the birth of partnerships and also the process of separation can be very helpful to the magician as they navigate their own fate.

In general, and in the mundane world, separation is the often the hardest thing for people to bear, and yet it is often a most significant event that brings new pathways, new beginnings, and evolution. Without separation and division there is no room for new patterns, new fate paths, and new understanding to grow.

Divination

When this card appears in a reading, it points to the end of something, a

disconnection from something, or the loss of something. It is the end of something that makes space for something new to appear.

Most of the time the 'separation' is permanent, but not always. However, what is consistent is that even if the separation is not permanent, then the change that it brings often is. The separation indicated by this card is not necessarily just one of losing a partner, divorce, or the ending of a relationship: it has a much wider meaning than that. It can be the separation from an object, the leaving of a place, or the end of a magical working or project that is then walked away from. It can indicate a major change in thinking or opinion, or the leaving behind of a part of yourself that no longer serves you. It is an ending, a loss that is necessary, and a break from something you were connected to.

How you read this card depends upon the question, the subject matter of the reading, and the position it lands in the layout. For instance, in a simple mundane reading, if this card lands in the position of dreams then it can indicate that the person is not getting enough sleep or that they have insomnia: they are separated from their sleep, and thus their dreams. Similarly, if this card falls in a position of 'unravelling' or falling way then it can indicate either that the emotional impact of a separation is lessening and leaving, or that the constant pattern of loss and separation in a person's life is now coming to an end.

In a magical reading, depending upon the question, it can be offering advice to walk away from something, or that something has walked away from the magician: a connection has been broken and it is time to move on. For example, if the magician has been working to protect someone from attack or danger, and the magician then checks through divination to see if that working has been successful, and this card appears in an inner position or endurance position, then it is likely that the working was successful: the victim has been separated from the danger.

When this card indicates a loss, one thing to remember is that by the nature of this card, the loss experienced will be fateful. It will be necessary for the good fate of the person in the future and will be a situation where the short term pain of separation will give way to long term contentment and a better situation. By letting go and not clinging, the person enables a new and better pattern of fate to evolve for them.

If a person clings to a situation of separation that is highlighted by this card, then it will inevitably bring suffering. The advice of this card is to trust and let go, and to move forward.

Keys

Loss, separation, let go, breaking of something, an end that brings new beginnings, end of an era, walk away, no, move forward.

62 Limiter

Meaning

The term 'Limiter' is a functional name for an inner power that is deeply connected with the Divine powers of creation and destruction, and also heavily involved in the complexities of fate patterns. It is one of those core powers that is inherent at all levels of existence from the deepest creation impulses, right down to the way that the physical body works.

In the card image, deep red lines move downwards until they hit a threshold. At that unseen threshold the thick lines fray and start to make shapes, like calligraphy.

The Limiter is like a fuse box: as power passes through it, the power is slowed right down so that it can take form and function safely. The Limiter power does this in the depths of creation by slowing the creative impulse down enough and filtering it, so that the power being filtered can take a myriad of forms. That inherent quality makes it a valuable ally in magic as magic is about filtering, weaving and directing raw power into something productive or balancing, and it is also about nudging fate patterns or bringing them into sharp focus. So having a power like the Limiter to work with allows the magician to first dam and then direct power into a vessel, structure or pattern so that it can 'do' something.

By nature of its 'slowing' ability, it also is naturally defensive: as a dangerous power or magical construct (i.e. curse, attack etc) barrels towards the magician, the Limiter slows it down enough that the magician can see it, react to it, and neutralise it. Because of this quality, the Limiter is one that is used in connection with the magical sword or blade.

The power of the Limiter can flow through just about anything, either in nature or by intentional action, and understanding this power better can also help us understand the frustrating twists and turns of fate, the complexities of life dynamics, and also help us to understand how our own bodies work. When a magician works with these sorts of inherent powers, it really helps if you can understand and spot where the power functions naturally and observe what it does. The reason for this is, if you understand the active principle of the Limiter in your everyday life, you will be far more likely to truly understand its function at a magical and also Divine level.

When you learn the usefulness of the Limiter, you will then discover that if and when it is needed in your life, if you trigger that power through your own actions

and self-limitation then the less fate, life and magic has to do it for you. It is always less painful when we engage these powers willingly in our lives than it is if lifefate has to do it for us, otherwise we are at the mercy of less predictable and potentially more destructive expressions of this power.

DIVINATION

When the Limiter appears in a reading, it indicates that something is being limited or slowed down. A simple analogy for present day (2022) would be Covid restrictions: the Limiter appeared in my readings in the 'home' position a couple of months before the first lockdown in 2020, and it certainly had me scratching my head as to its meaning at that time.

The limitations that are indicated when this card appears can be limits coming from your fate, or it can indicate a need for self-limitation as a key to moving forward. It can be a warning to slow down what you are doing, as one of the actions of the Limiter is to slow the speed of something so that it can form properly.

It can represent a block placed upon you for your own good, or it can indicate that the choice you are reading about will bring you to a limitation or place you in a holding pattern. It can also indicate a negative. For example, if you are asking if you will be accepted at a school or workplace and if the Limiter appears, then the answer is most likely no, or that it will not last, or that it will be deferred: essentially, that it is not the direction or place that you should be heading at this point in time.

If the question of the reading is about safety, protection, or threats and the Limiter appears (unless it is in a withheld position) then it is giving advice to put up boundaries, or limit something. A recent good example was a reading with a friend of mine. The Limiter appeared in a reading, and it landed in her home/hearth position. The cards around it were threatening, and the short-term outcome was loss. Two days later she realized that she always left a back window open. She decided to close that window and lock it, and then did the reading again: the short-term future was absolutely fine. All that needed doing was that window 'limiting' to stop her house being broken into.

The other way the Limiter can express in a reading is where it shows protection. If for example the reading asks 'am I safe'? and the Limiter is the outcome, then the answer is 'yes, you are safe, danger is being slowed down around you'. However, one thing to keep in mind with the Limiter as a protection is that it doesn't block out danger; it just slows it right down so that either the power is taken out of it, or so that you can see it. The advice of the Limiter with regards to safety is that you do your best to protect yourself during a dangerous time (locking windows, paying attention, not taking risks), and the Limiter will act as an early warning system while also scattering the risk to disarm it.

KEYS

Pause, self-limitation, imposed limitation, no, a small amount, protection, wait, sword, slow, slowed down.

63 ENDURANCE

> Be patient and tough; someday
> this pain will be useful to you.
>
> — Ovid

MEANING

A woman pauses, bowed over with a burden we cannot see. She is naked: she has only her skills and experience to clothe and protect her, and she leans heavily on her staff. She is surrounded by darkness, except for a light that is cast around her and that also lights the path where she has trodden. Out of the dark sky, two eyes observe. They do not look at her but at the path she has trodden: the eyes witness the light she has triggered by nature of her willingness to keep going.

The 'grinding' or endurance process is a normal part of mundane life and, it affects everyone at some point or other in their lives. Hence the sayings in English such as 'nose to the grindstone' which means working hard and not giving up, or describing someone as having 'grit': a substance which cannot be ground down. Endurance is what happens when we stand up to the challenges that life and fate throw at us. We do not crumple at the first difficulty; rather, we become determined to succeed. Endurance brings success, strength, conclusion, and ultimately, wisdom.

In magic endurance serves to strengthen. Without learning how to continue while under burden, or learning what our limits are, or learning to spot when we are under magical pressure, the 'inner' energetic muscles needed for advanced magic will not develop. Magicians are like energetic athletes: without training and being pushed, they will not develop the inner mental, energetic, and visionary capacity to achieve the finely balanced skills needed in serious magic. The grindstone power seeks to strengthen your vulnerability by pushing your endurance. You do not pour boiling water into a cracked glass.

As a magician you are never really pushed, worked, or ground down more than you can truly handle, and when you realize you have in all honesty reached your limit of endurance, and acknowledge that, then the pressure will start to back off. You have learned your limit: this is one of the most important lessons in magic, and also in life.

In life in general, the more a challenge is faced in the early and mid-part of your life, the less you will have to deal with it when you are older and less resilient.

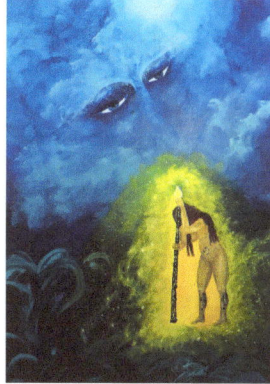

After you have been through a few rounds of endurance and you look back at some of your earlier experiences with this power, you will realize just how far you have come, how much stronger and wiser you have become, and how things that would have terrified you a decade ago now barely trigger a raised eyebrow from you. That is the gift of endurance: it changes you from a soft, squealing, easy-living and clueless individual into a hardened, focused, wise, and skilled master.

It is also wise to realize that in magic, a potential for brilliance is one of the triggers of endurance in a magician. A raw diamond is worth polishing and shaping; a lump of clay is not. The more potential someone has, the more their fate will put pressure on them to engage with endurance so that they can be polished.

One of the things that the magician never really sees while they are going through a period of magical endurance is how their magical work and determination starts to affect what is around them. This is illustrated in the painting as a light cast around the magician. As you work with magical endurance to evolve and strengthen, your deeper spirit starts to evolve more. This in turn slowly transforms that which is all around you: the land, the people, the creatures, and so forth. You also learn to be more patient and more compassionate with all humans, creatures, and beings when they really need it. Your own experience with burden and endurance lets you start to recognize the struggles of others.

Our energetic boundaries are not as fixed as we think they are: as we go through our transformations, so that power of transformation triggers within everything that is around us. As we light up, so does our world. This process is known in some forms of more ancient magic as our *harvest*: the grain has been winnowed and then ground down to flour that can be used to make bread. We are the grain that is transformed into something that nourishes.

Divination

The appearance of the Endurance card in a reading can elicit such reactions as 'oh, what is this about?' when we have not gone through such trials before. Once you have been through a few rounds of endurance, your reaction changes to something more like, 'oh shit...', and you start rolling your sleeves up to be ready for what is ahead.

Its meaning in a reading can point to a period that is coming or is present where you will have to plod, work, or fight your way through something. More often than not, the endurance process presents as something that has to be endured in order to achieve something.

What endurance does *not* mean is allowing yourself to be abused, whether by a company or a person. Such things must be walked away from as soon as it is humanly possible.

The need for endurance signified in a reading can be for a short period or a long time depending on what process is being triggered by this power. It can also be anything from having to simply build some work or personal discipline into your life at that time, or it can be a change of circumstances or life challenges that are really hard work until things settle down. Most of us hate change and it is usually difficult, but by getting through it in the best way we can, we open up new pathways and new patterns for the future.

We can often get clues about how our encounter with Endurance will play out by looking at where in a given layout's reading it falls. For example, if the Endurance card falls in a partnership position, then it can point to a period of relationship difficulties, hard work with a being or beings, or problems with working relationships. If it falls in a magical or inner position, then the need for endurance will be about a round of magical work that will be energetically difficult, or that the difficulty is coming from an inner source but playing out in your mundane life: that can be identified by difficult cards across the reading and the Endurance card in an inner position. It is saying, 'what you are going through or about to go through in your everyday life has deeper inner or magical aspects for your future'.

The appearance of the Endurance card in a reading generally says, 'this may be tough going for a while, but it will be worth it'. If it falls in a negative or withheld position in a layout, then it is saying that the situation will not really polish you, and so approaching it with the mentality of endurance (i.e. just getting your head down and plodding through it) is not actually the best approach.

There are times to endure, and there are times when we need to loosen off and not push ourselves. And there are also times to walk away from something because it would not serve any useful purpose for you or anyone else.

Keys

Necessary difficulty, challenge, endurance, strengthening, persistence, not giving up, being polished, transformation, discipline.

Extra

The understanding of the endurance and self-discipline dynamic in life has a long history, and is something the Stoic philosophers wrote about at length. If you wish to understand more about this dynamic then a good writer to read would be Lucius Annaeus Seneca, also known as Seneca the Younger, a Roman stoic philosopher. Here is a quote from his *Letters on Ethics*. While he is not talking about magic, you can see in his writings that he understands the necessity for strength development through self-discipline:

> Assuredly it is beneficial to set a watch on yourself and to have someone to look up to, someone who you think will make a difference in your plans. To be sure, it is much grander if you live as if some good man were always present and held you in his gaze. But I am satisfied even with this: let everything you do be done as if watched by someone.

Solitude encourages every fault in us.[1]

Another little magical extra for you: look up the art engraving called *Melencolia I* by Albrecht Dürer (1514 CE). It is a piece of art that is stuffed with magical symbolism that all points to a particular magical subject. In the etching, a Putto (a little angel) is sat on a grindstone, hunched over a slate, holding a slate pencil: they are learning their lessons at the grindstone. It is one of many important magical comments that Dürer hid in that etching.

64 Voice of Truth

Meaning

The Voice of Truth is a card that is deeply connected to the ancient and mystical concept of the heart spirit: the voice of our soul that dwells in our heart and speaks the truth on our behalf. This concept is highly developed in Ancient Egypt and appears in the funerary texts, where the heart spirit speaks to the scales of justice and tells truthfully of our actions and deeds.

In magic it is worked with in many different ways, and the most common is as 'that quiet voice within' that reminds us of our truth when we veer from our individual path. The poetic concept of a voice that speaks from our heart has a great deal of magical weight behind it. When we work in vision in the inner worlds, beings 'read' us in a variety of ways, and one of those ways is through what we perceive as 'the heart spirit'. This is the part of us where nothing is hidden, where our ideas, actions, attitudes, bigotry, and prejudices are all laid out for beings to see.

No one is perfect, everyone learns and evolves, and inner beings are very much aware of that in humans. But we cannot hide these parts of ourselves and our actions in the inner worlds. If we are trying to evolve and work on ourselves, then that shows, and most inner beings and inner contacts will cut us quite a bit of slack. If however a magician revels in misdeeds and ignorance, then most beings will give them a wide berth: the magician will attract only those beings who are similar to themselves.

The voice of truth is a card that indicates truth and balance, regardless of intent. And that is something that people can find hard to understand, as we are culturally primed to often accept intent over truth. Magically, truth is truth and intent is irrelevant: magic for the most part does not include human emotions or

---

[1] Seneca, 2017.

social niceties. It is through the development of self-awareness and self-knowledge, stripped of excuses and intents, that the inner voice of truth can strengthen in a magician. And without that self-knowledge and voice of truth, a magician eventually plateaus in their magical work as they are locked out of deeper magical explorations. The voice of truth is the key to deeper magical doors.

DIVINATION

This card often appears in a reading to offer an affirmative answer, and to indicate where the true path is, or leads. The truth indicated by this card is not just about whether something is true or not, but whether something is *right*, particularly for the individual. If the reading is about searching for the right path forward or which choice of action would be best to take and this card falls in a favourable position or in the near future position, then it points to the option being looked at as being the right way for a person at that time. Remember, fate works with time, and what can be not right for the longest time in someone's fate can suddenly become right and true as their way forward.

If the reading is looking at a magical situation and this card falls in a withheld or negative position, then it can point to the situation being not truthful, i.e., the being, magician, or working method is not right, is not truthful, or is not what it seems on the surface. This card gets right to the heart of something and indicates a balance and 'rightness'—or not, depending on where it falls in the layout.

The positioning in the layout is very important for this card, as it can indicate where the power is, where the truth is, and where the right path or focus needs to be at that time. If the card lands in a long-term future position, then it is saying that in the long term the situation in the reading, no matter how good or difficult it may be, will lead to truth: the current situation is a steppingstone in fate to get to that right way ahead, or to that truth.

It is a card of affirmation, of the right time, the right place, or the right person: it tells you whatever you are working with is good, truthful, or balanced for you at this time, and that lining up with that 'rightness' will release the blocks or 'knots' in the person's fate pattern.

If the card appears in a reading for a building or a place, then it is saying that some aspect of that place (indicated by the position in the layout) is solid, well balanced, and will be good for the job in hand.

Whenever it is in a withheld or in a negative or past position, the truth is not there or no longer there, or the place or person is not right or balanced.

KEYS

Right, yes, truthful, good, self-aware, balanced, helpful.

EXTRA

An extract from the Papyrus of Ani's Book of the Dead Spell 30.[1] Here we see an example of the concept of the heart, *ib*, being the seat of the voice of truth in a person, a voice that gives evidence of the deeds of a person:

> Thus says Thoth, judge of truth to the great Ennead which is in the presence of Osiris: Hear this word of great truth (from the heart of Ani). I have judged the heart of the deceased, and his soul stands as a witness for him. His deeds are righteous in the great balance, and no sin has been found in him. He did not diminish the offerings in the temples, he did not destroy what had been made, he did not go about with deceitful speech while he was on the earth.

> Thus says the Great Ennead to Thoth who is in Hermopolis; This utterance of yours is true. The vindicated Osiris Ani is straight forward, he has no sin, there is no accusation against him before us.

65 GIFT

MEANING

In magic, giving and receiving are highly magical acts that establish the magician as part of the community of spiritual beings, whatever type of beings they are. Hence at the early stage of magical training, the magician must first learn to give, to let go, and not cling on to anything. The first act of giving in magic opens the door to communion with the spirits, but it must be done unconditionally and not with the intent of receiving or establishing connection; rather it is about letting go. It is also about being willing to 'fill a gap' where there is necessity. This is the true root of both giving and receiving: giving is not about offerings or bribes, but about necessity both on the part of the magician and also on the part of the spirit.

This early magical act not only opens doors for the magician, but it also triggers a long and deep process of transformation for them. Often these days our cultures are about gaining more and more, as our social status is often measured by what we have and how much we earn. The more expensive things we have and the more money we have, the more respect and social status we gain. However, that cultural

---

[1] Von Dassow, 2015: plate 3.

signalling runs counter to the way the world of the spirits and magic works.

In the world of spirits, inner beings, deities, etc., and the powers within the land, the true treasure is *necessity*: do you have what you need? If not, then it is given to you. It also means giving when you have surplus to those, human or spirits, that are in true deficit: restoring balance.

The restoration of balance is the core element of magic, it is the foundation that all magic sits on, and it is a constant job to move towards balance, as true balance is fleeting. If you are part of the community of giving and receiving, which includes your magical acts, and if you are actively working magically to move something towards balance, then whatever you need that is in deficit comes to you. You give of yourself in work, and what resources you need come to you.

The magical dynamic of giving and receiving also plays out in the everyday life of the magician, hence in their early phases of magical training, the student is often prompted to give. Too many clothes sat unused in the wardrobe? Give them away. Have more money that you need as opposed to want? Give some to a homeless person or a good cause. And the giving must be without expectations of thanks or recognition, as such expectations turns giving into receiving. True magical giving wants nothing in return and is often tied into the paying forward of old energetic debts, thereby rebalancing your scales.

There is also much magic tied up in receiving with grace: judge not those who give to you, nor refuse when help or gifts are offered. Often in western cultures, receiving can be seen as being helpless, or in need, and as such can lower our social status and sense of independence. However, as a magician, receiving can help someone else rebalance their own energetic scales, and is a way for fate and spirits to get necessary resources to you even if you are not aware that you need them: there is as much power and grace in receiving as there is in giving.

And if, as often happens to magicians, you are given a gift that has ulterior motives behind it, accept the gift but understand that you are not beholden to the whims or wishes of the giver: giving and receiving is magically unconditional. If someone else wants to attach conditionality, then that is their 'karma', for want of a better word: you are not a part of that and do not act on it.

Unconditional giving and receiving is one of the main highways for energy and power to travel along, and in magic it is a critical dynamic to work within if you wish to successfully develop as a true adept magician. It is also a good and powerful way to live a mundane life, as the power also flows through the mundane world. Engaging in the dynamic of giving and receiving unconditionally triggers change out in the world. Like a tiny pebble cast into still waters, its ripples can grow and change everything in its path.

DIVINATION

When The Gift appears in a reading, it can indicate that what you need is coming to you in some form or other. This could be money, shelter, medicine, objects, energy, or something else. It is a card of resources: when the Gift shows up, resources will come your way.

If your reading is about what action you should take and the Gift appears, then it is telling you that you must help someone with resources, or let something go by giving it away. Sometimes our energy can get blocked up, and by giving something away, it releases that blockage and energy can start to flow back and forth again.

If the reading is about a specific magical act or contact with inner beings or spirits, then it is warning you that you need to give a gift as a part of your contact work. Sometimes it is obvious what you need to give and sometimes it is not. When it is in connection with deity work, the most powerful way to give is in vision by putting your hand into your pocket, and whatever you take out of your pocket is what you give. If that happens to be the keys to your car, then in the physical world out of vision, you need to get rid of your car.

Such a dynamic can be terrifying, but often there is very good reason behind it. For example, staying with the car keys, if the deity asks for a gift and your car keys appear in your hand, the letting go of the car is often connected with fate. You may be fated to have a serious crash in that specific car: giving it up changes your fate. The deity gets the energy released from the act of giving, which is what a lot of giving is about, and the magician avoids a potentially deadly event: instead, they just have to contend with an event that is a bit stressful and inconvenient. You can always get another car, but that specific car must go. If you are not in a financial position to get another car, and you have given up your car in response to a magical vision, then another car will find its way to you as a gift.

In mundane readings, the meaning is more or less the same as the magical meaning: giving and receiving resources without expectations or strings attached. That can be anything from receiving monetary help as a gift (not a loan), or a special object. It can also mean medicines, as this card is about a resource that is necessary.

Sometimes it can indicate a gift that is not a necessary resource, but the act of giving and the love with which it is given can brighten your day and make you feel loved. So in a way, it is a necessary resource!

Keys

A gift, getting what you need, resources, giving where needed, receiving, medicine, support, help, release your surplus to those who need it.

Extra

If ye disclose (acts of) charity, even so it is well, but if ye conceal them, and make them reach those (really) in need, that is best for you.[1]

---

[1] Extract from Surat Al-Baqarah:2.271 *The Noble Quran*. English translation by Muhammad Hibib Shakir (1866-1939) Cairo, Egypt.

If there be among you a needy man, one of thy brethren, within any of thy gates, in thy land which HaShem thy G-d giveth thee, thou shalt not harden thy heart, nor shut thy hand from thy needy brother.[1]

66 Lightning Strike

Meaning

This card is directly related to the Serpent of Chaos card. This card is the lightning strike that limits the Serpent of Chaos and puts it back in the box. In both this card and the Serpent card, the lightning hits the ground with two forks: this is mirrored in the two-pronged stick that traps the serpent in ancient Egyptian magic, which is known as the *Was* staff.

The card represents a power that is an expression of a natural force: the storm and the lightning. These are powers that can suppress the dynamic of chaos when it rises from the Underworld and runs rampant in the living world. The power of the storm and lightning in the ancient Egyptian magical religion was personified in the deity Set: a powerful and at times terrifying god, but one who has the power to pin the Serpent of Chaos, Apep, and send him back down into the Underworld. Hence the *Was* staff with its forked bottom was the magical staff of power of place. If you can get chaos under control, then you have order.

In magic, we work with storm powers to suppress the power of chaos when it overflows into our world, but it is a long and hard task. Often the power of chaos emerges because our collective societies have become unbalanced enough to produce a ripe environment for that power to move freely.

In their full power, the storm deities are terrifying and are often connected with war or violence as well as storms. How we respond to the manifestations of these powers has a powerful bearing on whether the chaos will be subdued or not. Chaos brings division, conflict, and a breakdown of any order, both in nature and in human societies. If we respond in kind, then we become part of the problem. However, if we respond with necessity in search of balance, then the turbulent powers of the 'storm' will become focused and flow through us to overcome chaos. However, it is not a 'one hit' situation, rather it is an often long, drawn-out struggle. This is something that we can observe throughout history and also in cultural mythologies.

[1] *Deut.* 15:7.

This dynamic also plays out in much smaller and at times individual ways, particularly for magicians. When we drift into situations, actions, or behaviour that over time open us up to the insidious creep of chaos, we are given warnings through our magical work, through our dreams, and through our observations. If we do not spot them or choose to ignore them, then the creeping chaos will spread out in our lives like a slow-moving shadow. It is never a sudden event; rather it is a slow unravelling that is facilitated by our inaction.

When we finally choose to take action, often it is a difficult and at times painful action which has to be initiated by a sudden change in what we do. Sometimes we trigger that for ourselves, and sometimes fate does it for us: the storm gathers around us and the 'lightning strike' event often comes without warning. It can be a sudden loss of our job, our health, or our stability, or the sustaining of an injury: whatever it is, it gives us a chance to change, to step back, and to see where we were heading. If we facilitate it for ourselves by making a necessary but often sudden change then it will be less painful, as this puts us in control to some extent.

The most important magical aspect of this card is its complexity. When we are faced with something we do not deeply understand, then we think very much in polarized terms: a thing is either good or bad. The Lightning Strike is not so simple: it is a weave of complex and often opposing powers that ultimately are productive for the magician.

Divination

Like all cards, how this card is interpreted depends upon what the question is and the layout position it falls in. This card can indicate a sudden event that on the surface can seem to be a disaster, but which in fact is clearing the ground for you and suppressing something that is of ultimate threat to you. It is an event not to be feared; it is an event that you will need to step through in order to reach the more balanced situation that awaits you.

If this card comes up regarding a magical working, then it indicates that the power you are working with may take on a form that is much more powerful than you expected. It will do so for a good reason. Sometimes we set out with a magical working or act to achieve a specific goal, but we are not aware of the deeper inner powers that are gathering around us that can flow through our magical working in order to achieve a wider goal. The magical working provides a coming-together of focused fate points that the Lightning Strike can operate through. We may have intended to do a ritual or visionary working to achieve one thing, but the conditions created by that magical working also work perfectly for a power to flow through that will suppress or pin a destructive or chaotic power that is rising in the land or society around us.

This card can also appear when there is the need for sudden action, like an action that is not planned (and therefore is invisible) but one that strikes straight to the heart of what you are doing or trying to achieve. If you are undertaking difficult magical work or trying to defend or shield from something and this card appears in a relevant position, then it is advising you to act in way that is unplanned and which therefore could not be anticipated.

The Lightning Strike is a power or action that cannot be foreseen by another, as it has no warning as to its timing or strike location. Often it is an action that is outside of the norm for the individual who is taking it. An example of this would be to use a form of magic that is not in your usual repertoire or is completely outside of your tradition. The act is not prepared for; it is simply done.

As the Lightning Strike is also a pinning action, the appearance of this card in a magical reading can indicate that the action needed is one of pinning. This is most likely to come up in a reading that is about a difficult image, being, or object, usually in the area of magical work that is to do with clearing, exorcism, and removal. In such cases the image or object is pinned by driving a large iron or copper nail through it, and then destroying it with fire. When this process is indicated for a being, the magician first draws or paints the being to exteriorize it, and then pins the image along with using utterance as the pinning is being done, and then the image is burned.

Pinning can also be used on a patch of land that has hostile, destructive, or chaotic powers and beings flowing in it, the presence of which is seriously threatening living creatures and humans. The pin is usually iron or copper (on occasion it can be obsidian) in the form of a double- or triple-bladed instrument that comes to a clear long point. In the absence of such a specific instrument, a long, strong, and thick iron nail can be used. It is used with utterance and magical patterning to suppress the volatile power and send it deeper into the Underworld. A highly ritualized and effective form of this action can be seen in Tibetan Buddhism: it is often used on the land before a temple is built in order to suppress and transform those volatile land powers.

Occasionally this card can appear as a warning of an impending dangerous storm that could present danger to the reader. This is more likely if the card is surrounded by difficult cards and the near future looks, well, destructive... This possibility can be checked by using a yes/no layout. If the card is indeed warning of a storm that is a threat to you, then while the timing of such can be difficult to get from a reading, it is nevertheless a warning to prepare. Ensure that your home is ready and that you have the necessities to hand should you need to get out of the storm's way. I have had warnings a year before a storm struck, one that was so bad that we had to move and live somewhere else. The further away the storm is in timing, the bigger it is likely to be. Big events in the future show up earlier in readings: often a year or two before they happen.

In mundane readings, this card is about 'things that strike out of the blue': unexpected sudden events for either good or bad which will have a bearing on your fate and future. If you look at where the card lands in the layout, then it can give you a fairly good idea of what sort of event it will be, or at least what area of your life it will affect. Because this card can bring good or bad sudden events, when it appears in a reading, just make sure you pay a bit more attention to safety, and don't take risks.

This card can also appear in mundane readings when something needs dealing with in a sudden and unexpected way. If you are under oppression or in a really bad situation and this card comes up, then it is advising you to act without planning, without warning, and in a way that would be unexpected.

If the reading is about a building, then it can indicate issues with the electricity, or the possibility of an electrical fire.

KEYS

Sudden unseen event, necessary destructive event, dangerous storm, something needs pinning, a need for sudden unexpected action, electrical issues, natures response to chaos, protection of fate path.

67 SPLENDOUR

MEANING

Splendour is one of the simpler cards in the deck. It has a pretty straightforward meaning: success. I chose the word Splendour rather than success in order to illustrate the subtle inner aspects of this card, which involve the recognition of the beauty and splendour of nature in its success. While we may sometimes consider particular aspects of nature to be weird, failed, or difficult, the actual physical genetic structures of everything in nature are constantly evolving patterns of success. And when we look at nature, at the landscape, the creatures, and the sky, at times the splendour can take our breath away.

When something comes together, works well, and is successful, we celebrate the splendour of it as well as the success. And while we can easily fall into the modern marketing trap of 'everything successful is handsome or beautiful', which is not the case, it is pertinent to observe that something successful, be it physical, energetic or a concept, also has a harmony to it. The bits all come together to make a whole, and the endurance of the hard work behind success finally locks into a pattern that is harmonic and coherent: that is the splendour I am reaching for in the meaning of this card.

Success doesn't just happen, either in a mundane sense or a magical sense. Sometimes it can happen by accident, or by fate, but whatever is behind a success usually includes a process of weeding, failure, trying, trying again, and so forth, either by the person or by fate. That moment when success is realized is the moment where for an instant everything is beautiful, everything is great, and the world is full of splendour. This may last only for a second or two, but it is an energetic feeling that expresses success.

The overall meaning of this card is not only success, but the splendour of achievement. Whatever it is may be a failure in the eyes of some, but for the individual, they see and feel the splendour of their achievement. It is also a measure of seeing the splendour in life around them, the harmonious splendour of great architecture, and the splendour in the first steps taken by a toddler. It is the recognition of greatness in everything from the tiniest achievement to the completion of a world-changing creation.

DIVINATION

In divination, this card can be a simple and mundane indication of the success of something, and where it lands in a layout indicates the ground zero of that success.

But it can also indicate the splendour and beauty of a hidden success, a completion or achievement that may go unnoticed by many, but which has not gone unnoticed where it counts.

It can also have layered meaning, where two different meanings converge into one: this most often happens in magical readings. For example, if a magician is looking to see if a particular option for magical work would be successful, and this card appears as an outcome, then it is saying, 'yes, it will be successful, but you also need to see the beauty in the success in order for it to manifest itself'. That means seeing the many roads, efforts, beings and powers that all converge into a harmonic pattern in order for something to be achieved successfully and taking joy at seeing the beauty of all those component parts, while also giving respect where it is due.

If the card falls in a 'place' position (e.g. hearth/home or inner worlds), then it indicates that is where success will be achieved or found, or where it has sprung from. If the reading is a directional reading and it is looking for a lost object or person, and this card appears in a direction, then it indicates the general direction where whatever is lost will be found. Then the reader can narrow down that general direction into sections, distance, and degrees, in order to further pinpoint whatever is missing.

It is also an emotive card that indicates joy, not only in success, but in simply being alive. It is that moment when you realize just what an amazing and beautiful place this world is, despite its grubby and negative side. It is a positive card, a cheerleader, and a round of applause for something. When it appears in a reading, you have done well, and your splendour has been noticed.

KEYS

Yes, success, achievement, joy, beauty, respect, harmony.

68 True Justice

Meaning

People often view justice as something that serves them as individuals, something that 'rights' what they feel has been 'wronged' in their lives. This view is one of mundane, temporal justice: a justice which depends upon the culture and society a person lives in. It also depends on the emotional maturity of the individual. Temporal justice is different to Divine or True Justice (though temporal justice does include an aspect of Divine Justice). By Divine I do not mean anything religious or connected to any particular religion; rather it is Divine because it is a universal power that flows through the whole of creation and destruction.

Magically, it is easier to understand if you realize that there are two levels of justice. One is 'Divine' or universal justice, and the other is temporal justice. The former is a pattern entwined with time and fate and is the balance that nature flows through in true cause and effect. The latter is how a society organizes itself, and how we function as day-to-day humans. The two are not separate, but the deeper into magic you go, the more you see how True Justice and balance trumps the power of temporal balance. The former gives us what is necessary, and the latter gives us a sense of closure (whether justly so or not). One of the important aspects of magic for magicians is learning how to bring those two dynamics together in their life and work.

Justice is not something you pray to or do rituals in order to trigger for you; it is something that you allow to flow through you by nature of your own deeds. The cause and effect of True Justice has its roots in your own actions and in your fate choices. This is not to say the victim of injustice is to be blamed, not at all: what it means is that our everyday actions, our everyday give-and-take, affects how our fate patterns constantly reform and adapt. How we react to injustice, and how we uphold justice in our own actions, defines how the scales will seek to balance themselves.

Honesty, integrity, and balance are the key features when working magically with justice, and where the magic needs approaching in harmony with Universal Justice. This can manifest in ways such as securing and vigorously defending a boundary (thereby passively flowing in accordance with fate patterns) but not crossing your boundary and attacking (thereby actively creating new fate patterns), and maintaining the balance of Justice in your own actions regardless of the unjust actions towards you by others or other beings: let fate deal with the assholes. This can be hard, as we are wired to want to see justice done, but magically you have to learn to walk away from that urge. What is important is upholding your own honesty and integrity to the best of your current ability: doing so will protect your own fate pattern.

It may not change our fate, but it does change how that fate expresses to us as a direct experience. The deeper you get into magic and mysticism, the more you begin to understand the complexity and delicate nature of True Justice, and how elusive it can be.

DIVINATION

When Justice appears in a reading, it indicates that the dynamic of Justice and balance is active in our lives. How it relates to us depends largely upon the subject matter of the question, and where it falls in a layout.

If it appears in a magical reading, then it can be speaking of the reharmonisation of something, of bringing something into balance. It can also be a warning to ensure that the magician upholds Universal Justice in their magical work. Upholding True Justice in the face of injustice brings with it a level of protection, while also maturing your fate pattern. In practical magical terms this can be advice on how to handle a particular situation, or how to approach a particular power or being.

The appearance of this card can also mean a successful conclusion to something, and that conclusion is something that balances your current fate pattern: something has come full circle and, for good or bad, is now complete.

If a magical question is about, 'is this the right way to approach this magical working' and the True Justice card appears in a favourable position, then the answer is 'yes, you nailed it'. Where it appears in the layout can show where the 'fulcrum' of the balance is situated, be it in the family life, magical work, fate pattern, dreams, and so forth.

When this card falls in a withheld position in a layout, it is saying that justice is being withheld, whether by some magical force or by the actions of the people involved. Different choices will need to be made to free up that power of balance.

Depending upon the question and the position this card falls in, it can indicate a process of rebalancing that is currently happening. For example, if you are sick and you do a reading to look at your health, then the True Justice card can indicate that the body is going through a rebalancing process, or that it has reached a stage where the healing can now begin.

When this card appears in a reading about a building, and the question is magical, then it can point to the harmonics of the building's architecture and its strength, and also indicate that the energies of the building are clear and balanced. If the question is temporal, then it can indicate that there are legal issues that may need careful attention, but if the card is in a well aspected position, then it should all turn out well. If, however, the card falls in a difficult position, such as an endurance or withheld position, then it is likely that legal disputes or contracts will be a major problem.

Staying with the theme of buildings and places, if the magician is using readings to look into the energetic history of an old building or site, and this card appears, then it can indicate that it was once a place of judgement or law, whether in a magical, universal, or a temporal sense. For example, stone outcrops that were ancient altars and that were aligned to the magical pattern of 'threshing floors' are often represented in readings by the card True Justice.

Ultimately this card expresses our own 'harvest': the weighing of our deeds and lessons in life, the fruits of our harvest such as our Work and children, and the legacy we leave behind when we die.

In mundane readings, this card usually speaks of temporal justice: it can represent law enforcement, a court case, a legal contract, a settlement, or the conclusion of a dispute. If the card falls in a negative position then justice will not be upheld.

This is a card of rebalancing, of coming into harmony, of dues being paid and disputes settled, and it can indicate that the subject of the reading will be confronted with justice and will have accept a just decision.

Keys

Truth, justice, balance, harmony, law, harvest, results of actions, cause and effect.

VII. Dynamics and Powers II

69 UNRAVELLER

MEANING

The Unraveller is a life and magical dynamic of loosening and ultimately unravelling. Just as endurance tightens us up and brings us strength and discipline, so the Unraveller loosens, weakens, and eventually makes things fall apart.

Sometimes when things are too tight or uptight, or too solid and heavy, this stops forward progression and brings stagnation. This is where the magical dynamic of the Unraveller triggers and starts to slowly unwind that solidity and fragment it.

The action of the Unraveller is usually slow, so it can go unnoticed for a long time before it is recognized. Disciplines fall by the wayside, critical thinking is rejected in favour of fantasy, selfishness and self-centeredness creep in, and everything in a person's life—relationships, work, and magic—starts to go wrong.

In magic, the Unraveller triggers either when the magician has become too disciplined and is blocking themselves, or when they start to become unbalanced and 'play' with their magic, or when they feel they have the 'right' to do anything and work with anything. But magic is not a game, and when magicians start treating it as such their unravelling often manifests first in their mental health. The usual disciplines of the mind that keep things in check, like moods and behaviours, start to fragment, and the magician starts lashing out or becoming highly egotistical. At that point the magic usually shuts down for them, and they are left interacting with their fantasy and ego.

The dynamic of the Unraveller is one that plays out not just in people but also in places, buildings, situations, fate patterns, and magical patterns. It is the first stage of something composting, where something unwinds before it falls apart and dies. Like most magical and energetic dynamics, its early-stage action can be useful when something needs unwinding a bit and unknotting. The trick is to not let it go too far, as that ultimately destroys.

When people come to magic, they think it is all about specific very glamourous weapons like swords and blades, pins and poisons. However, it is the life patterns that run through everything that are the most powerful magical tools, helpers, and weapons, and the Unraveller is one of them. Like all true poisons, working with the Unraveller is a matter of potency, not substance. Everything is poisonous in certain doses, and everything is medicinal in certain doses. This is where the true skill of magic comes in: the alchemy of energetic doses of power.

Divination

When this card appears in a reading, think very carefully about how you interpret it so that you don't scare yourself or anyone else. It needs to be read in the context of the question and the subject matter.

Here is an example. The reading is about a threat, or a difficult struggle, and your question is: 'how will I get through this situation?' The Unraveller appears in a near future position. That is saying, 'the way you are dealing with the situation is unravelling you'. This could indicate depression, a mental health breakdown, physical sickness, or erratic behaviour that is ultimately not good for you. A change of approach to dealing with the struggle is needed. However, if the question is 'how will this situation come to a conclusion?', then the question is about the situation, not an individual person. The Unraveller lands in the near future position in the layout, and it is showing that the problem or situation will slowly loosen and dissipate over time. It is not a fast conclusion nor a clear end; rather it is a slow and steady breaking up of a situation that will resolve in time (if there is a good card in the long-term future position). You see how the question posed has a major bearing on how a reading is interpreted?

The main thing to remember when you see this card is that it generally signifies that something is falling away or falling apart.

In mundane readings it means the same, just usually with less power behind it, as magic always amplifies situations. For instance, if you are about to go on a long journey for a few weeks and the Unraveller appears in your reading, then depending upon where it falls and what the question is, it could signify that while you will be safe, there may nevertheless be lots of inconveniences: delays and mishaps that cause you to 'unravel' a bit, usually by stress, exhaustion, or losing your temper. When you see something like this, then you can be prepared: just assume that things will go wrong, have backups of documents, funds, etc., and just expect delays.

When the Unraveller happens to us rather than happening from within us, the best way to deal with it is patience, preparation, and paying attention to details, since basic discipline (Endurance) counterbalances the Unraveller's looseness.

Of course, when the Unraveller power is flowing through you and you are slowly unravelling because of a prolonged situation, or stress, or illness, then engaging discipline and Endurance can be very hard indeed. The best way to pull out of the Unraveller is to find one small thing, one simple discipline, where you can take back control, and do it no matter what. This could be a simple as sticking to a bedtime. It doesn't matter what it is: you just have to engage with a simple, doable discipline. Doing this engages Endurance, which I magically call the Grindstone, and step by step this will inch you back from the Unraveller. The Unraveller loses its power where there is discipline, and small steps eventually make a long road.

Keys

Falling apart, falling away, loosening, breaking up slowly, crumbling, unwinding.

70 Defeat

Meaning

Defeat is something we all experience as a part of life, and so too on our magical path of development. Whether that defeat is temporary or not is up to us. The angel observes the shattering and painful defeat of a human they watch over. They cannot intervene, as defeat is a step upon the ladder of magical and spiritual development. The angel waits, keeping vigil with the human, and witnessing their defeat.

If the human eventually rises off their knees and gets back on their feet, then the angel will walk with them to the next trial, lesson, or success that their fate path has as a possibility for them. Defeat is an experience that we can learn from if we are willing to do so: if we rise and forge on then the process of fighting back in the face of defeat will give us strength. Defeat teaches us our limits, which is of the upmost importance in magic, as without understanding our own personal limits of endurance or the limits of our ability we are likely to seriously injure ourselves. And worse than that, not understanding your limits can lock you of magic: if you try to work a level of power that you are incapable of holding, then you will 'blow a fuse'. Essentially you become locked out of magical contact and are unable to reach any power beyond your own life force.

However, if a person strengthens and matures through the tests of defeat then they will become toughened to the knocks of life and magic. They learn to know their limits and instead of overstretching those limits, they learn to work within their own limitations by crafting and refining their skills. Magically, this makes a person 'compact' as a magical force, and also skilled with laser-like precision.

If you spend your life hopping from one skill to another without truly mastering any of them then you will become the master of nothing. However, if you work on

195

at least one of those skills over a long period of time, then you will become a true master of that skill. It is the same in magic: of all the different skill sets within magic, no magician is master of all of them. But they will become a true master of at least one of them if they know their limitations, which means to know oneself: a major requisite for adept magic. Their eventual level of mastery will come from their refusal to give into a series of failures and defeats, and from picking themselves up and trying again each time.

Divination

The card of Defeat can appear for a number of reasons. If for example you are doing readings or asking advice about a particular option for something and Defeat is the outcome, then the answer is obvious: you will fail if you follow that option. Defeat can be a good card for filtering out possibilities when you are looking for the best way to approach something.

If however the outcome of the reading is good but the Defeat card is prominent in the reading, then it is likely that you will have to go through at least one failure before finally succeeding. Such an option should not be dismissed if the Defeat card is a part of the process, as it means that you will go through various trials that will potentially teach you many things on your journey to success in the endeavour you are working on. Often on a magical path, while we are focusing on success in one action, the process of getting to that success is littered with lessons that will teach us about other, different skills or experiences that we had not even thought of.

If Defeat comes up in a reading about one's life or magical path, then think very carefully before you decide to change the direction of your fate path. Not all defeats are things we have to go through, and when we look at such things using divination, it is wise to think very carefully about whether it is necessary to continue on a path that includes defeat. It could be painful, shattering even, but also good because of what it could teach you. It could also divert you down a 'side road' on your path that you would miss if you tried to avoid the defeat. But then there are also times when it is not necessary to put oneself through the wringer: the trick is knowing what to avoid and what not to avoid.

If for example you were thinking of moving to a different area or moving house and you did a reading which showed Defeat as the outcome, then such a thing is really not worth exploring any further. Simply look for somewhere else to move to, and also consider staying where you are and spinning your wheels for a while.

If you are doing a reading about your magical or life path, and you are looking at different options for some reason and Defeat appears as an outcome in all of them, then that is a strong indicator that no matter what choice you make, a time of defeat is an aspect of your fate pattern at that time. In such a case, forewarned is forearmed. With such a strong fate point, there will be a reason for going through that defeat. When it arrives, be ready to learn from it, and use your perception to spot what needs learning, what needs letting go of, what needs self-reflection on limitations, and most importantly, look for the seedling of a new chapter in your fate.

Often crushing defeat hits us when there is a whole new episode of fate development waiting ahead of us. But first we must go through the dark night in order to learn our limits and have things stripped away from us that no longer serve a purpose. When we have learned what we need to learn and we have been moved to where we need to be, then the dawn starts to break and a whole new vibrant chapter begins in our lives. But we only get to that new chapter if we do not give in. If we climb back up off our knees and get walking then the new chapter will slowly unfold. If we stay on our knees in defeat and self-pity, then we will be stuck there for the rest of our lives.

Keys

Failure, loss, no, not now, bad timing, being tested, need for strength, know your limits, temporary collapse, pause, midnight/dark before dawn.

71 Voice of Untruth

Falsehood flies, and the Truth comes limping after it.

— Jonathan Swift[1]

Meaning

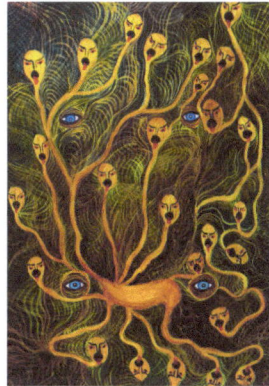

In magic, the Voice of Untruth can be a problem indeed. It usually manifests through unscrupulous or manipulative beings talking to and fooling a magician, or, it can manifest through using divination that is being manipulated by a being for its own agenda. When a magician starts working with inner contacts and beings, it can be difficult for the magician to truly know what it is they are talking to, and only experience can remedy that. A healthy dose of scepticism that filters and analyses, but does not block, is always a good thing to have in magical work.

The Voice of Untruth is both an action, and a conscious magical inner dynamic. Sometimes these two aspects are separate, and sometimes they come together. Lying is an action undertaken by choice in order to gain something or manipulate someone. The magical inner dynamic of untruth is where a conscious power seeks and finds a human who is a cracked vessel and fills them. The being can then utter untruth

---

[1] Jonathan Swift: Anglo-Irish author. Quote from his article in The Examiner, 1710.

through the person in order to facilitate a situation whereby the being can either feed energetically from a large group of people (by creating a 'false messiah'), or it can seed widespread chaos and destruction through social and/or political manipulation.

Everyone and everything has an agenda, good or bad; and when that agenda is 'bad' the Voice of Untruth often becomes part of it. In terms of magical inner contact, a good way to ascertain whether truth or lies is coming from a being or inner contact is their presentation and what they are saying. When someone or something appears in a grand way, elaborately dressed in a fancy outfit, and tells you that you are the next messiah or the greatest of adepts, or that you have special powers, or that they can give you special powers, then you are listening to the Voice of Untruth. If a being or inner contact appears in an ordinary way or barely appears at all and tells you that you are an idiot and need to take responsibility for yourself, then that is more likely a Voice of Truth...

Humans are easily glamoured. When someone or something appears larger than life and appears to have power and be in control, when they are saying what the crowd wants to hear and it is appealing to the crowd's darker or lower urges, then you are witnessing the inner dynamic of the Voice of Untruth uttering through a cracked vessel. This weakness in humanity is manipulated not only in the magical world, but also the mundane world: we are attracted to glitter and gold, not moss and earth.

When the Voice of Untruth gains traction in someone, or a community or group, it becomes a power that isolates, divides, and normalizes cruelty while justifying it. It becomes the door-opener for the power of chaos. This happens in magical groups and in societies. The Voice of Untruth is not a person; it is an actual power dynamic that flows where and when it can. Once it gets a grip on an individual or group, then it triggers the Unraveller dynamic. At that point, things start to very slowly unravel and fall apart, as people no longer know what is true and what is untrue. This in turn triggers people to stop considering it their responsibility to figure out the truth for themselves: instead, they passively accept the lies from whatever person (vessel) the Voice of Untruth is flowing through.

The other way the Voice of Untruth can manifest in magic is through ancestral inner contact. It is easy to get a romantic view of ancestors as 'all-wise' spirits that have their best intentions for us. But there are times that this is not true. Look at your own family, and also at the members of other people's families: there is usually a mix of good people, bad people, indifferent people, and sometimes just downright nasty people. That is humanity, and often the nasty and stupid outnumber the good. It is the same with ancestors who have stayed connected to this world for one reason or another. One particularly common situation is where someone is trying to worship or do magical work with an ancestor, but the ancestor spirit has moved on (or was never there) and a parasitical being has stepped to masquerade as them. This being will then interact with the magician to make energetic connections and feed off their life force.

Some cultures got around that problem by using their religion or cultural system.

Ancestors become mixed in with mythic ancestors and heroes (such as in Chinese culture): this creates a pattern that filters out the worst of ancestor interaction issues. The pattern acts as a filter for the most part, so that what gets through to the living magician is a mixture of blood ancestors, mythic heroes, and what the west would call 'the gods'. It is a very interesting and useful system.

DIVINATION

This card's appearance in a reading is warning that something or someone within the situation is being deeply untruthful and misleading, and not in a small way. It is a warning of manipulation, fantasy, imbalance, and ultimately viciousness.

The only two places in a reading where this card is ever positive is in a withheld position, in which case it is saying, 'there is no untruth in this situation', or if it is in a past position, which indicates that the lies have now ended. But that past position could also be saying, 'this may be okay, but it is built on a foundation of lies.' In such a situation something good could come out of something bad, but it is still wise to tread carefully.

If the reading is about a situation where choices have to be made, and the current reading is asking about one particular option, and this card falls anywhere in the reading, then regardless of the outcome it is not the greatest of options and it would be wise to search for another approach. Serious lies infect and undermine any situation, and this card is not about 'little white lies', but about intentional manipulation, misinformation, and misdirection. A choice that has such a dynamic embedded within it is a recipe for unravelling and chaos.

This card can also come up in a personal reading if the person is accepting convenient lies because it serves them, and they are kidding themselves it is 'truth' or that it is okay because it serves a good purpose. Fooling oneself in such a way never ends well: again, it triggers an unravelling dynamic within the person and they start to rot from the inside out.

In mundane readings, the meaning of this card is simple; lies, untruth, misinformation, and covering up the truth. It can also appear if someone is cheating on their partner, or if someone is repeatedly stealing or ripping off a close friend or partner. It can appear in a company reading if someone is embezzling from the company, or if the company has a spy in its midst who is passing on trade or economic secrets.

This card is not about the withholding of truth, which can sometimes be necessary for a variety of reasons. It is about deeply embedded untruths with a nasty agenda behind them.

There are times when this card can appear when it has nothing to do with lies as such: here it tells of an imbalance that brings 'untruth' along for the ride. A good example would be drug addiction. It can also show up for physical dependency, which is not the same as addiction.

KEYS

Lies, misinformation, misdirection, manipulation with untruths, spying, stealing, cheating, addiction.

EXTRA

Here is an extract from an interesting article written for Niemanlab (Nieman Foundation Harvard University) by neuroscientist Rachel Anne Barr. In the wider article, she explores neuroscience research in brain activity and fake news, and also false memories. Although this is a very short extract from the original article, it is available in full online (at this point in time) and is worth reading if this is a subject you are interested in. It is directly relevant to magicians in lots of different ways.

> The first job of fake news is to catch our attention, and for that reason, novelty is key. Researchers Gordon Pennycook and David Rand have suggested that one reason hyper partisan claims are so successful is that they tend to be outlandish. In a world full of surprises, humans have developed an exquisite ability to rapidly detect and orient towards unexpected information or events. Novelty is an essential concept underlying the neural basis of behaviour and plays a role at nearly all stages of neural processing.

> The primary region of the brain involved in responding to novel stimuli – the substantia nigraventral segmental area, or SNVTA – is closely linked to the hippocampus and the amygdala, both of which play important roles in learning and memory. While the hippocampus compares stimuli against existing memories, the amygdala responds to emotional stimuli and strengthens associated long-term memories.

> This aspect of learning and memory formation is of particular interest to my own lab, where we study brain oscillations involved in long-term memory consolidation. That process occurs during sleep, a somewhat limited timeframe to integrate all of our daily information. For that reason, the brain is adapted to prioritize certain types of information. Highly emotionally provocative information stands a stronger chance of lingering in our minds and being incorporated into long-term memory banks.

> The ability of fake news to grab our attention and then highjack our learning and memory circuitry goes a long way to explaining its success. But its strongest selling point is its ability to appeal to our emotions. Studies of online networks show text spreads more virally when it contains a high degree of "moral emotion," which drives much of what we do. Decisions are often driven by deep-seated emotions that can be difficult to identify. In the process of making a judgment, people

consult or refer to an emotional catalogue carrying all the positive and negative tags consciously or unconsciously associated with a given context.[1]

72 Binder

Meaning

The Binder is a core universal force that affects everything through nature, and which comes into sharp focus in magic. The Binder is a force that captures and binds up that which is overforming, overproducing, or is otherwise out of control. The Binder does not destroy; it simply takes something out of circulation and 'locks it up'. It does not block; rather it restricts.

If the power of the Binder were not in creation, then everything would overgrow and breed endlessly until everything was dead. The Binder is a power that is like a worker: it gravitates to where there is overgrowth and triggers the power of restriction. In magic we see this as part of the natural order, and in this deck the opposite power to the Binder is the Light Bearer. Where the Light Bearer brings light, utterance and life, so the Binder restricts those expressions so that a balance can form. That restriction can be a slowing down, or a winnowing, or a full restriction if something should no longer be in circulation.

In Kabbalah the Binder is known as Gevurah, which is the second of the seven Divine middot.[2] It is associated with the holding back of Divine utterance thereby restricting creation and life. Hence its name is Gevurah, which means 'strength', as only Divine strength can withhold the light which gives life to the world. This is the source of the old saying that 'what protects a person from death is their fate.'

The power of the Binder runs through everything in the physical world as well as through the inner worlds. If you are a magician and you pay attention in your everyday life, then on close inspection you will see how the actions of the Binder sometimes trigger in small ways. In retrospect when you look back at that time, you will see how that restriction brought your body or life back into balance.

The Binder can also bring death if it is engaged with in life beyond what is necessary. Too much severe fasting beyond normal limitation, for example, can eventually kill a person: *severity* is the key word with the Binder. There is a

---

[1] Barr, 2019.

[2] Middot: seven Divine traits that make up the lower seven sefirot of the Kabbalistic Tree of Life. The seven Middot are the powers that bring formation to the physical world.

connection between the Binder and death. It is not a death card, but it is a power that can lead to death when taken too far: constriction eventually throttles the life out of something. The Binder restricts the light, breath, and ultimately the life of something, whereas the Light Bearer brings light, breath, and ultimately life.

Divination

In divination, this card indicates a form of restriction, and it blocks a way forward. It shows a path forward being constricted to the extent that it will not work, or it indicates that something has been restricted for a purpose.

In magic, the Binder is a core power along with the Light Bearer: they are two opposing powers with the magician between them as a fulcrum. When the magician keeps contraction and restriction in balance with expansion and release, it brings a stability to their magical work. And when these powers are worked with in magic, it will start to manifest through your everyday life in small ways so that you can engage with them and act with restraint and/or expansion in how you live your life. The more these core powers are worked with in a mundane way, the more they will become second nature to you in your magic.

In mundane readings, this card is also about restriction or 'blocking up'. How it is read depends heavily on the subject matter of the reading and the question posed. It can indicate a blockage in something or someone, either physically, emotionally, or mentally, or it can indicate a heavy restriction: this could be anything from actual imprisonment to not being able to think clearly or being locked out of something or somewhere.

Another meaning of this card is *self-restriction*, where you choose to take yourself out of a situation for your own good. A good and common example is where people, and magicians in particular, take themselves off social media for their own mental, emotional, and energetic health. If this card appears as an answer to a question of 'what should I do?', then look at the aspects of your life where you are getting drained, threatened, or are overindulging, and then self-restrict. If we act to identify and self-restrict or bind up that which threatens us, then not only do we grow stronger, but we also follow a pattern of behaviour that our biology uses, which gives it more energetic power.

One other meaning of this card is *constriction*. It is a bit of an obscure side meaning of this card, but it can come in useful in health readings, and also in 'search' readings when looking for someone or something. If this card is an outcome of a reading in a search situation, then the missing person is either imprisoned, trapped and bound, or is stuck in a constricted space like a narrow tunnel, tight cave, etc.

Keys

Restriction, bound up, restrained, imprisoned, trapped, removed from circulation, constriction, no, don't, unable.

A physical example of binding can be observed in the condensation of DNA. While genes make up approx. 2% of DNA, a large percentage of DNA is made up of old viral DNA that has integrated into our own. However, our body adds a chemical modification to the viral genetic sequences called methylation. This chemical causes the DNA to condense and bind so tightly that the viral genes can longer be accessed and used.

73 DANGER

MEANING

Danger can come in many forms, and we confront danger every day of our lives often without realizing it. Driving a car or walking down a street can be dangerous, but these don't bother us: we quickly and unconsciously do 'risk assessments' as we go about our lives.

However, there is another type of danger, a danger that is filled with power, be it a violent storm, an accident, war, an adversary, and so forth. The danger of this card for magicians generally has two expressions. One is a wider danger that is not directly connected to you and will affect far more people than just you. The other is a danger that is a 'junction point' in your own fate where an innocuous event can be filled with power that then makes it dangerous for you.

The wider aspect of danger often comes in the form of dangerous storms, earthquakes, natural events, war, building collapses, community infections, or car pileups: essentially anything that threatens life and limb and that would happen regardless of whether you are there. It is the sort of danger you can plan to get out of the way of, if you are aware that it is coming.

The 'junction point' danger for a magician, something I call a 'hotspot of fate', is something that is far more complicated than an obvious danger. There are times where fate paths or patterns collide with unfortunate timing, and where inner destructive power finds a crack that it can fill. These events rely heavily on time, specific people, places, astrological patterns, and buildups of inner or magical power. It is being in the wrong place at the wrong time around the wrong people which allows a minor event to become filled with enough power to become a major event. Such junctions are not just destructive: they can be creative, too. But in relation to this card, such a junction is dangerous. The ins and outs of fate and danger are too complex to include in a book like this, but this at least gives you an idea.

Here is an example of a fate hotspot: a magician does a complex magical working that has built up a lot of power. There is a waiting period during the magical working, so the magician goes out to buy food at the local store. That day there is a planetary conjunction, which in the chart of the magician squares off against some difficult natal planets in potentially dangerous positions and houses. All of this creates 'bad energy weather', so to speak, for the magician. The magical work is not finished but paused, so there is an unstable inner power still orbiting around the magician. The magician wears a bright hat that is their favourite hat, and off they walk to the store.

A person driving a truck spots the red hat and likes it, but in looking, loses their concentration. Something in the back of the mind of the magician tells them to stop and look in a store window, so the magician stops and looks. The truck driver manages to quickly get a good look at the hat as the magician has paused, and the driver suddenly realizes they have lost concentration. The driver manages to slam on the brakes just before hitting the car in front. If the magician had not listened to that voice in the back of their mind, then the gaze of the driver would have lingered for just a few seconds more while the magician was walking. That lingering distraction would have caused the truck driver to slam into the car which would have shunted it forward onto the crosswalk where the magician would have been standing if they had not paused.

The fate junction point, or hotspot, which is a buildup of power waiting to out itself, was made up of the fate paths of the driver, the driver of the car in front, two other people standing at the crosswalk, the magician, the magical pattern put on pause, and the spot of land that the path and road was on. The hotspot was defused and dissipated by the magician doing an act that was not planned until a second before it was done: looking in that store window. And that is how the danger of fate hotspots are often averted: by sudden unplanned change.

If the magician had by some chance done a divination reading before going out, then regardless of the subject matter, the Danger card would have featured in a prominent position to scream 'danger!' at them.

DIVINATION

This card is a clear warning of danger. The level of danger, small or major, can usually be discerned from what the reading is about. By small I mean that it will not kill you, but it is possibly unpleasant and could potentially have a longer-term knock-on effect in your life.

Whatever the reading is about, when this card appears in anything but a withheld position, it means that whatever path of choices and actions you are taking, a danger is present for you that you most likely need to avoid.

If the Danger card appears in a reading but the near future and longer-term future cards look okay, then it is likely that the danger is fleeting or must be walked through. Sometimes a small or brief danger is a necessary step that takes us from one fate step to the next.

When this card appears in a reading with other negative, destructive, or dangerous cards around it, think very carefully about what you are doing, where you are going, and what you are planning. Look to see if that picture changes in a reading if you make a different choice or change direction in your actions. If the danger still appears, then it is likely to be a wider danger rather than a personal one. In such a case, think about where you live and what sort of disasters can happen. Then use readings to narrow down where and when the impact is likely to hit. Ensure you are ready to deal with a dangerous natural event like an earthquake if you live in an earthquake zone, and during the time of danger do not take risks either in life or magic: drive carefully! Being aware that danger is ahead is half the battle and makes dodging it much easier.

If the reading is about a planned magical act or working and this card appears, then you are missing something that puts you in danger, or it is totally the wrong time to do that work, or it is heavily unbalanced and will backlash on you in a dangerous way.

If the reading is about a mundane relationship, then it can indicate that the relationship is not only in danger, but also that it is potentially a danger to you from an inner health, energetic, or emotional aspect.

This card is always a strong caution, and every time it appears in a reading, make sure you photograph or write down the reading, along with the date and the exact question that was asked. Later in time when you look back at it, think about what subsequently happened around you or to you: this will give you a good idea about how this card works for you as an individual.

If this card keeps appearing in all of your readings and falls in different places, then it is likely a warning about a destructive energetic tide that is flowing through your area or land. This makes it a warning to take no risks and not to do anything unbalanced or silly, as the tide will fill any weakness in anyone or anything and bust it right open. Such tides can be as short as a few weeks, or, rarely, can last a few years.

KEYS

Danger, destructive potential, warning, change plans, take no risks, be sensible and be attentive to what is happening around you.

EXTRA

This card was a strange painting to do as a contacted painting. Like some of the others, it started to build up a few days before I started it, and though I had a specific image in my head, what came out was something completely different. I had planned a threatening animal in a storm, but this dude showed up instead and no matter how hard I tried, this image forced its way through. I felt surrounded by danger as I painted it, and I had a really bad feeling about it. I could only play one track of music throughout the time I painted it, and that was Mars, from Holst's *The Planets*.

I started it on the 22nd of February 2022, and two days later Putin invaded Ukraine: then it all started to make sense. What I was painting was the power and consciousness of a destructive force that had found a suitably corrupt and power-hungry human to move into and express itself through. I had inadvertently tapped into the inner pattern of outer events that were on the cusp of expressing themselves.

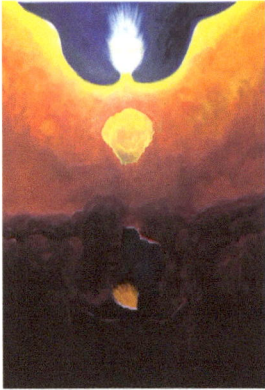

74 FALL

MEANING

The Fall is a dynamic that in everyday life is for the most part a minor thing, but in magic it becomes more focused and potentially serious. In Abrahamic faiths, The Fall is about angels who transgress and are subsequently cast out of heaven. The magical meaning, however, is much less simplistic, and has nothing directly to do with angels.

The deepest dynamic of The Fall is connected to the card the Test, whereby the magician or mystic reaches deep into the Mysteries and through request or circumstance is 'judged' or 'weighed' in life by Divine powers. If that 'weighing' is too 'heavy' because they still have work to do, then they are cast back into their life fate pattern to continue with their evolution. It is a junction point in an individual's fate pattern whereby their measure of life has not as yet been fulfilled, and even if they wanted or welcomed death and judgement, they are rejected from it. The Yorkshire plain-speaking meaning of this card is 'stupid but saveable'.

This dynamic surfaces within the life of some magicians when they are edging closer to the deepest inner Mysteries which, upon their death, disengages them from the cycle of rebirth into life. As they start to immerse in those deep Mysteries, they can be tempted to let go and lose themselves within them, which brings death in a way that is counter to their fate pattern.

One of the adept achievements in magic is to be able to edge close to the deepest mysteries and yet remain anchored in life in a mundane and magical way. This is really important for a magician who is reaching for immersion in such mysteries, as the deeper process of soul evolution happens when the magician balances their access to the deepest accessible mysteries in life with remaining anchored in the physical world of mundane life. This dynamic was deeply misunderstood in Christian western mysteries for a long time, where philosopher-magicians and holy mystics welcomed death or even tried to force it through starvation, self-harm or magical means. The inner result was the opposite of what they expected and wished for.

A lesser version of this dynamic is 'going back to square one': here the actions and intentions of the magician become imbalanced to such an extent that they are ejected from the pattern of magic without being barred from it. They have to start again, often living through reiterations of challenges that were magically triggered as learning events.

It is a cause-and-effect dynamic whereby the further you intentionally walk along a path of evolution in life and magic, the narrower that path gets. Stupid decisions taken out of laziness, emotion, or temptation that are dangerous for others, and when you really do know better, kick you off the path. You have to climb back up from the fall and find a part of the path that is stable enough for you to walk on again. It can be a harsh lesson indeed, but it is a very necessary one that brings wisdom, clarity, and knowledge if you are willing to learn.

It is more severe than a simple defeat, and less severe than a magical or second death event. The Fall is where you are given a second chance, but those chances are limited. If you continually screw up badly when you know better, then at some point, you fall.

DIVINATION

When the Fall appears in a reading, always approach it in the context of the subject matter, question, and position it falls in.

Its overall message is one of destroying what you have achieved by a serious lapse of judgement, laziness, or downright stupidity. The appearance of the card can be a warning that you are about to do this, or it can indicate that the fall has already been set in motion: which is meant depends very much on the question and where the card lands.

For example, in a magical reading, if this card falls in the inner worlds position in a layout, or in the near or long-term future, then you are about to do something that will lead to your downfall. If it falls in the first position, the relationship position, the fate cycle position, or the endurance position, then it is likely that the dynamic has already been triggered. If the reading is about a magical working or project and this card appears, then it is saying that the project is doomed from the start, as it has an inherent weakness that will trigger its collapse. In such a case it is worth doing alternative readings to look at different approaches, timings, and powers, to see if there is a better way of doing it.

If the Fall has already been triggered, then you are left with two choices: wallow in your 'fall from grace' and spend the rest of your life licking your wounds and blaming others, or get back up, start again, and this time resolve to not make such a big mistake again.

If the card appears in a mundane reading, then the above is also relevant but more likely to be less severe. The more you have achieved and the higher you have

207

climbed on your path, be it in your career, relationship, studies etc., the more you have to lose and the bigger the fall will be.

It can also appear in less dramatic circumstances when you are about to do something that is stupid and that could be far more trouble, and trigger more loss, than it is worth.

It is a card of loss of status, loss of position, lost progress, lost work, rejection, becoming an outcast, and having to start all over again. As such it is a card of failure, but not permanent failure: this is a failure that offers you the opportunity to learn a harsh lesson and rebuild yourself. If you do choose to 'rebuild' then it is likely that you will be far more successful than if you hadn't fallen in the first place, providing you put your heart and soul into whatever it is you fell from. And this time, you will be more likely to pay attention, not get lazy, and not cut corners.

Keys

Rejection, loss of status through one's own actions, outcast, failure as a result of stupidity, bad lapse of judgement, lost progress through stupidity, back to the beginning.

75 Serpent of Chaos

Meaning

The serpent pictured is an illustration of the Serpent of Chaos and destruction. Although it has sharp teeth and is deadly, it is also beautiful in a strange way with its iridescent skin. This illustrates how this power can appear alluring to some, so much so that they ignore its teeth and venom. This is important to understand with this power, which is deadly indeed, yet can be hypnotically attractive: its power and beauty can draw people in. This translates in the real world to an alluring power and glamour that is truly poisonous, but people want its power, so they ignore how deadly it is. Its venom can be witnessed out in the world in the form of lies and mistruths that affect whole nations. As such it is linked to the Voice of Untruth.

Obviously it is not a real serpent: rather it is a power that rises out of the Underworld. But when that power appears in dreams and visions, it often appears as a vast or beautiful serpent.[1] There are many serpent powers that flow through

---

[1] A power that appears as a serpent is a visual vocabulary that says, 'this power is very old, much older than humanity'.

the Underworld. Some are destructive, others are protective. The serpent of Chaos is the deadliest of the destructive serpents.

The Serpent of Chaos is a theme that appears in a variety of cultures around the world. Chaos is a condition without any order, without any fulcrum of balance, and where nothing follows any coherent form or pattern. In mythologies and the stories of various religions, chaos reigned supreme in the absence of any order at the very beginning of creation, and ever since the living world began it has tried to assert its power here.

From a magical perspective this power emerges from the Underworld when the right conditions come together in the surface living world: then it attempts to destroy the order of nature, and of living beings. For us humans, it attempts to destroy our individual, communal, and national order and balance.

This dynamic of destructive chaos is sometimes depicted as a serpent or sometimes as a dragon. Most of its various cultural depictions of involve a person, saint, or deity 'pinning' or spearing it with a forked stick or a spear, or controlled or contained by lightning or the shape of a lightning flash. The Serpent of Chaos is rarely depicted on its own without containment: wherever it appears in ancient and classical stories or images, there is always something in the image or story that contains or pins it. To have a depiction of this power without containment, from a magical perspective, gives it a window that it can reach through into this world.

The power of chaos unleashed in the world seeks to open out and seed destruction by filling the living with chaos so that they slowly destroy themselves and everything around them. Notice that the power does not directly strike; rather it poisons everything that it can reach and 'infect'. This power fills those who are far from balance and pushes them to destroy while also unravelling those it infects. It gives power and energy to a person that it fills as its vessel so that it can continue spreading its chaos into other willing vessels.[1]

In the card's image, the serpent is contained in two different ways: one is the red lines which show a magical containment pattern, and the other is the lightning. The red line of magical patterning crosses in such a way to limit the top and bottom of the serpent, but it cannot fully contain the being. It cannot be fully vanquished as it is a natural power inherent in the planet: it can only be subdued for a while. The lightning ends in a fork: a two-pronged action of power that pins and subdues the serpent, putting it back to sleep in the Underworld. Hence mythological depictions of the serpent or dragon being subdued often include lightning, a two-bladed sword, or a stick with a forked bottom.

The venom of the Serpent of Chaos can be observed in the world in a communal way by seeing groups or even whole populations that appear to 'lose their mind or rational thought' to become driven by a collective mindset that is incoherent, destructive, and twisted. No amount of logic gets through: the group mind delves into humanity's darkest depths and dwells there. This can be observed in history when a population under such venom tips beyond the normal 'revolutionary' wish

---

[1] A vessel, in magic, is a person, place or thing that can be filled with energetic power.

209

for change, instead sets out to destroy anyone or anything that gets in their way or does not think like them. It brings about a collapse of any order, and the society essentially 'turns on itself'. From a magical perspective, when this being is fully active in the world, it is often accompanied by a mass of parasites and also tends to coincide with destructive tides that are flowing out into the world.

What provides a person with a measure of immunity from becoming 'infected' as a vessel of this power is recognizing their weaker base self, and instead of suppressing it, constantly working to evolve themselves and to create and seek their own balance. The serpent always seeks out the weak, who are like empty vessels, in order to spread its venom. Knowing yourself, knowing what is right and true for you as a unique soul, and understanding the dogma of cultural norms around you will help you avoid this crazy power. But also, be aware that it is not 'morals' or 'saintliness' that protects from this power: it is self-knowledge and common sense. If you have bare legs and feet and you are walking in viper territory, then you run the risk of being bitten and becoming very ill indeed. If you wear boots and thick pants then you are far safer. Common sense and self-knowledge are always the key to magical protection.

The venom of the Serpent of Chaos is energetic. What holds your energetic integrity and protects you from parasites and such serpents is your energetic and emotional balance. In the natural tides of the planet, what keeps this power under some level of control are the lightning strikes.

Divination

When this card appears, it warns of the possibility of the presence of this power and that you are in danger from it either personally or through its infection of the people around you.

It can also be a warning that you are leaning too far towards your baser side and need to reevaluate how you are functioning in life. Watch particularly where you are putting your mind, as it is through the mind that this power spreads it venom.

The appearance of this card is always a warning that you are in danger of being badly duped. In magical readings it can point to a very destructive, venomous power that appears to you as somehow 'almost too good to be true'. It is far more dangerous than a parasitical being and is also much harder to get rid of, so do not be tempted by whatever it is offering.

The warning of this card is about losing your own balance by allowing what you know or suspect is not true or right to gain a foothold in your mind, and using your mind to play out fantasies in which you would not indulge in real life. The mind is always the first foothold that this being gains. If you wouldn't mass shoot people you don't like, then don't fantasize about it: such fantasy creates a crack that allows this being in.

This card can also warn that someone is 'glamouring' you: they will tempt you with offers of position, money, power or control, or feed you misinformation that can be dangerous to you. They can often appear as larger than life and in control,

210

and will appear to know what they are talking about. In the same vein, it can also indicate a cult or cult-type situation where brainwashing can occur.

In a health reading this card can indicate poison, venom, or an aggressive condition that can gain a hold of your whole body if you do not deal with it promptly.

KEYS

Danger, chaos, degeneration, evil, destructive Underworld force, being glamoured, brainwashing.

EXTRA

If you want to look up the older understanding of this power, then here are some starter points for you in your research:

In the mythology of the Nordic countries, the serpent of chaos is known as Jörmungandr[1] in the skaldic poem *Ragnarsdrápa*[2] and in the *Prose Edda*.[3] The power that can overcome the serpent power is Thor, the god of storms, lightning, strength, and protection.

In Egyptian mythos the serpent of chaos is called Apep, who is brought under control by the deity Set, the power of the storms and lightning. Set is a volatile power of the desert and the deity that protects the solar god Re as he passes through the Duat.[4] In late Egyptian mythos Set becomes merged with chaos, but that is a Greek influence which often confuses people in their research. Look for the older Egyptian mythos for an understanding of Apep and what that power does.

Indian Hinduism has Vritra which is the chaos serpent in the *Rig Vida*.[5] Vritra is controlled by Indra, a powerful deity whose powers include storms, lightning, and water, and who is the slayer of obstacles.

---

[1] Also known as Miðgarðsormr: the serpent of Midgard.

[2] Ragnarsdrápa (Ragnar's poem) a Scandinavian text from the 9th century CE.

[3] *Prose Edda*: Iceland 13th century CE.

[4] Duat: the Egyptian Underworld.

[5] The *Rig Veda* is a series of Sanskrit hymns that is one of the four sacred Hindu texts that makes up the Vedas: approx. 1500 BC.

76 Destruction

Meaning

Destruction is a natural force which is a part of the cycle of creation and destruction. In nature, destruction serves to clear away that which is overgrown, overdeveloped, or is weak and failing, in order to make space for something new to grow. It is a constantly flowing act of nature that keeps life and death in some sort of balance.

From a magical perspective the above is also true, and it is termed *necessary destruction*: destruction which serves a long-term purpose. Necessary destruction is rarely total destruction; rather it is destroying what needs to be destroyed. It is a raw power that has no intent other than to express itself, and it finds its way to express itself through weaknesses. When the conditions are ripe for destruction, it fills and blows apart all of those weaknesses.

Magicians, like every other human and living being, have a series of creative and destructive events in their lives: this is just part and parcel of being alive. For a magician, the key is to spot the destructive power building up, and to try and spot where and what it will express through in the world around them. By doing that, the magician can avoid the worst impact of most destructive tides and events: they can dodge, withdraw, move sideways, and do whatever is necessary to get out of the path of the destruction.

However, if the destruction is building up specifically for the fate pattern of the magician, then it is up to them to spot that potential through divination, to see where the weakness is that is attracting that destruction, and to remedy that weakness however they can. It is better to 'destroy' or get rid of something that is weakening us than to have the inner force of destruction do it for us.

It is important to learn how to observe one's habits, to recognize the things we cling to, to spot our physical and psychological weaknesses, and to address such things. A lot of the destructive buildup within our own fate is facilitated by our inability to let go of something and move on. That could be belongings, people, beliefs, places, a career, or a destructive habit. By intentionally addressing such an inability and working on it, the impact of destruction upon our fate is lessened.

Developing the ability to let go of something and move on disengages a large percentage of destructive potential in our lives and fate. What we end up with are lesser elements of destruction in our lives when they are necessary, but not a total destruction. And once you have walked through that disaster and come out the other side, there will be a time when you can look back and see that without that destruction, you would not have developed properly.

Like all things in life, destruction is complex and has no easy 'off-the-shelf' answers. However, with careful thought and the willingness to adapt, destruction can be avoided or at least modified. Destruction brings necessary change, and it is often harsher when it has not been voluntarily engaged with.

The key to all of this magically is not to fear destruction but to realize that at the right place and time it serves a good, if somewhat painful purpose. Learning to not fear destruction, but to work with it, and also to walk with it, is of paramount importance to all magicians. Sometimes a magician has to mediate destruction to a place or time by carrying that power within them and simply 'showing up' where needed. In this way they become a catalyst for necessary change. But they can only carry the inner power of destruction if they have first learned to deal with it and accept it in their own lives, otherwise mediating it can magically destroy them.

DIVINATION

The level or intensity of the destruction indicated when this card falls into a reading depends upon the question and the layout position it lands in. For instance, if you were doing a reading about whether you should do a particular magical action and this card came up in an outcome position, then the answer would be 'nah, that would be a bad idea, it would backlash on you'.

If however you had a nagging sense of impending doom and you did a reading to look at if you were in any danger, and this card came up in an outcome position, then it is a warning that destruction is flowing around you and you need to either prepare if it cannot be avoided, or you need to identify where or how in your life it is going to express, and then see what actions you can take to dodge it.

This card can also 'slow burn' in readings. If in your general personal readings over a period of time this card keeps appearing, particularly if it lands in a central position, then it is a warning that something is slowly destroying you and it needs attending to. That can be anything from a bad diet to a contaminant, or a hidden illness. Using divination you can look at various aspects of your life at present: your health, work, environment, etc., to see where Destruction and other 'bad' cards make a major appearance. That will help you decide on an appropriate reaction.

The key to any destructive force showing in a reading is not to panic and act out of fear, but to take a deep breath and look carefully at what is going on, and look for the 'window when the door is shut'. For example, if after further divination you identify the destruction is to do with your job, then you can look further to see if it is something overall to do with the company (a fire, a bankruptcy), or specifically with your own job. If the latter is the case, then the first step to disengage the destruction is to accept the possibility of losing your job and immediately start looking around for alternatives. The more you are willing to be open to change, wherever that change may take you, the less of an impact the destruction will have on you. It can often be the disaster that 'makes' you: the scramble for an alternative job can take you down fate paths you would never have walked down otherwise, and that can eventually end up being far better for you.

Sometimes the remedy for this card in a reading can be very simple. If the destructive pattern is not directly related to your actions but is an overall wider fate issue that is building up, then a simple act like changing a routine action, or not going to a planned place, can be enough to discharge the buildup or to dodge it.

This card's severity can be identified through the context of the reading's subject matter, question, and time span. The Destruction card showing up in a 'how is my day or week going to be' is more likely to point at having a bad day or banging your leg or arguing with an idiot on the internet. If it is a long-term reading, then it is something to take a bit more seriously.

If the question is about a building or place, then whatever you are planning to do with that space is not a good idea and would end in disaster. If it shows up in a reading about potential house to buy, then walk away from the deal, as it would be a disaster that would be hard to recover from.

Key phrases

Loss, destruction, dangerous imbalance, destructive behaviour, make a major change, painful rebalancing, catastrophe, natural disaster, get out of the way.

77 Magical Death

Meaning

The meaning of this card has its roots in ancient Near Eastern mythos and survives in two forms which point to a dynamic that is of the utmost important to adept magicians and teachers to this day. It is connected to the magical practice of self-imposed silence: not speaking of that which should not be spoken except to a mind of equal understanding.

As a magician advances in their work and development, they discover things for themselves, and they have visionary and magical experiences that change and evolve them. The hallmark of these changes and experiences is that they come as unexpected gifts: they are not gained by study or learning. It is tempting, for lots of reasons, to teach these hallmark experiences to others so that they too can evolve. However, while the teaching dynamic is good for magicians in their early stages of development, to teach the deeper mysteries or convey them to others who have not discovered these experiences for themselves is a terrible thing.

Why is it a terrible thing? Because the evolution of a soul comes not from knowing about something, but from directly experiencing it for themselves, unprompted, unguided. This follows their natural fate path, and as such the experience arrives when it is the right time and place for that unique individual. If a teacher outlines some of the deepest mysteries and these subconsciously prompt the student to 'have' the same experience, then it is not their own unique experience; it is merely a copy of the teacher's experience. That 'copy' experience wipes out the fate possibility of the student having their own unique experience, which in turn limits their evolution: it cuts down the young plant before it has had chance to grow for itself.

This is known in Kabbalah as 'cutting down the plantings'. It is the worst 'sin' against another human being that a magician can do, as it stifles or ends the path of evolution for that soul for this lifetime. And when it is done intentionally or in gnosis, such action can trigger the 'Magical Death'. The defence mechanism of the mysteries that triggers when the magician oversteps in such a way is an angelic dynamic. It is not a being that you can talk to or that judges you; rather it is a power that triggers through simple cause and effect.

It is a power that protects the deeper mysteries not because they should be some special secret that only a chosen few should know, but because of the damage that forced exposure could cause to an evolving soul. You can destroy your own path if you wish, that is your choice, but to damage the path of evolution for another is a crime beyond all others.

Sometimes it is done without thought; at such times, warning shots are given. Sometimes it is done out of ego: 'look what I know that you do not'. This can elicit either a warning shot or a full strike, depending on the severity of the situation. But when it is done in full knowledge and with the intent to limit another soul, that will trigger a full strike.

A full strike will remove a person from their inner connection to magic and everything around them, and then it will start to break them down bit by bit through physical or mental illness. Upon death, they become nothing: the Other. An ancient Egyptian would call this 'suffering the second death'. This is illustrated in the image for Magical Death. First, I painted a magician; then I painted the angel. Once the two 'players' were facing each other, I had to destroy the magician by painting an unrecognizable dark lump over them so that no part of the humanity was left. When I finished and stepped back, the mess showed faint and distorted faces in agony.

In everyday magical reality, a full strike is rare indeed. However, warning shots can occur frequently if the magician is repeatedly overstepping the line out of ignorance. This can physically manifest as a sense of 'burning': getting very hot, a very red face, and the body feeling like it is on fire. If and when such a sensation occurs, then it is wise indeed to stop what you are doing or saying, adjust, reel back

215

in, or wipe out what has been written that caused the burning. It is also wise to then analyse carefully what could have triggered such a response, and why it happened. Learn from it, adapt, and do not repeat the same mistake.

The Magical Death is deeply connected to the Binder, which is a manifestation of the Kabbalistic Sefirot Gevurah. The ultimate aim of the Magical Death is to withhold and potentially destroy the path forward of something which needs limiting because of its actions. When you think about that carefully, and if you understand Kabbalah, then you will understand why the Magical Death is so deeply connected to the fifth Sefirot.

Divination

When this card appears in a reading, it is always a warning of self-destruction as a result of one's own actions.

In magical divination the appearance of this card in a reading is a strong warning that lines are about to be crossed that should not be, or that the actions of the magician have the potential to destroy the future of another person or thing in a way that will trigger the magical death for the magician. It is a warning of ignorance that has consequences for the magician, and those consequences can be mild or highly dangerous depending upon what is being done.

Occasionally this card can appear if the magician themselves is about to damage their own path of evolution through pushing themselves into areas of magic that are not conducive to, or are downright dangerous to, their own spiritual evolution at that present time. This is something difficult for people who have grown up in a meritocracy to understand. Development and evolution in magical and spiritual paths is not linear: everything in magic has its own time for each individual.

In mundane readings this card can indicate a self-destruction or self-harm through the abuse of power or position. Its meaning is the self-destruction as a result of such an abuse of power: it does not indicate the act of abuse itself. This destruction can come through the justice system, from community rejection, or by the abuser triggering a self-destructive action or psychological implosion. It can also indicate suicide in some instances. It can also indicate the potential death of someone as a result of action taken that is known to be forbidden (for good reason) or dangerous.

If the reading is about a building or place and this card appears, then it indicates that the place is either going to be condemned in the not-too-distant future, or that its structure is potentially going to collapse.

If this card appears in your reading, then think very carefully about your actions and words, both now and what you have planned for the near future.

Keys

Stop, danger, harming others, exposing a secret, punishment, burning, crime, be silent, unwise, danger of being destroyed, condemned.

EXTRA

Here is an extract of the cryptic Kabbalistic tale of the *Four Rabbis and Pardes*:[1]

> ...Now, these four sages were some of the greatest of their generation. They were extraordinary in wisdom and piety, as is known, for they were able to see with RuachHaKodesh, and they mastered the discipline of Maaseh Merkava, the Work of the Chariot.
>
> Rabbi Akiva warned them; When you enter near the stone of pure marble, do not say 'water, water,' since there is actually no water there at all, and it is written, He who speaks falsehood will not be established before My eyes.[2]
>
> The Four men entered the Pardes;[3] Ben Azzai, Ben Zoma, Ben Abuyah, and Rabbi Akiva. Ben Azzai looked and died. Ben Zoma looked and was harmed[4] Ben Abuyah chopped down the saplings. Akiva entered in peace and departed in peace.
>
> What is the meaning of Ben Abuyah destroying the saplings? Of him scripture says: Do not let your mouth cause your flesh to sin. The authority was granted to Metatron to erase the merits of Acher: Ben Abuyah became Acher, the Other who has no place in creation (second death). A heavenly voice was heard: Repent, O backsliding children!' All may repent from their sins, except for Acher.

---

[1] *Babylonian Talmud*: Chagigah 15a.

[2] Magically, this can be interpreted as saying, 'you are going in vision through the realm of death'. When such work is done, there is often a physical urge for water, which is part of the death mysteries. So we would interpret this as saying that the four rabbis went into Pardes via the death vision.

[3] Pardes: the Hebrew word פַּרְדֵּס literally means 'orchard', and is used to indicate paradise or the heavenly realm.

[4] Ben Zoma gazed and was stricken with insanity. Regarding him it is written, "You have found honey, eat moderately lest you bloat yourself and vomit it". *Proverbs* 25:16.

78 Empty Vessel

Meaning

I painted this image in the way a child would, because the bottom line of this dynamic is immaturity. Like in all arts and magic, there is always a set of people who furnish themselves in the outfits and trappings but do not truly understand what they are doing, or why they are doing it. For them, doing magic and acquiring its trappings is more about assuming an identity and a status that they can wield as a weapon or to attract money, sex, or power. Such people are easily spotted in magic, as they put all their time and energy into the 'look' and the 'toys' such as fancy wands, cool looking outfits, and glamorous looking swords. They can talk a good talk to a beginner, but most of what they come out with is parroted from books or simply made up.

They never manage to actually penetrate magic or even dip a toe into its waters, as they have no self-truth and no self-awareness. They quickly become parasited as their foray into magic is often simply a path to abusing others or a way to make money, which leaves them wide open to parasitical manipulation.

There is an old saying: the empty vessel makes the most noise. This is very true in this situation. The empty vessel is someone that is often highly manipulative, and yet charming and can project authority. They can often impress beginners with fancy rituals and words, but there is no magic there: it is all show.

In magic this type of person correlates closely with the fool or idiot: they will never step onto the path of magic in their lifetime, and hence their sum is zero. They are not on the Path of magic and never will be, no matter how much they want to be.

Out in the mundane world the same dynamic applies. True emptiness is a nothing that will always be nothing, and it can be a negative force that swallows that which is vulnerable, like truth. When the powers of chaos rise in humanity, the easiest vessels it can flow through are the empty ones, the people who are unthinking, who have no self-awareness or self-truth, or who are lifelong immature selfish idiots. The powers of chaos can flow easily through such people and can fill them with a power that inflates their ego to the point of being dangerous. Because they are empty vessels, a chaotic being (think demon) can easily take control of them and operate through them. Usually such a being is not only looking for an empty vessel, but particularly one with potential access to power: the boss of a large and powerful company, or someone with an access route to politics, a public platform, or weapons. Often the empty vessel has arrived at their current position of power not by means of their skills but through money or connections.

However, with empty vessels, it is not always destructive beings that can 'inhabit' and drive them. I have come across empty vessels that are driven or operated by beings that are working to uphold fate patterns, or to facilitate the life of another person, such as through financial or emotional support. The fateful person and the empty vessel cross paths, and an angelic being fills or operates the empty vessel in order to protect, support, and uphold the fateful person. It took me a while to get my head around that one, but I have now witnessed it enough times to recognize it.

Divination

The appearance of the empty vessel in divination points to foolishness, ignorance, stupidity, and speaking without knowledge or thought.

If the reading is looking at a magical system or person and this card appears, then it is saying that there is nothing magical there: it is all show and no substance.

Should the card appear in your own magical readings, then it is warning that you may be fooling yourself, that what appears to be magical is not, or that you are being conned or are actually conning someone even, if you did not intend to.

It can also point to a foolish act: if you are doing a reading about an intended magical working and this card is prominent in it, then what you are proposing to do is foolish, stupid, and/or could harm you. It is not a bright idea and will not work magically. Sometimes readings can be sarcastic, and the appearance of this card can be telling you that you are an idiot and need a slap around the back of the head. Don't be shocked if this happens, as it is normal: all magicians (myself included) have been called an idiot by divination more than once. If this does happen, then just step back and look at what you are doing and what your intentions are in order to find out what you are being an idiot about.

The numerical pattern of this card is zero, so this card can also function as a 'no', empty, nothing, or 'doesn't exist'. The deepest root of this card magically is the emptiness: not the Void which appears to be empty but from which all things flow, but true emptiness.

If this card appears as a descriptor card for someone in a mundane reading, then do not fall into the trap of feeling that you can 'save' them or 'educate' them. An empty vessel is always such, and they can become an energetic black hole that will suck the life out of you.

This card can also point to loss of brain function if the reading is about an old person. Dementia slowly 'empties' a person's memory until they have little left: in such cases, the Empty Vessel card can appear for them. This is even more likely if it lands in the 'head' position of a health reading. If this happens, then tread carefully with your interpretation, as it could point to other things also.

Keys

Idiot, no, zero, nothing, bullshit, stupidity, empty, a shell, loss of function, loss of memory.

Extra

This is an extract from The Basic laws of Human Stupidity[1] by Carlo M Cipolla.[2] Although this extract is about humanity in general, with careful reading and thought it will become clear how relevant this extract is to magicians and how they operate out in the world. It is a bit long for an 'extra', but well worth reading and thinking about both in magical and mundane terms. It is also entertaining to read...

The probability that a certain person will be stupid is independent of any other characteristic of that person.

In this regard, Nature seems indeed to have outdone herself. It is well known that Nature manages, rather mysteriously, to keep constant the relative frequency of certain natural phenomena. For instance, whether men proliferate at the Northern Pole or at the Equator, whether the matching couples are developed or underdeveloped, whether they are black, red, white or yellow the female to male ratio among the newly born is a constant, with a very slight prevalence of males. We do not know how Nature achieves this remarkable result but we know that in order to achieve it Nature must operate with large numbers. The most remarkable fact about the frequency of stupidity is that Nature succeeds in making this frequency equal to the probability quite independently from the size of the group.

Thus one finds the same percentage of stupid people whether one is considering very large groups or one is dealing with very small ones. No other set of observable phenomena offers such striking proof of the powers of Nature.

The evidence that education has nothing to do with the probability was provided by experiments carried on in a large number of universities all over the world. One may distinguish the composite population which constitutes a university in five major groups, namely the blue-collar workers, the white-collar employees, the students, the administrators and the professors.

Whenever I analyzed the blue-collar workers I found that the fraction σ of them were stupid. As σ's value was higher than I expected (First

---
[1] Extract from Cipolla, 2021: ch.2.
[2] Carlo M Cipolla (1922-2000): a former Professor of Economics and Fulbright Fellow UC Berkeley USA.

Law), paying my tribute to fashion I thought at first that segregation, poverty, lack of education were to be blamed. But moving up the social ladder I found that the same ratio was prevalent among the white-collar employees and among the students. More impressive still were the results among the professors. Whether I considered a large university or a small college, a famous institution or an obscure one, I found that the same fraction σ of the professors are stupid. So bewildered was I by the results, that I made a special point to extend my research to a specially selected group, to a real elite, the Nobel laureates. The result confirmed Nature's supreme powers: σ fraction of the Nobel laureates are stupid.

This idea was hard to accept and digest but too many experimental results proved its fundamental veracity. The Second Basic Law is an iron law, and it does not admit exceptions. The Women's Liberation Movement will support the Second Basic Law as it shows that stupid individuals are proportionately as numerous among men as among women. The underdeveloped of the Third World will probably take solace at the Second Basic Law as they can find in it the proof that after all the developed are not so developed. Whether the Second Basic Law is liked or not, however, its implications are frightening: the Law implies that whether you move in distinguished circles or you take refuge among the head-hunters of Polynesia, whether you lock yourself into a monastery or decide to spend the rest of your life in the company of beautiful and lascivious women, you always have to face the same percentage of stupid people: which percentage (in accordance with the First Law) will always surpass your expectations.

VIII. The Mystagogus Layout

Essentially, any good layout will work with any deck, and any good deck will work with any properly constructed layout. The layout shown on the next two pages does not require the use of this deck: it can be used with any magically coherent deck. However, when used with the deck it awakens a much wider scope of divination.

The *Mystagogus* deck and layout interact magically as well as in terms of communicating information for divination. Each layout position is an aspect of a certain card in the deck, and when that particular card also appears in a reading in any layout position, you have an extra layer of information that you can access. Say for example that the Daimon card appears in the reading, and the Wind Spirits card also lands in the Daimon position. You would then read the Daimon card in relation to the position it landed in *together with* the Wind Spirits card in the Daimon position, since the shared natures of the positions and cards have produced an additional set of connections.

The Mystagogus layout came out of this specific deck. It follows the pattern of the lightning flash, a shape and highway of power that has deep and ancient roots in the magical mysteries. The lightning flash of the layout also passes through three spheres or orbits of influence. The first orbit is the here and now: the mundane world and the influence of the past. From there the lightning flash passes into the second orbit of fate dynamics. Then it passes into the third orbit of inner powers and inner connections. Finally, it answers the question.

For magicians, this pattern also has a layer of meaning within it that illustrates how inner power travels and expresses itself from the perspective and experience of the human. It also illustrates the balance of oppositions in power dynamics for the magician: if you spend time looking at the various positions and meditating on them, then you will start to see various meanings surfacing, and especially patterns of cause and effect. Finding the connections between the positions that sometimes cross over the lightning flash will particularly help you to get a deeper reading on important issues.

POSITION MEANINGS

1. Progenitor: what the story is about.

2. Endurance: what must be overcome for success/growth.

3. Unravelling: what must be let go of or loosened up, or what is falling away.

4. Partnership: what you are closely interacting with or what is having a direct influence.

5. Hearth: home, family, tribe.

6. West gate: what is now fading into the past but can return.

7. North Gate: what is now long past and will not return, but has relevance.

8. Fate Weavers: the current individual's fate pattern that is active.

9. The Path: what is moving forward, active and positive.

10. The Binder: what is withheld, is not active nor should be.

11. The Gift: help that comes to the situation.

12. Underworld: the adversary of the situation.

13. Dreams: what is happening in sleep and dreams. Can also be a position of visionary work.

14. Inner Worlds: what is flowing to the situation from the inner/spirit worlds.

15. Daimon: advice offered on what actions are needed for success.

16. Danger: what is dangerous and can inhibit or stop progress

17. East gate: short term future, the path ahead.

18. South gate: what will come to be in the longer term future as a result of the current situation.

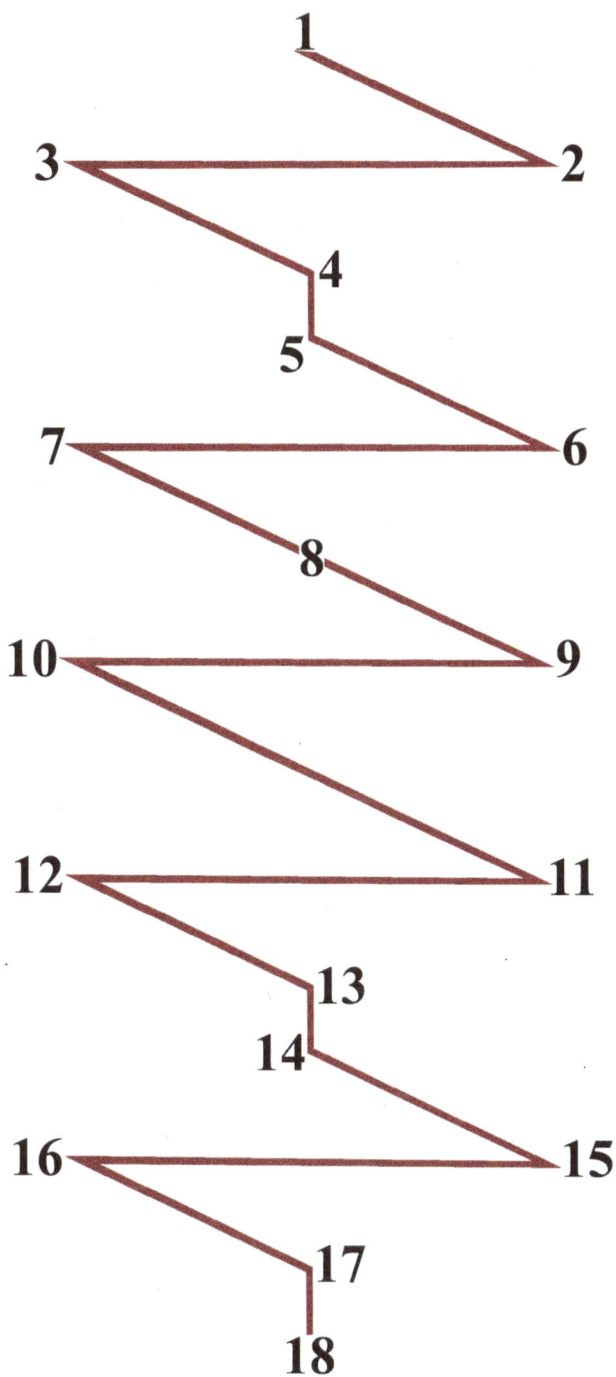

Cards, Magic and Music

THE PASSIVE USE OF MAGICAL IMAGES

Sometimes cards or the image of the card can be used passively in magic to bring a certain energy or vibe into a space for a while. This only works as a part of process; it is not like throwing on a switch and walking away, rather it is about the placement of that image, your awareness of it, and your occasional conversation/interaction with it.

The effects are subtle but are enough to nudge an energy into a different level of tuning in a space. A good way to measure the effects of the image is to work with it placed in a room for a few weeks, keep notes, and then put it away for a week and observe the subtle difference.

Not all card images of this deck are suitable for such use, simply by nature of the power they bring into a space, or because their influence is something that should come from yourself. Below is a list of the most common reasons to use a card this way, and a list of the cards that would be suitable for that reason.

Choose very carefully from the list: go for the one that really speaks to your heart, not your mind/agenda. Each card has a different approach and perspective, and the power will influence you first before it flows into any situation around you. Because of that, it is important to choose wisely: do not get out True Justice if you are looking for justice and yet you behave in unjust ways towards others, whatever the motivation.

A card/image should be chosen carefully, and most importantly, it should be *necessary*. It is pointless working with an image that is not needed at that time, as it will do nothing. Contacted images switch on where there is a deficit that can be addressed by their energy if it is truly needed. Just ensure that you place the card or image where it will not be handled or messed with. And only work with one card at a time. Never be tempted to think that 'more is better': to do so can get pretty messy for all concerned.

Passive use of magical images does not work like active magic, as in it doesn't just suddenly fix something. Rather, its influence slowly grows as a presence, and its action unfolds slowly over time. The more you keep an awareness of the image, the stronger its pattern will align to your fate pattern. Visionary magicians can also use an image passively as an inner gateway into a contact or place.

Here are some card suggestions for particular issues:

For Protection Angel of the Web, which is the card back design. Threshold Guardians, Perception (will warn you and watch for you), Defence, Hidden Knowledge (to hide behind), Inner Desert (only if you are a magician and one that works with balance), or Daimon.

For Peace (in self) Wisdom, Phanos, Purification, Awakening (only if you are willing to face yourself), Progenitor, Hearth, Sanctuary, Sacred Place, Water of Life, Light Bearer.

For Healing Fate Weavers (to strengthen and protect your fate pattern), Purification, healing, Wisdom, Phanos, Hearth, Sanctuary, Sacred Place, Water of Life.

For learning The Student, the Path, Dreams, Perception, service, Star Gazers, Chariot, Inner Desert, East Gate, Inner Library, Underworld, Wind Spirits, Balance, Ancient One, Companions, Oracle, Divine Servants, The College, Endurance, Voice of Truth.

For guidance Fate Weavers, Awakening, The Path, Daimon, Dreams, Wheel, Perception, Service, Utterance, Creating, Loadsharer, Leadership, Inner Desert, Wisdom, Phanos, Wind Spirits, Companions, Divine Servants, Light Bearer, Voice of Truth.

For Justice Fate Weavers, The Path, Perception, Service, Defence, The Test, Voice of Truth, True Justice.

DISCOGRAPHY

For those interested, these are the CDs (yes, I am old school) that were used while I was painting. Sound, vibration and utterance have a strong influence on contacted work when the music is approached magically. Most of the time the images 'chose' the music themselves: I could not paint until the right music was found and played. Some paintings wanted the same CD or even same track on repeat, and others changed day by day as the painting changed/developed. A small number of the paintings were painted in silence for magical reasons, and some were painted with only the recording of a bell on repeat.

In no particular order:

Tridion. Arvo Pärt Stephen Layton (Conductor). Hyperion Records LTD.

> Progenitor, Phanos, The Path, East Gate, Sacred place, Water of Life, Light Bearer, Divine Servants, Separation, Splendour, Defeat, Magical Death.

Armenian Spirit. G Minassyan & Armenian musicians/ Hesperion XXI. Alia Vox (record label).

> Creating, Hearth, Ancient One, Companions, Secret Commonwealth, Partnership, Lightning Strike.

The Saint and the Sultan. Pera Ensemble. (only used CD 2). Berlin Classics.

> Fate Creation, Awakening, Daimon, Loadsharer, East Gate, Sacred Place, Water of Life, Light Bearer, Progenitor, Divine Servants, Separation, Splendour, Defeat.

Armenie 1: Chants Liturgiques du Moyen Age et Musique instrumentale. Ocora label.

> Magic, Silence, Star Gazers, The Test, East Gate, Underworld, The College.

Requiem: Coronation Mass, Ave verum Corpus. Mozart. Peter Schreier (Conductor). Decca.

> Harvester, West Gate.

Voices: Chants from Avignon. Benedictine nuns of Notre-Dame de l'Annonciation. Decca.

> The Student, Dead End, West Gate, Sanctuary, Endurance.

Stravinsky conducts Stravinsky: Petruska & Le Sacre Du Printemps CBS Records.

Dreams, North Gate, Nature, Underworld, Wind Spirits, Firestorm, Companions, Unraveller.

Voices of Light Richard Einhorn, Anonymous 4. Steven Mercurio (Conductor) Sony label.

Service, The Four Creatures, South Gate, Profane Place, Underworld, Light Bearer, Oracle, Separation, Endurance, Lightning Strike, Unraveller, Magical Death.

The Planets. Holst. Herbert von Karajan (conductor). Decca.

Fate Weavers, Danger, Wheel, Firestorm, Partnership, Limiter, Lightning Strike.

The Music of Armenia Vol 1: Sacred Choral music Mihran Ghazelian (conductor) Celestial Harmonies label.

Wisdom, Akh, Inner Library, Sanctuary, The College.

Caithrèim – Ceol agus Amhràin ò Dhràmai an Phiarsaigh www.cic.ie

Perception, Leadership, Nature, Ancient One, Companions, Threshold Guardians.

Peer Gynt/Holburg Suite/Sigurd Jorsalfar. Greig. BBC Scottish Symphony Orchestra. Naxos label.

Underworld, Nature, Wind Spirits, Water of Life, Secret Commonwealth, The Gift, Splendour.

Ancient Voices/Vox Sacre. Anonymous 4, Soeur Marie Keyrouz. Harmonia Mundi label.

Chariot, Akh, Obscure Path, Sanctuary, Ghost, True Justice, Magical Death.

Quràn Recitation: The Music of Islam, Vol 10. Celestial harmonies label.

Utterance, Hidden Knowledge, The Test, Phanos, Foundation Stone, Balance, Divine Servants, Voice of Truth, True Justice, Binder.

The Music of Armenia vol 5, Folk Music. Celestial harmonies label.

Hearth, Wisdom, Nature, Companions, The Gift.

Japanese Drums. Masaya Takashino. Arc Music label.

The Healing, Defence, West Gate, Choppers, Limiter, Danger.

The Music of Islam. Produced by David Parsons and Professor Margaret Kartomi. Celestial Harmonies Label.

Inner Library, Oracle, The Gift, The Fall, South Gate, Limiter.

Fatala. Gongoma Times. Womad Recordings label.

Wind Spirits, Ancient One, Threshold Guardians.

Traditional Turkish Sufi Music: The Sun of Both Worlds. Dü-Şems Ensemble. Arc Music label.

Inner Desert, Foundation Stone, South Gate, Wind Spirits, Oracle, Ghost, Limiter, True Justice.

Bibliography

Barr, R. A. (2019), "Galaxy Brain: the Neuroscience of How Fake News Grabs Our Attention, Produces False Memories, and Appeals To Our Emotions", *NiemanLab* (Nov. 21, 2019).

Beekes, R. (2010), *Etymological Dictionary of Greek*, 2 vols., Leiden and Boston: Brill.

Bohak, G. (2006), "Catching a Thief: the Jewish Trials of a Christian Ordeal", *Jewish Studies Quarterly*, 13, 4, pp. 344-362.

Charles, R. H. (1913), *The Apocrypha and Pseudepigrapha of the Old Testament in English*, Oxford: Oxford at the Clarendon Press, vol. 2.

Cipolla, C. M. (2021), *The basic laws of human stupidity*, New York: Doubleday.

Cresswell, J. (2014), *Little Oxford Dictionary of Word Origins*, Oxford: Oxford University Press.

Forget, J. (ed.) (1892), *Avicenna, al-Ishārāt wa'l-tanbīhāt (Pointers and Reminders)*, Leiden: Brill.

Hesiod (1914), *Homeric Hymns, Epic Cycle, Homerica*, Loeb Classical Library, 57, translated by H. G. Evelyn-White, London: W. Heinemann.

Homer (1919), *The Odyssey with an English Translation*, Loeb Classical Library, 104, translated by A. T. Murray, London: W. Heinemann.

Khan, H. I. (1996), *The Mysticism of Sound and Music*, rev. ed. Boston and London: Shambhala.

Kline, A. S. (2013), *Lucius Apuleius: The Golden Ass Book XI*, available at https://www.poetryintranslation.com/PITBR/Latin/TheGoldenAssXI.php.

Kristensen, B. M. (2004), *The Living Landscape of Knowledge: An analysis of shamanism among the Duha Tuvinians of Northern Mongolia*, København: Institut for Antropologi, Københavns Universitet.

Lane, E. N. (ed.) (1996), *Cybele, Attis and Related Cults: Essays in Memory of M.J. Vermaseren*, Religions in the Graeco-Roman World, 131, Leiden and Boston: Brill.

Legge, J. (1891), *Tao te Ching by Lao-tzu*, Sacred Books of the East, 39, Oxford: Oxford University Press.

Lichtheim, M. (2006 [1975]), *Ancient Egyptian Literature Volume I: The Old and Middle Kingdoms*, Berkeley and Los Angeles, California: University of California Press.

Maure, F., J. Brodeur, D. Hughes, and F. Thomas (2013), "How much energy should manipulative parasites leave to their hosts to ensure altered behaviours?", *Journal of Experimental Biology*, 216, 1, pp. 43-46.

McCarthy, J. (2017a), *Quareia the Apprentice*, Exeter: Quareia Publishing.

— (2017b), *Quareia the Initiate*, Exeter: Quareia Publishing.

— (2020a), *Magic of the North Gate*, Exeter: TaDehent Books.

— (2020b), *Magical Healing: A Health Survival Guide for Occultists, Pagans, Healers and Tarot Readers*, Exeter: TaDehent Books.

McCarthy, J., M. Sheppard, and S. Littlejohn (2022), *The Book of Gates: A Magical Translation*, 2nd ed., Exeter: TaDehent Books.

Murakami, H. (2006), *Kafka on the Shore*, Vintage.

Myungjoon Lee, M. A. (1994), *Plato's Philosophy of Education: its implications for current education*, PhD thesis, Milwaukee, Wisconsin: Marquette University.

Noble, M.-S. (2020), "Philosophising the Occult", in *Philosophising the Occult*, Berlin: De Gruyter.

Poulin, R. (2007), *Evolutionary Ecology of Parasites*, Princeton, New Jersey: Princeton University Press.

Richardson, A. (2009), "Dion Fortune: Moon Priestess", *Journal of Magic and Ritual*, 9, 9.

Schlechter, S. and C. Taylor (1899), *The Wisdom of Ben Sira: Portions of the Book of Ecclesiasticus from Hebrew Manuscripts in the Cairo Genizah Collection*, Cambridge: Cambridge University Press.

Seneca, L. A. (2017), *Letters on ethics: to Lucilius*, Chicago, Illinois: University of Chicago Press.

Simpson, W. K. (1966), "The Letter To the Dead From the Tomb of Meru (N 3737) At Nag'ed-Deir", *The Journal of Egyptian Archaeology*, 52, 1, pp. 39-52.

Speth, G. W. (1893), *'Builders' Rites and Ceremonies: Two Lectures on the Folk-Lore of Masonry*, Delivered by G. W. Speth to the Members of the Church Institute, Margate, On the 30th October and 13th November.

Summers, K. (1996), "Lucretius' Roman Cybele", in Lane (1996), pp. 337-366.

Von Dassow, E. (ed.) (2015), *The Egyptian Book of the Dead: The Book of Going Forth by Day: Being the Papyrus of Ani (Royal Scribe of the Divine Offerings)*, 3rd ed., San Francisco: Chronicle Books.

Quareia
A New, Free School of Magic
For The 21st Century

Advancing education in Mystical Magic
and the Western Esoteric Mysteries.

www.quareia.com
schooldirector@quareia.com

Quareia is a practical magical training course founded by Josephine McCarthy and Frater Acher. It is a complete and freely available course designed to develop a student from a complete beginner into an adept. There are no barriers to entry: the course is accessible regardless of income, race, gender, religion, or spiritual beliefs. Quareia is aligned to no particular school or specific religious, mystical, or magical system; rather it looks at and works with various magical, religious, and mystical practices that have influenced magical thinking in the Near Eastern and Western world from the early Bronze Age to the present day.
The entire course is free and openly available on the Quareia website.